Gnosis, the Mysteries and Christianity

Andrew Welburn is a fellow of New College, Oxford. He is author of several books on the Romantic tradition, and also of *The Beginnings of Christianity*.

For Jacqueline

Gnosis, the Mysteries and Christianity

An anthology of Essene,
Gnostic and Christian writings

Selected and introduced by Andrew Welburn

Floris Books

First published by floris Books in 1994
© 1994 Andrew Welburn

British Library CIP Data available

ISBN 0-86315-183-3

Printed in Great Britain
by BPC Wheatons Ltd, Exeter

Contents

Acknowledgments

This volume complements, and in many respects runs parallel to my earlier work, *The Beginnings of Christianity*. Here I attempt the difficult task of taking the reader inside the sources of ancient Gnosticism and the Mysteries which stand so enigmatically as handmaidens to the birth of the Christian religion, and still point out to us hidden depths of its spiritual significance otherwise largely lost. I draw upon the insights of a large number of scholarly and spiritual writers, referred to extensively in the notes. In the introductions and linking passages I have tried, in a limited way, to set the scene and to place the text in the process of the esoteric reinterpretation of the Bible's prophecies by the Essenes, the spreading of ideas which brought the wisdom of the Mysteries in new forms back to the Mediterranean world, and the new fusion of the sense of mythic-divine encounter with the facts of history which took place in Christianity. Understanding those processes has become, I suggest, the most pressing concern in the modern consciousness. The deliberate veiling, by the ordinary Church tradition, of the way that Christianity came into being, has led to the inevitable resurfacing of the difficult questions which now seem to so many to leave only the choice between a new mythical naturalism and subjectivism, or the outright denial of the spirit (whether inside or outside the establishment of the Church). In these texts, as in Christianity when seen in the light of its connections with them, myth and history come together in extraordinary and exciting ways — offering us insights into our own situation and its needs as much as into their original setting and Christian origin.

I have chosen translations for their merits, including sometimes for their truth to the obscurity and imperfect understanding shown by a pious Father of the Church when summarizing the *gnosis* of Simon the Magus or the intricacies of *The Book of the Blessed*. Here the annotator must work overtime. Elsewhere, as with the Dead Sea Scrolls, I have been able to find versions with real poetic quality, rather than the vague 'biblicism' of so many renderings.

The texts from the Dead Sea Scrolls in the translation by T.H. Gaster are reprinted by permission of Martin Secker and Warburg; the *Poimandres* in the translation by R.M. Grant from the text of

Nock-Festugière, by permission of HarperCollins; the *Apocalypse of Adam* in the translation by G. Macrae and D. Parrott, by permission of E.J. Brill, Leiden; the *Gospel of Philip* in the translation by K.H. Kuhn from the German version of M. Krause, by permission of Oxford University Press. Some of the commentary-material appeared originally in the form of articles in *The Threshing Floor*.

My thanks go to Mona Bradley, for typing so many of the texts in the early stages of the book; to Christopher Moore, of Floris Books, for shepherding the progress of the work to its fulfilment; and to Jacqueline for her enthusiastic yet exact reading of the typescript. Remaining errors and imperfections are necessarily my own.

Introduction

Answers without questions

The origins of Christianity are extraordinarily hard to discover, and at least since the Reformation have been the subject of hot debate. In modern times the fascination has only increased, and sweeping theories have alternated with more cautious and traditional assessments in the twentieth century as striking new discoveries opened up fissures in the very fabric of theology.

It may seem surprising that despite the accounts of the Gospels in the New Testament, the Book of Acts and the writings of church historians like Eusebius from the early centuries, so much about early Christianity should remain obscure. Surely, when the Gospels describe the teaching of Jesus, his conflict with the Jewish authorities and the Roman imperial power, his death and the subsequent appearances of the risen Christ to his amazed and sometimes incredulous disciples, we know all we need to know about the factors which created a new religious movement and eventually swept away the ancient, pagan world? Certainly the Church preserved these records from the earliest times and made their contents the basis of its claim to impart salvation. But the problem which emerged to vex the Church in later centuries is precisely that the records are chosen, arranged, even modified to fit the subsequent perspective of the Christian message. That was only natural. The Church preserved them for its own purposes, not as treasured items in a museum but as part of the urgent struggle to win souls. Yet in doing so, the Christian authorities deprived us of some of the keys to understanding the Gospels and the writings of the earliest Christians such as Paul and John. Some of the crucial ideas underlying all of Christian thought are not explained in the tradition but stand, as it were precipitated before us as a *fait accompli.* The result is that the transforming agency, the spiritual experience of the first Christians who felt the 'world turned upside down,' eludes us. And if we cannot understand that, if at the very

point where the Gospels promise to bring us into the very presence
of Christ something has been lost, then how is Christianity possible
in the modern world that can no longer live, blindly, by unquestioned tradition?

Let us take an example. The Church proclaimed Jesus as the
Messiah, the Lord's anointed foretold in the Jewish scriptures.
Christos is in point of fact the Greek word which likewise means
'anointed,' the rendering into the language of the Gospels of the
term Messiah. In all the Gospels, Jesus is called by this name and
his claim to fulfil the Jewish prophecies is urged in many passages.
His miraculous birth, according to Matthew, was itself the fulfilling
of an utterance by Isaiah. His miracles, his sufferings, his overcoming of death, according to the evangelists, all proved that he was
indeed the Messiah, God's Son. So familiar has this assertion
become that it is easy to overlook an all-important fact. The Jewish
prophecies concerning the Messiah contain nothing about a
miraculous birth, nothing about a miracle-worker, nothing about
suffering and death — above all, nothing about a God incarnate.
The Jewish Messiah, still awaited by the orthodox in Judaism, is to
be a great and powerful leader of the nation sent by God. He will
be a religious teacher, making clear at last the apparently contradictory meanings of the scriptures and scrupulously obeying the Law.
But he is nowhere said to be God, or the Son of God, in any of the
prophecies. As for the passage in Isaiah, it is notorious that it speaks
only of a 'young woman' who will bear a child of great sagacity.
The term 'virgin' is rather brought in from the fulfilment than the
other way around. Somewhere in the stages of the Gospel tradition
before it reached us in its present form, the notion of 'the Messiah'
had been radically transformed. This new idea of the Messiah was
brilliantly realized in the Gospels' portrait of Jesus, but it bears such
little resemblance to the Old Testament prophecies that Jewish
religionists have never taken Jesus' claim to their fulfilment at all
seriously.

Now take a contrary case. When Paul describes the redemptive
work of Christ in his letters to the early communities, he speaks
about the grand design of the Fall and Salvation, of the sin of the
First Adam and of the Second Adam who restores our lost relationship to God. He speaks of the 'Old Adam' within us — and since
Adam means 'man' he evidently means our essential nature, which
is rescued and redeemed by the 'New Man' or Christ, who may also

become the 'Christ in you.' Once again it is easy to assume the viewpoint of later times. Christian theology, in the wake of Paul, has built a great edifice upon this fine antithesis of Fall and Redemption, the Adam in whom all sinned, the Christ in whom all are made alive. We take it for granted that the story of Adam in the Book of Genesis played a similar role in Judaism, presenting a humanity fallen and in need of rescue by a merciful God. How can one then fail to see in Christ the one who came to play just that part? But not at all. Judaism read the account in Genesis as a hymn to the greatness and goodness of the Creator, an idea which is one of the very cornerstones of Jewish thought. By comparison, the story which explains the presence of imperfections such as disease and death, and human frailty, is hardly referred to anywhere else in the Old Testament and did not substantially affect the estimate of Jewish teachers that human beings were perfectly capable of attaining to righteousness before God by obeying the God-given Law. Once more the pattern of 'fulfilment' can hardly be explained by the situation in the Old Testament. There is no suggestion there of an Adam in us all; no mention of an Adam who is to return at the end of time or of 'Paradise regained.' Again, these ideas have come from some source which had already transformed the Jewish materials, enabling Paul to present Christ in a powerful way as part of a cosmic balancing process, equal in effect to the original act of creation — which continued to hold its privileged position in Judaism nonetheless.

Thus the Church has preserved documents which furnished the foundations of Christian thought; but it did not preserve the original context, the background of ideas from which they emerged, and so leaves much uncertain. The most perilous aspect of Protestantism has turned out to be this uncertainty of context. Removed from their role as supporters of the Catholic tradition and made into authoritative documents, the Gospels have turned out to be oddly unstable guides, and scepticism has found many easy inroads into the Protestant establishment. And yet the situation is also an exciting one. Especially in the most recent times, we are not without startling indications that the context of original Christianity can be rediscovered, and that it has an unexpected relevance to the contemporary predicament. There have been in the twentieth century two major discoveries of written texts — the one in caves near the Dead Sea, the other in the cliffs at the edge of the Nile — which have opened

to our probing modern gaze something of the spiritual life in the
world of Christian origins. They have shown factors at work in the
tale which would never have been predicted from a knowledge of
Christian and Old Testament tradition — factors which had raised
novel questions in searching and religious minds in the centuries
before Christ. Things which seemed marginal or about which almost
nothing was known have surfaced and even taken a central role. It
turns out that expectations about the coming of the Messiah, about
a new direction in human history, and much more, had indeed been
transformed since Old Testament times. And that transformation
had to do with a religious world that later Christianity was anxious
to play down, and to dissociate itself from rather energetically: the
world of the pagan Mysteries.

Writings from the sands

The writings presented in this book all come from the period of
Christian beginnings. Some of them are non-Christian Mystery texts,
recording the secret knowledge or *gnosis* which was taught to
the initiates after they had been through an arduous (sometimes
dangerous) preparation. An example of a purely pagan Mystery
would be the *Poimandres* in our Chapter 5. It is attributed to the
divine scribe or divinized man of Egyptian tradition, Hermes or
Thoth. Yet it contains some striking analogies with earliest Christianity (such as a creative Word recalling the Gospel of John) and
with Judaism (such as a hymn containing formulae used in the
Synagogues).

Other texts come from Judaism itself, and from the period
immediately before the time of Jesus. The Essene writings from the
Dead Sea Scrolls are the most prominent instance. If anything could
be expected to clarify the inner reality of the world in which Jesus
lived, such writings must surely be the ones to do so. Yet so unlike
the usual idea is the world they reveal that most theologians have
backed away from the consequences of the truth they suggest. The
Judaism of the 'Righteous Teacher,' like that of Jesus, was strongly
opposed to the pious ideas of the Pharisees; the Teacher's followers,
the Essenes, considered that the Temple in Jerusalem had been
profaned and polluted — they might well have supported Jesus in
his 'cleansing of the Temple,' and his allusions to a 'true High

Priest,' implicitly unlike the present dynasty, would have met with their approval. Yet theology has backtracked on the notion of a close link, because the Judaism of the Teacher and his followers was a visionary reinterpretation of the Bible with Mystery-rites, esoteric teachings, secret gatherings and special techniques of 'illuminated' reading that made the biblical text refer to their own present and future fate.

Other writings included in the present selection come from the borderlands of the Jewish territory or from groups who were clearly in touch with pagan Mysteries as well as with the Jewish tradition. And again, similarities to the Gospels or to what we know of earliest Christianity through its liturgy are glaring. Some of the writings come from Samaria — that centre of rivalry to orthodox Judaism which preserved its own ancient version of the Bible's books of Moses, its own Temple on Mount Gerizim and its own expectation of a Messianic prophet. Even today some of the Samaritans still hold to these alternative versions of the ancient biblical faith. In Jesus' time, Samaria was the home of Simon the Magus, an esotericist whose *Great Annunciation* is full of strange ideas about a Messiah-with-a-difference who is a 'Great Power' of God. Simon's later disciples thought he himself might have been that 'Seventh Power'; but other sources record that Simon acknowledged Jesus' claim. The shocked orthodox Fathers of the Church regarded Simon's theology, however, as the source of all error in Christian thought, and Simon himself as the primal 'heretic.' Yet his ideas are often like those of the Essenes. Was the Church again trying to forget a formative stage of the Christian tradition? Jesus broke the Jewish taboo and spoke to Samaritans like the woman at the well; might he not have been in touch with Samaritan thought?

Still other writings come from Christian times. The twentieth-century discoveries in the Egyptian cliffs at Nag Hammadi show, however, that the early 'apostolic' traditions were not all similar to the ones that survived the filtering by the Church which produced the standard historical view. The *Gospel of Philip* is not a gospel like the lives of Jesus which we know from Matthew, Mark, Luke or John. It is a book of loosely related Christian thoughts, describing the bases of the Christian life and alluding constantly to the 'Mysteries' which Jesus established and, it claims, performed. Scholarly researches show that these Mysteries are related to pagan Mystery-rites — but also to the sacraments of the Catholic Church.

In fact, the *Gospel of Philip* has more and more come to be seen in the mainstream of Christian liturgical development. Among other Mysteries, it seems to resemble those of the ancient Iranian light-god Mithra, well-known in the Roman Empire though originating further east; but closer to the terrain of Christian origins, *Philip's* ritual patterns are closely reminiscent of a semi-Jewish group — the Mandeans, who were active in Palestine in Jesus' time. Once more the similarities suggest that Mystery-connections need not mean that we are far removed from Jesus' own environment. But for the moment we need not try to argue for definite links. It is important to appreciate, rather, that these are writings which reflect the influences and ideas of the centuries close to Jesus and the religious culture of his own country or its immediate neighbours. By contrast, the Old Testament prophets lay far back, and wrote in a language (classical Hebrew) that was no longer spoken, its place long having been taken by Aramaic.

Let us therefore list the writings to be presented in detail, noting for the present simply their likely provenance in space and time.

The Mandean Mystery

Preserved in the *Canonical Prayerbook* of the Mandeans, the semi-Jewish group just mentioned. This remarkable sect survived from biblical times into the twentieth century, though in order to avoid persecution from Jews, Christians and Muslims, they had to retreat into the marshes of Iraq and Iran. Experts consider this 'initiatory recital' to be one of the oldest parts of their scripture, and since we know that the Mandeans were baptizing in the Jordan valley around Jesus' time, there is no reason to doubt that it was being used there in substantially the form it has today. The Mandaic language in which it is preserved is nothing more than a dialect variation of the Aramaic tongue which Jesus spoke.

The Essene Mysteries: from the Dead Sea Scrolls

In 1947 a Bedouin shepherd accidentally stumbled upon a cave outside Qumran, by the Dead Sea. It contained a variety of ancient scrolls, with texts from the Bible, Hebrew poems, prophecies, visions and other works, whose importance and character were only gradually to be unravelled. Eventually the texts revealed a picture, uncertain and fragmentary in part but generally accepted by scholars in the field. They had been written by the scribes of the Order of

Essenes, in the century or two before Christ. The term Essenes is never used in them; but the ideas expressed agree so well with ancient historians on the Essene teachings that little or no doubt remains.

The teaching in these texts is based for the most part on the Bible, and biblical texts form the greater part of their bulk. There were also, however, works by Essene seers which include the powerfully written poems included here. They describe from the personal experience of the author, the spiritual process of initiation into the Order and its secret teachings — or, it may be better to say, the author's spiritual vision formed the basis of the Order and its esoteric content. For the writer is probably none other than the 'Righteous Teacher' who is referred to, or alluded to in riddling terms, by other of the documents. Later (see pp.?ff), I give my reasons for believing that he was active around 100 BC. (Some scholars would put him earlier, c.175). His writings mention the landscape of Qumran, to which he withdrew and which became the spiritual centre of Essenism. At the same time, there were other Essenes living in the villages up and down Palestine and in Jerusalem. The Essene movement continued to be very active into early Christian times.

The Testaments of the Patriarchs

Fragments of these books were found among the Dead Sea Scrolls. They probably belong, however, to a phase in the history of Essene thought prior to its expression at their centre in Qumran. There are indications of earlier links with Damascus, in Syria, and recent scholarship connects the *Testaments* with Syria too. These works contain prophecies about the Messiah — unorthodox ideas with cosmic symbolism and a dual reference to Priest and King, worked out in detail in the Dead Sea Scrolls whose fuller explanation first made the obscure foretellings of the *Testaments* make real sense. The text is preserved in full in a Greek translation, utilized here; the Qumran fragments are in Aramaic. The original writings probably date from around 150 BC. Before they reached modern eyes, however, the texts were interpolated by a Christian with details of the prophecies' fulfilment by Jesus. There is other evidence too that some Christians at least had their expectations of the Messiah modelled on these esoteric and mysterious *Testaments* — as we shall see.

The Great Annunciation *of Simon the Magus*
The text of this extraordinary work is preserved (in order to be refuted) by the early Roman bishop Hippolytus in his comprehensive attack on heresies, the *Refutatio omnium haeresium*. Although hostile, Hippolytus was usually accurate in his account of enemy doctrine, and quoted substantially from his sources, often word for word. In Book VI of the *Refutatio* he includes the text in Greek of the *Megale Apophasis* or 'Great Annunciation' attributing it to Simon the Magus, the Samaritan teacher contemporary with the apostles. No more than Jesus, however, will Simon have written down his thoughts in literary form: that would be done by his pupils, and there is evidence that they formulated the present text in the cultural setting of Alexandria — the capital city, as it were, of ancient religious and philosophical search. Such features as the quotation from Homer, for example, almost certainly came in at that stage. In fact, many Gnostic ideas from Syria or Asia Minor first found written expression in the literary metropolis of Egypt. Simon is otherwise known from legends and shorter historical notices; but since the teachings of the 'Great Annunciation' bear a significant relationship to the poetic symbolism of the legends, its Samaritan character and basic authenticity are secure. Frequent similarities to the thought of the Essenes as well as to Christianity indicate that its content is compatible with the background of a first-century Magus.

The Poimandres *of Hermes the Egyptian*
A celebrated text from the Hermetic tradition, the *Poimandres* is the first tractate of the *Corpus Hermeticum* which was rediscovered at the time of the Renaissance amid great scholarly excitement. It was translated into Latin by Marsilio Ficino and published in 1471. It has been translated many times since, but often from bad texts or in eccentric editions (such as that of the Oxford scholar Walter Scott). It is included here, however, because the new picture of manifold links with the culture of its time evinced by early Christianity is strikingly illustrated here. A document from the pagan Mysteries of Hellenized Egypt, the *Poimandres* includes a meditation on the creation-story from Genesis (whose inner meaning is 'a Mystery hidden until this day,') a creative Logos, and a powerful affinity with the light-mysticism of the Gospel of John, as well as with Christian Gnosticism. Other related Hermetic documents include references to baptism, the need for repentance or *metanoia* ('transfor-

mation of mind') which echo the words of John the Baptist in our New Testament Gospels. On these and similar grounds, the work can be dated to the first century AD. It has Egyptian prototypes (e.g. in the fragments of Nechepso), but plainly shows the effects of the developments in spiritual thought which were at that very time creating Christianity. It adds the perspective of the Mysteries themselves. That perspective was to continue unchanged in the Gnostic forms of Christianity which grew up over the next century, and were subsequently extirpated as 'heresy.' But its connection was earlier. It has links with the early tradition of Jesus' sayings in the *Gospel of Thomas*, with the proclamation of the Baptist in which Jesus too joined (according to Matthew), and a shared background with the Gospel of John — the Gospel now thought likeliest to come from someone close to Jesus.

The Apocalypse of Adam

A new chapter in understanding the backdrop to Christian origins was opened in 1945, when Egyptian *fellahin* scraping minerals from a cliff by the Nile at Nag Hammadi stumbled upon an ancient collection of Gnostic books. Impounded for decades by the Cairo Museum, the texts were finally translated into English and published in 1977, making a volume of several hundred pages. One part of the discovery had been smuggled to Europe earlier, and was bought by the Jung Institute in Zurich; that part included the *Gospel of Thomas*. The rest of the thirteen 'codices' (bound papyrus books) contained Christian, Hermetic, and pagan writings, mostly unknown before. They most likely formed the library of a Valentinian Gnostic group active in Upper Egypt in the fourth century AD. (Other theories are: the collection of a heresy-hunter, to furnish the documentation for his refutations; or, the unorthodox reading of the monks in the Pachomian monastery — unlikely thought!) On the assumption that it is the library of a Gnostic cell, we may note again the boundary-crossing character of their reading. Many of the books, it is true, represent the special teachings of the several Gnostic sects which were well established from the second century onward. But others reach back to the phases of Christianity before the entrenched positions had emerged — e.g. the *Gospel of Thomas*, with its collection of the sayings of Jesus, still without much indication of context (that came later, as the tradition spread to new readers who as yet knew nothing of the background). Others again may reach back into the world of Jewish esotericism of pre-Christian times, when it was already in touch with the Mysteries. One such case may be the *Apocalypse of Adam*.

The *Apocalypse of Adam* purports to contain revelations made at the beginning of history by Adam to his son Seth; that is not a usual claim in Gnostic literature, for which the Gnostic seer usually claims the authority of his own vision alone, but it is a pattern found in some Essene books and related apocrypha. Moreover, the apparently Christian features of the work which have impressed certain scholars turn out to be less Christian on close examination. There is a Messianic figure, who contends against the powers of Darkness, suffers and then receives 'glory and power'; but there is no suggestion that his suffering has any redemptive character. The final victory of the prophet, or Illuminator, in his climatic appearance among the 'kingdoms' of humanity, does not make any mention of the Christian paradox of the crucified one. The model is an overtly heroic one, analogous to that of the patriarch-prophets of the Essene traditions, or even more to figures from Zoroastrian legend or the pagan world. More probably then, the *Apocalypse* shows ideas which point towards Christianity rather than assume it, and it is best to hold to the original conception of Alexander Böhlig that it comes from a pre-Christian baptizing sect — the Essenes, or Mandeans or related to both. It might be dated to the first century BC. With its links to the Mysteries of several lands, its widening spiritual perspective and sense of the imminent appearance of the Illuminator-Christ, it may well turn out to be the most important of all the new texts for an understanding of Christian origins.

The Book of the Blessed *by Justin the Gnostic*

Another text preserved by Bishop Hippolytus in his *Refutatio*, the *Book of Baruch* (a name really meaning 'the Blessed' in Hebrew) seems to take up the threads of the *Apocalypse of Adam*. Although it has long been known as an unusual variation on Gnostic ideas, it was previously hard to relate the work or its author to any specific line of development — though Gershom Scholem pointed to early kabbalistic connections. Since, however, the *Book of the Blessed* also makes explicit reference to the Gospels and the Christian fulfilment by 'Jesus, the Son of Man,' it belongs to the Christian continuation of the *Apocalypse*'s prophetic vision. Nothing is known about Justin, its reputed author, except what Hippolytus tells us here, and that is very little. He was probably active at the end of the first century or beginning of the second century AD. He may have lived in Alexandria, since he is familiar with cult motifs from a special Mystery of Isis — but he is familiar with so many myths and Mysteries that no hard and fast conclusion may be drawn about his starting-point.

The Gospel of Philip

One of the 'new Gospels,' like the *Gospel of Thomas*, the traditions in the name of the apostle Philip were at first assumed to be Gnostic ideas. In support of that view, it was possible to point to those like Marcus, the pupil of Valentinus, who practised rituals suggestive of those in the *Gospel* and taught similar conceptions. Subsequent analysis shows, however, that Marcus' special teachings mark a divergence from Valentinianism, and probably stem from a different tradition which he found already flourishing: a tradition very like that of the *Gospel of Philip*. The latter's resemble also the mainstream liturgical development of the Church's sacraments, at an early stage when they are close to the forms of the pagan Mysteries and to those of the Mandeans. Much of the evidence points to Antioch, one of the major centres of earliest Christianity, and for a time the centre of Paul's life and work, as the community in which the rites assumed this form. (Some influence of Pauline ideas can be traced). Probably then Gnostics like Marcus were going back to a primal form of Christianity, and interpreting it with the aid of Valentinian thought, rather than developing a 'new Gnostic system.' Other Gnostics, like those who owned the Nag Hammadi library, preserved the *Gospel* without Valentinian additions. But there is no evidence in the *Gospel* that its addressees were a minority group. Controversies over doctrines are mentioned; but the only other denominations are Hebrews and pagans. If there is Gnosticism in the *Gospel of Philip*, it had not yet been isolated and pushed out of the Church. It is still present as a part of the way the experiences of the ritual-sacramental life of the Christian could be understood.

A date is hard to establish, since the loose compilation of the elements from the apostolic tradition and elsewhere gives few fixed points of reference. Dating on the assumption that it was post-Valentinian has probably been too late. Some point in the second century probably represents the juncture at which the collection was fixed.

The Secret Gospel according to Mark
A further discovery in 1958 — this time at Mar Saba in the Judean desert — brought a short text which comes closer still to demonstrating that the suppressed history of Christian origins would alter our view of the Gospel tradition itself. It contains a passage supposed to come from the original version of the Gospel of Mark; and several scholars have supported its claim. With its mention of Jesus' baptizing activity, and its new telling of an episode hitherto only mentioned in the Gospel of John, it has the potential to make us rethink many of our suppositions about the historical setting and the interconnections between the strands of evidence about Jesus himself.

An alternative Christianity?

The Fathers of the Church wished to place Christianity beyond question, beyond comparison, by covering up certain aspects of its early, formative stages. Accidental discoveries, and the revaluations they have produced, have raised once more some of the questions about Christian origins they hoped to have laid to rest forever. The Dead Sea Scrolls from Qumran have shown us the intense spirituality of a mystical sect, the Essenes: Jews who rejected the conventional worship in the Temple, and conventional Jewish society, setting up their own ideal community in the desert in anticipation of an apocalyptic 'new age' to come, and interpreting the Bible anew under the guidance of their 'Righteous Teacher.' The 'Coptic Gnostic Library' from Nag Hammadi has revealed to us the writings of early Christian seers, Gnostics and other visionaries whose understanding of Christianity was disconcertingly unlike that of the victorious Fathers of the Church whose version survived to become orthodoxy. The impact of these discoveries has been far-reaching, even if muffled from the public ear. Much of our understanding about early Christianity has been thrown into uncertainty, and the crisis is only now coming to a head.

Many of the documents assembled in this book derive from the discoveries at Qumran or Nag Hammadi, or they are similar documents which have taken on new meaning when placed in the perspective which those discoveries provide. In presenting them I have tried to choose writings interesting and valuable in themselves

— some, for example, are poems of considerable beauty and power — but also to take further a trend of interpretation whose force has gradually been increasing over recent years. When the Gnostic writings from Nag Hammadi were first investigated and the results made known, it seemed immediately apparent that already by the second century of Christianity there were those who resisted the power of the Church. The 'Gnostic Gospels' such as the *Gospel of Thomas* provided them with an alternative vision with which to challenge the Church organization and its canonical 'four Gospels only.' They furnished the basis of a full-blown 'alternative Christianity' often with much more appealing attitudes in such matters as the role of women, individual experience, ritual and Church authority. The Gnostic Gospels breathed an air of inner authenticity and rebellious assertion of spiritual freedom. Hitherto, historians had only known about the Gnostics from the unfriendly summaries given in the Fathers, mainly for the purpose of stamping them out as heretics, and a few late writings such as the *Pistis Sophia* which seem to scrape together ideas and traditions no longer fully understood. But now the Gnostic Gospels spoke across the centuries for a Christianity that many felt had more to recommend it than much handed down by the Church. At the very least they tilted the balance drastically back after two thousand years of suppression.*

Yet it often happens that the deeper import of things emerges only gradually. As the 'new Gospels' were studied further it began to seem possible that the Gnostic Gospels were more than a fascinating 'alternative interpretation' of the Christian message which had posed a challenge to orthodoxy in the second century (and several times since). At first it was still assumed, for instance, that the *Gospel of Thomas* — one of the earliest of the Nag Hammadi texts to attract public interest — had been the treasured Gospel of a special group, at loggerheads with the mainstream Church and asserting their own ideas. That, after all, was how the Fathers had described the Gnostics: as deviant groups each following some different seer, each with their own pet notions. The *Gospel of Thomas* was found to contain many of the ideas that they had ascribed to the infamous heretics or at any rate many passages which could be interpreted in conformity with them. Only gradually did a different approach gain ground. It was opposed by many of the more

* See the account given by Elaine Pagels, 1980.

orthodox Christian scholars, for whom the recognition of an alternative version of Christianity in the second century was less of an embarrassment than the further possibility emerging out of the fog — namely, that such gospels as *Thomas* were not heretical alternatives to the Gospel tradition of the Church's New Testament but actually parts of its own earlier history. Nevertheless that view has come to seem more and more certain.

The *Gospel of Thomas* contains sayings *(logoi)* attributed to Jesus, and its opening words make the claim that the apostle Thomas preserved and wrote them down. The first and most momentous saying is the following:

> He who finds the interpretation of these words shall not
> taste of death.

Many of the sayings were already known from the New Testament. *Thomas* includes several of the parables, for instance, and some sayings against the scribes and the Pharisees and other materials which are easily recognized. It was all too easy, therefore, to presume that *Thomas* was dependent on the more orthodox tradition, but had branched off from it by ascribing to the sayings a mystical 'interpretation' and claiming for their special knowledge *(gnosis)* an authority deliberately different to that of the Church. Not so. It turned out that the form of the sayings quoted in *Thomas*, especially the parables, could not be derived from the versions in the canon. Minor differences of wording tended rather to suggest that *Thomas'* version was earlier, less polished by literary transmission, more probably close to the original form. As for the unfamiliar sayings also quoted in *Thomas*, scholars recognized allusions to them in the letters of the earliest Christian writer Paul.

Furthermore, it has long been recognized that the Gospels which we have in the New Testament are the end-products of a complex process. In the days of the apostles we know that the Christian message was taught orally. Sayings of the Lord were repeated with particular reverence, and in due course collected together in written form. The next step came when the setting of the sayings began to be described for those who did not already know — something that had hardly been necessary for the apostles and those who had heard them speak. Eventually the Gospel developed into the form we know from Matthew, Mark, Luke and John. For a long time, however, the term 'Gospel' referred to the Christian message, and was applied as the name of a kind of literary work only much later.

Now, *Thomas* is almost entirely made up of sayings of Jesus, with only the most rudimentary indications of a situation in which he spoke. It is hard to avoid the implication that it is not a deviant offspring from the canonical Gospel tradition; it is one of their ancestors. Although the Gnostic Gospels may have ended up in the hands of special groups as the Fathers assert, those groups did not create them. They were carrying on an earlier phase of the Christian tradition which the Church was anxious to leave behind and their subsequent sectarian role was in large part thrust upon them. Looked at from this perspective, the potential of these 'apocryphal' gospels becomes suddenly enormous. For they may actually restore the missing context of the earliest Christian proclamation, the spiritual experience which transformed the older expectations of a Messiah out of all recognition.

Of course, we need to exercise a good deal of caution. The texts which have been restored to us by archaeology are if anything strikingly diverse. They do not present us with a unified picture to set against the orthodox portrait of the founder of the Church. That indeed seems to be the first lesson they have to teach: the hammering out of a single doctrine was a late achievement, not the starting-point of Christian evolution. In the beginning all sorts of ideas are evoked in order to try to understand the overwhelming Event. A kind of individualism marks the earlier stages of the tradition, as if every line of history gains its unique fulfilment and higher meaning in Christ. Only afterwards was it insisted that there should be one 'right belief' *(ortho-doxia)*. That is why it is important that we look again at all the evidence together, not just the apocryphal gospels, not just the canonical writings: all must be re-immersed in the melting-pot of the beginnings, so that we can understand how the different versions arose. We may then understand too why the Church had to cut its ties with that spiritual ferment of ideas and hopes, and insist upon its own unique right — understand, though not condone the path of persecution on which it then tragically embarked.

Esoteric teachings

The clear boundaries which emerged in retrospect hardly existed in
the exciting world of Christian origins. And they have had to be
softened, sometimes dissolved altogether in order to reconstruct the
inner reality implied by the new gospels. Christianity superseded
Judaism, announced the demise of the Law and the rule of God's
grace. As for the Gnostics, it was reported that they had purged
Christianity still more thoroughly of its lingering admiration for the
Jewish scriptures. One of the most important revolutions, however,
in the picture to come out of the Nag Hammadi discovery is the
realization that trends like those of Gnosticism had in fact already
been infiltrating Jewish spirituality, in all probability long before the
rise of Christianity. Far from standing at opposite poles, the earliest
Jewish Christianity and Gnostic Christianity share much common
ground, and the Gnostic writings show rich connections with the
visionary and apocalyptic writings of later Judaism and the
beginning of the kabbala or Jewish mystical lore. Even more
disturbing, they show that the boundary dividing Judaeo-Christian
ideas from the pagan world — held to be utterly impassable by the
orthodox tradition, for which paganism was the great enemy to be
overcome — was at one time flexible or open to a creative give-and-
take.

One feature of all the newly recovered writings we have mentioned so far, for example, is their secrecy. All are presented as
esoteric knowledge: and this is a feature which links them not so
much with the Old Testament or Judaism, but with the pagan
Mysteries — cults which imparted profound religious experience
and often a direct vision of a God, and an assurance of salvation
after death to their initiates. Indeed, the Nag Hammadi library of
works used by a group of Christian Gnostics is surprising not least
in that it contains a number of pagan writings, such as those
attributed to the Egyptian Mystery-god Hermes Trismegistus, with
their characteristic oath:

> This is the oath: I make him who will read this holy book
> swear by heaven and earth and fire and water and seven
> rulers of substance and the creating spirit in them and the
> unbegotten God and the self-begotten one and the one
> who has been begotten, that he guard the things that

> Hermes has said. And those who keep the oath, God will
> be reconciled with them and everyone whom we have
> named. But wrath will come to each one of those who
> violate the oath.

But in the Christian writings too the esoteric, Mystery-atmosphere is noticeable.

Moreover, we can detect behind the traditions of nearly all the Gnostic and esoteric writings, outwardly concerned with the structure or evolution of spiritual worlds, or the mysteries of creation, underlying patterns of ritual process. There are allusions to purifications, baptisms in water and baptisms of the mind, investiture with priestly robes, symbolic acts of 'enthronement' and union with angelic or divine ambassadors of the higher worlds. This lavish backdrop of sacramental and ritual life is alien to the Old Testament world: but it suggests immediately the Mystery cults of the rest of the Near East, Egypt and Babylon, and the pagan cultures of the Mediterranean. One especially rich example, the *Gospel of Philip*, may throw light at last upon the sources of Christian sacramentalism, about which the canonical New Testament has virtually nothing to say — and also upon the particular Mystery-stream which flowed together in some secret way with emergent Christianity. At any rate, this channel of communication joining early Christian literature, Judaism and the pagan rites shows us a solution to the 'gap' between the older prophecies and the Christian fulfilment. Between the Old Testament and the Christian fulfilment lies a stage in which ideas such as that of the Messiah, or of the 'inner Adam,' were elaborated, transformed and spiritualized by esoteric groups. The immediate forerunner of Christianity was not the Judaism of the prophets and the scribes, but an esoteric Judaism like that of the Essenes or of others whose descendants were to become Gnostics.

Does this help explain too the current of rumours that have come down to us, that Christianity itself is essentially an esoteric religion? That its deeper meaning was imparted to 'those with ears to hear'? The *Gospel of Philip* speaks of baptism and the Eucharist in Christian life, but also of 'something which is higher than these.' And what of that passage, never really explained, in the first of the letters of Paul to Corinth which grandly asserts:

> For we speak a wisdom among the initiates, a wisdom not
> of this aeon, nor of the world-rulers of this aeon who are

> passing away. We speak a theosophy in a Mystery, an
> occult wisdom which God ordained before the
> aeons ... (2:6f)

Perhaps the newly discovered writings will help us break down the
barriers here too.

Even before the discoveries at Qumran and Nag Hammadi had
opened out for us this esoteric domain, there were some who saw
the connections they now so abundantly document. While most
theologians tried to ignore the fact that the Jesus of the Gospels had
little to do with the orthodox expectation of the Messiah, for
instance, a classical scholar opined that:

> The idea of a son of God born to save the world is
> essentially a Greek idea. All the Greek-speaking
> populations of the Levant were permeated by the old
> agricultural worship of the Renewal of Life in the New
> Year after the dead winter. The Renewal was of course
> conceived as a person. He was the fruit of the marriage of
> earth with Heaven through the spring Sun and Rain; a
> son of God and an earthly Kore or maiden; a babe who
> will become King and make all things new ... He was to
> save the life of the world, and above all to save man's
> soul. All the philosophy of the Hellenistic age is tinged
> with a mysticism which comes chiefly from a sublimation
> of this agricultural New Life, combined with the desire for
> *Gnosis*, Knowledge of God or union with God, of which
> there were germs in Plato and intense developments in
> the Egyptian and Oriental Mystery-cults.*

It proved highly difficult, however, to bridge the historical gap
between pagan Mystery and the Jewish teacher-reformer we know
from the Gospels, even in Matthew's account of the miraculous
child born of a virgin. But now in the *Gospel of Philip* we find such
passages as:

> If it is fitting to utter a Mystery, the Father of the All
> united with a virgin who came down, and edification
> illumined him. On that day he revealed the great Bridal
> Chamber. Therefore his body, which came into being on
> that day, came out of the Bridal Chamber. As he who

---

* Gilbert Murray, in A. Loisy, *The Birth of the Christian Religion*, London 1948,
Introduction.

came into being from the bridegroom and the bride, so
Jesus established the All in it by means of these.

Here the birth of the child is a mystic event, re-enacting the
generation of Adam from the Spirit and the 'virgin Earth,' and so
making the world new. Jesus reveals the mystic rebirth in the Bride
Chamber, the initiation-chamber which becomes, like the Mithraic
cave, an image of 'the All.'

Were the practices of the Philip-community marginal or deviant
types of Christianity, 'syncretistic' blendings of orthodox Christianity with pagan rites? Or do we have in them a clue to a phase when
the boundaries were not yet established, a formative phase, when
Christianity had not yet repudiated its origins in the Mysteries? The
sacraments mentioned in the *Gospel of Philip* have been studied in
detail, and rather than a marginal form of Christianity they suggest
a place in the mainstream of development. And whereas some of its
ideas suggest what the great heresy-hunter Irenaeus tells us about
Gnostic secessionists, 'there are others where the closest parallels are
to be found not in Irenaeus' discussions of Gnostic theories but in
his own Demonstration of the Christian faith.'* As for the Mystery-
significance it attaches to baptism and its account of resurrection,
there seem to be signs of the influence of Paul. After all, Christian
baptism has repeatedly invited comparison with Mystery procedures:

> In the Eleusinian mysteries, for example, there was an
> official in charge of such rites, called a *hydranos*. A marble
> relief from the fourth century BC depicts a goddess,
> probably Persephone, in this role, pouring water from a
> phial over a young, nude figure; it cannot fail to remind
> us us of the earliest pictures of Christian baptism, six
> centuries later.†

Attempts to link Christianity to the Mysteries have sometimes led
to sweeping conclusions, e.g. that Jesus never lived but was a
'nature myth' or things of that sort. But one scholar who drew
exactly the opposite conclusion has managed to dominate a surprising amount of twentieth century New Testament thought. Rudolf
Bultmann realized that the Mystery-connection need not lead away
from the historical situation of Jesus' world. He noticed in particular

---

* R. McL. Wilson, *Gnosis and the New Testament*, Oxford 1968, p.97.

† Wayne Meeks, *The First Urban Christians*, Yale 1983, p.152.

the ideas about a 'secret Adam' and a myth of salvation preserved by the semi-Jewish community called the Mandeans. Their secret scriptures spoke of a series of incarnations of this Primal Man, or of his emissaries and apostles who appeared among humankind as teachers or 'revealers.' The Mandeans still survive in parts of Iran and Iraq today, and they still practise rites of initiation including baptisms which often suggest what we know of the earliest Christian usage. Historical analysis does indeed support the view, however, that they had their origin among the esoteric and Gnostic sects of the Jordan valley around the time of Christ. Did they provide the Mystery-background of Christianity, the cosmic myth invoked by Paul? Much in the Gospel of John also has an uncanny resemblance to some of their ideas. But the attempt to explain everything in Christianity from the Mandeans soon brought dis-satisfaction among scholars. Only now have the new discoveries brought a denser, richly coloured picture in which the Mandean connections may fall into place. (The *Gospel of Philip* quotes from one of their secret scrolls, for example.) More enduring was the basic response to the realization that a myth had been present at the heart of Christianity: the programme of 'de-mythologizing' has been relentlessly pursued by many theologians anxious to rescue Christianity for the modern man.

In its own way this is just as extreme as the dismissal of Christ as nature-myth, and some are coming to question whether the essence of Christianity really remains when we strip away the language in which the early Christians expressed themselves. De-mythologizing shows up our own unwillingness to understand a consciousness other than our own, to respond to ideas at the very point where the older expectations and prophecies were being transformed and Christianity was coming into being. It asserts an unwillingness to enter into them except in so far as they lead to our own accepted ways of thought and assumptions which we do not wish to see challenged. Yet Christianity is, and ought to be, a challenge. And we are being challenged by the power of a myth, joined to the historical events of Christian origins — all the more so now that the Gnostic and esoteric element in the picture has been graphically restored to us. This fusion of myth with the unique events of the life of Jesus may be the most brilliantly original achievement of Christianity. Hence before we approach our documents in more detail, we should pause to consider the work of

a thinker who proposed an alternative path to de-mythologized
Christianity, though it is one which takes account of the changing
consciousness of man and does not urge us to retreat into the
mythic past. Rudolf Steiner argued in his book *Christianity as
Mystical Fact* that Christianity had deep roots in the pagan Mysteries
as well as in the Jewish religion. But he did not therefore conclude
that Christian belief had somehow to be rescued from its mythological sources.

He realized that the questions about the background of Christianity could never be shelved finally in the way the early Church had
wished. Even if no discoveries had been made to bring them to our
notice, modern consciousness would not have been able to acquiesce
in the uncertainties which the situation produced. In fact, the crisis
had been looming since the Reformation and he foresaw the end of
the line that has now been reached by some Protestant theology.
The supposedly absolute authority of the Bible has there led to
almost total scepticism; the incomparable text has turned out to be
a myth as well. But Steiner pointed out that the study of the
Mysteries enables us to see what the sacred mythologies actually
meant to the initiates. We can comprehend the experience which the
Mysteries conveyed, and which Christianity transferred to historical
events — to the actual life and sufferings of Jesus. We shall often
have cause to refer to his insights. What he suggested was not a
reduction of Christianity to the ancient Mysteries that had gone
before. He argued that there must have been a process of reinterpretation, with gradual stages, which led to the more individualistic,
personal relationship to God that emerged in Christianity. The
Church had tried to fix that relationship in a particular form. But its
potential might actually by no means be exhausted.

The discoveries of the Dead Sea Scrolls and the Gnostic library
from Nag Hammadi have gone far to affirm such a view of Christianity historically. In the writings of the 'Scrolls' from Qumran we
see already in the Judaism at the time of Christian beginnings a new
rapprochement with the Mysteries: esoteric rites, spiritual discipline
and the experience of 'illumination,' combined with the Law and
with the Jewish emphasis on community. The texts from Nag
Hammadi show us a 'Mystery'-form of Christianity, with Jesus as
the cosmic divinity — and above all, the mythological imagination
surviving in its most vivid and vital form, on a scale which no-one
would have dared to predict from the references to the Gnostic

'systems' that had come down *via* the Fathers of the Church. The transitional stages which Steiner had assumed are now most richly documented, and in their own way exhibit the playing out of just those issues of mythology against history, cosmic reality against individual identity, which Christianity fuses into its 'mystical fact.' Most startling of all, however, a short fragment from a 'secret Gospel of Mark' (which may simply be the original form of our Gospel in the New Testament) connects Jesus himself with Mystery activities.

The drama of the modern consciousness, then, may be being enacted in its historical origins here in these documents from apparently obscure religious movements whose very existence was almost disguised by the later orthodoxies of Judaism and Christianity alike. Their rediscovery may mean that we can understand for the first time our own spiritual situation, and by resolving it into its original clarity once more we may even be able to take a step further in that evolution of consciousness which, according to Steiner, is still going on.

The selections I have made here aim at conveying the inner reality of the esoteric experience: the intense struggles of the Essene to live in the 'age to come' which is already there for his higher consciousness, the visionary illumination of the Gnostic and the cosmic scope of his 'awakening.' They are also texts specially connected to emerging Christianity, and do not attempt to cover every aspect of Gnosticism or anything else. However interesting some of those developments were which led in other directions, the amazing diversity of images found a strong counter-pull in the unique historical event which took place on Golgotha, and it is that — anticipated in the Messianic prophecies yet overturning their assumptions of a triumphant leader with that of a dying God, foreshadowed in cosmic imagery yet happening as an individual agony — which anchors the fantastic brilliance of the inner life of the Mysteries in earthly terms to give an new impetus to man's spiritual life.

1. The Mandean Mystery

The scholarly research of the first half of this century, prior to the epoch-making finds just mentioned, had already found in the little sect of the Mandeans one small window into the esoteric world which linked the pagan Mysteries with the Jewish world. This glimpse proved exhilarating, indeed too much so for many as we can see from the 'Mandean fever' which infected New Testament scholarship in the 1930's. We realize nowadays that attempts to trace everything back to the Mandeans must give way to a recognition of their place in a more complex picture: but the excitement was essentially the thrill of recognizing in their esoteric theology something that formed part of the immediate backdrop to Christian origins. Their writings are still vitally important, because they show us better than anything else which has survived the nature of the Mysteries in the very region and almost exactly the time of Jesus' own life.

The Mandeans take their name from the Semitic word *manda*, knowledge or *gnosis*. Today they form a small and ever-shrinking community of believers in parts of Iran and Iraq, with their own religious literature and customs, their own dialect of Mandaic (closely related to Aramaic, the spoken language of Palestine at the time of Jesus, now extinct) and their own traditions about their history. Virtually nothing was known until the early twentieth century about any of these, mainly on account of the secret, esoteric character attaching to their teachings. Lady Stefana Drower was responsible for winning their trust and obtaining access in the end even to their priestly scrolls, when she went out to learn their language and explore their beliefs. Her books about them still form an invaluable source of fascinating information.*

Subsequent analysis of their sacred texts and traditions has confirmed the basic accuracy of their tale. The nature of their language confirms that they did indeed once reside in the region of the Jordan valley, and agrees with the idea that they were there in the time of Jesus. The 'historical' parts of their books, which are

* See Lady Stefana Drower, *The Mandaeans of Iraq and Iran*, Oxford 1939, and especially her *The Secret Adam. A Study of Nasoraean Gnosis*, Oxford 1960.

really legend based on oral tradition later written down, describe
their flight to escape persecution in the chaotic time following the
Roman conquest of Jerusalem, and there is no reason to doubt that
this furnished the motive for the move to the east. In addition to
material deprivations and horrors after the fall of Jerusalem in 70
AD, Judaism reacted to defend itself by concentrating religious
authority in 'orthodox' teachings and teachers, the Rabbis. The
exciting phase of openness and the meeting of ideas was over.
Mandaism's 'position as a minority opposition evidently led to the
persecution of the community and finally to its emigration from its
native Jordan territory,' writes a modern expert, Kurt Rudolph, 'to
the east, to begin with in Harran and the Median hill-country, then
in the southern regions of Mesopotamia.' The early Christian
community may have had to flee for identical reasons to Pella in the
Transjordan. It would be a mistake to suppose, however, that the
two groups would have had much sympathy for each other. The
only knowledge of Christianity evinced by the Mandean scriptures
is hostile knowledge. It may be that they knew Jesus only as one
who had betrayed Mysteries similar to theirs, and so portray him as
a false prophet:

> And he was called by the name of 'good-for-nothing
> Messiah' and he led them all astray and made them like
> himself, who perverted the words of light and changed
> them into darkness.

Despite the many resemblances to Christian rites, therefore, we may
assume that there has been no Christian influence on the Mandean
community. Their evidence stands independently pointing to a
common background in the Mysteries of Palestine.

Other elements in Mandaism on the other hand are undoubtedly
later accretions. Studies have demonstrated that Mandean traditions
concerning John the Baptist are secondary — they probably
originate from a time when persecution again loomed, now from
their Arab neighbours, and it was necessary to claim descent from
some prophet mentioned in the Qur'ān with honour. That must be
why John's name is always cited in the Arabic form *Yahya*. The
notion that the Mandeans might turn out to be disciples of John the
Baptist who clung to their original master, rejecting Jesus, has sadly
had to be abandoned by serious scholarship. In reality the sources
of their esoteric ideas are much older. Their highly elaborated rituals
centre around baptism, it is true, but they look back directly to

pagan Mystery rites, especially those of ancient Babylon. There already we know that there were purifications, washings and anointings, connected with themes of cosmic ascension or of descent into the underworld and rising to life. The old Babylonian wisdom-god Ea guarded the springs of 'living water' which welled up from the *apsu,* the abyss from which all things originated. The initiate-king played the role of Ea's divine son Marduk, the creator, in a New Year Festival at Babylon which included certain rites per-formed in secrecy in a special holy place or 'House of Creation.' And according to the myths retold at the Festival, the god or king died and was temporarily imprisoned in the 'underworld moun-tain,' the hollow interior which on a related but different plane of symbolism could be seen simultaneously as the belly of a cosmic monster who had swallowed him up, or as a cosmic womb from which he would be reborn and 'ascend into heaven' before his father Ea.* The central Mystery-themes are woven together: the inner process of death and rebirth, a new beginning; the fight with the monster which leads to victory over the forces of chaos within and without; the ascension, or expansion of consciousness which gives to the individual experience a cosmic significance. All of these are echoed in the Mandean Mystery, which also retains the sym-bolism of royalty. Every initiated Mandean is called a 'king,' though his crown is a 'crown of light,' the shining aura rather than a crown of gold. Many of these strands can be seen in a beautiful and profound poem recited by the initiate, now included in the *Canonical Prayerbook.* According to Lady Drower it is also one of the oldest parts of their liturgy.

The initiatory recital tells how the soul was 'raised up' to new life through a baptismal Mystery. The waters of baptism are still called 'jordan,' even though the community has now wandered far away from its original home. The rite features a sacred meal of bread and 'wine' (unfermented grape-juice), and a kind of ritual of adoption wherein the initiate is placed on the knees of the Father. By means of similar gestures the initiate-kings of ancient Egypt and Babylon were adopted by the gods and as 'sons' ruled in their cosmic power.

* See the fine account of the festival in H. Frankfort, *Kingship and the Gods,* Chicago 1978, pp.313ff. The text of the poem which was recited at the celebrations is translated by N.K. Sandars in *Poems of Heaven and Hell from Ancient Mesopotamia,* Harmondsworth, 1971. The inner dimension of the poem is discussed by Rudolf Steiner, *True and False Paths,* London 1969, pp.33ff.

Then there is spoken 'the name of the Mighty Life,' which is a Mandean circumlocution for God, who as in the Gospel of John is Life and Light. All this takes place in the sacred enclosure and the cultic hut which the modern community, mindful of more prosperous days, still refer to grandly as a 'Temple.' In the text it is called the 'House of Life,' and is an image of the cosmos, again picking up archaic Babylonian ideas and terminology: the initiate 'looks up to heaven,' i.e. to his cosmic origins, when he stands within it. That is the source of his strength, which he needs to overcome the initiatory ordeals.

He looks back to his origins in another way too. The Father who takes him to the waters of rebirth is said to 'plant' him, and the picture evokes another aspect of the Babylonian temple. 'It is clear, for instance,' writes F.H. Borsch in a wide-ranging study,

> that several Near Eastern temples had in their precincts a *garden* (the garden of the gods) in which were located the tree and waters of life ... Many times the king is pictured holding a twig or plant in one hand, while in the other he grasps a cup or vase of water. Occasionally we see him watering his tree of life. He is so closely associated with these that he can even be identified with them and himself be seen as the tree under which his people find protection and as the source of the life-giving water.*

That 'Paradise' or garden of the gods which the Bible tells us was lost in earthly history could still be found, it seems, through the inner quest of the Mysteries. The king remained as a link between the world of the gods and ordinary mortals. Later, when other individuals as well as the king were granted access to these things and the Mysteries were gradually 'democratized,' the adepts still used this symbolism of the living source of water, welling up from hidden depths, and the 'plant' or 'tree' of Paradise which grows again in the soul of the initiate. Through death and rebirth it is possible to find again the primordial reality, the source of growth and renewal lost in external life. And in some versions, the idea grew up that in the 'age to come' Paradise would appear again for all to see: that would be when the ultimate king, the Messiah, came into the world. For the Mandeans, however, such an 'historical' reinterpretation of the myth does not come into consideration. For them, these are realities only accessible to the initiated, to those who

---

* F.H. Borsch, *The Son of Man in Myth and History*, London 1967, p.98.

have entered into their own depths and discovered there the truths to which the symbols point.

That of course requires courage, as well as inner discipline and knowledge of the forces that are unleashed; and if not rightly controlled, the energies which initiation taps may indeed wreak psychic havoc. The myth for that reason provides the adept with a prototype, the divine model. In the Mandean Mystery, the Father himself goes before the 'Soul' of the seeker, entering the underworld mountain, the elemental fire and the 'sea' of waters and calling upon it to follow. Behind the pattern we still recognize the figure of the king-god Marduk, who himself died into the mountain and was reborn, the king being the representative or 'father' of his people. At each stage the ordinary consciousness or lower self of the initiand shrinks back in fear, thinking only of its own survival and unable to comprehend how it might really be enriched and deepened by throwing itself into the new experience and obeying the Father's call. But at each stage its timorous voice is overcome by the deeper-lying determination of the seeker, and above all by his trust in his heavenly origin and his patience in waiting for God's grace to bring the right moment for the achievement of his goal.

It is very striking, throughout the visionary recital, that the experience is not recounted from the viewpoint of a single consciousness, in the modern subjective or personal sense. The individual undergoing it is at the outset a clamouring diversity of voices, all of which are in some sense himself and yet are each something greater or lesser than himself. The call of the Father is in one sense his own higher self urging him to risk everything to become what he is divinely intended to be — hence what he finds through initiation is less God in the abstract than 'the life of my Self' which shares in the divine life. The cowardly voice of fear is also in a certain way himself, yet less than himself since by obeying it he would never find the courage truly to be anything at all. Another self and another voice is the Soul which recounts the ritual experience, rhythmically repeating the formulae for each variation and affirming the effectiveness of the Mystery process; still another is the questioner who begins each section — he may be a priest intoning the question, but the question must become that which a man takes up and asks his own soul before there can be any answer! Thus all the 'selves' are partly inside, partly outside the seeker, and his quest is to still the clamour of these competing voices and find the deeper unity, the 'life of my Self' in its cosmic dimension: as part of 'the Mighty Life' in whose name the ritual is acted out.

The Mystery points back to an earlier kind of consciousness, less individualized than our modern self-awareness, more based on the sense of belonging in a larger whole and sharing in a universal life. The festivals associated with the Mystery-rites expressed the same ideas in popular form, and the initiates deepened them into direct spiritual perception of the common ground of life. The initiates were by no means estranged from the popular religious and social life through their 'secret' rites: they were indeed the source from which it sprang and took its rejuvenating power. The Mandean Mystery still has this archaic character, and held together the wandering community over many centuries. It is pre-eminently a Mystery of the Father, the universal model. Christianity was to bring the modern kind of individualism into the Mystery-experience, putting it in some ways on a different plane. At the same time, its themes of death, rebirth and cosmic ascension, its baptismal rites and cultic meal of bread and wine remarkably foreshadow Christianity, and in the recently discovered *Gospel of Philip* we have evidence of a direct link between the Mystery and Christianity itself.

The Mandean rite cannot be explained purely out of the Babylonian background, however. Its symbolism of Light and Darkness, its much-used symbolic handshake which signifies 'redemption,' its ritual banners and many other details point to a further major influence: the dualistic Mysteries of ancient Iran. The elements of fire and water in the Mandean Mystery evidently stand for the cosmic polarity. For at least in the version of the Iranian teachings ascribed to the Chaldean prophet Zaratas it was said:

> that there are two original causes of things, father and mother, and that father is Light and mother Darkness, and that of the Light the parts are hot, dry, not heavy but light and swift; but of Darkness, cold, moist, weighty, slow; and that out of all these, from male and female, the world consists.

Similar ideas underlie the Mysteries which in pagan form spread through the Roman and the whole Mediterranean world under the authority of the old Iranian god of light, Mithra or Mithras. In fact, when we look at Mandaism and the Mithraic Mysteries we observe many obvious similarities in their rites and customs as well as in their cosmological teachings. The Mysteries of Mithra likewise are

a blend of Babylonian as well as Iranian ideas, with water-rites analogous to baptism involving light-symbolism and anointing with oil,
a sacred meal that was so like the Christian Eucharist that it severely
embarrassed the proselytizing Fathers of the Church, and others such
as the *dexiosis* or ritual grasping of the right hand which reminds us
even more strongly of the gestures performed by the Mandeans.

We have then a complex of Mystery-ideas, developing from
Babylonian foundations but influenced powerfully by Iranian
concepts, spreading out into the Mediterranean world around the
time of Christian beginnings. Starting from similar premises, the
Mysteries evolved in different ways. Mithraism assimilated many of
the characteristics of Greek and Roman religion, for instance, and
eventually developed its own synthesis of rites and images,
organizing itself as a 'secret brotherhood' (though one that was
ostentatiously loyal to the Empire). There are signs that Mandaism
too was part of a successful movement, and analogies e.g. with the
description of the cult among the Sabaeans of Harran in later times
suggest that this type of Mystery was once more widespread. The
Mandeans are significant too in bringing together the streams of
Judaism and the Mysteries, and we shall discover how fruitful that
encounter was to be when we come to look at the writings of the
Essenes, who practised many similar rites and share in particular
the influence of Iranian Mystery-language with its polarity of Light
and Darkness. In the case of the Mandeans, however, the Jewish
encounter led in the end to an apparent collision of values and
goals. The startling way in which the themes of the Bible are
reworked from a completely different viewpoint in some of the
Mandean scriptures points straight to the world, which we shall also
explore, of Gnosticism.

Was Christianity also a part of this spreading of ideas? If we are
not afraid to acknowledge the 'myth' in Christianity, but understand
its reality in the inner life and experiences of the Mysteries, we need
not flee from such a recognition. Yet it is only by understanding the
inner reality of the ancient teachings that we can grasp their role in
the obscure process of Christian origins. At any rate, the initiatory
recital of the Mandeans gives us a starting-point in the presence of
the Mysteries in the Jordan valley at the time of Christ. That
presence may not be in itself the answer to the riddle of Christianity: but it is a first and, in the light of all the new evidence, an
extremely consequential clue.

Source: The Canonical Prayerbook of the Mandaeans, *No.30. Translated from Mandaic by E.S. Drower.*

1. 'The Life' is a standard Mandean expression for the absolute Being; in his utter transcendence he is often called 'the Great Alien Life.' He sends his divine messenger Manda d'Hayye ('Knowledge of Life') to impart salvation through the forms of his Mysteries. In the *Gospel of Thomas* Jesus is repeatedly called 'the Living One,' or 'Son of the Living' (Prologue, 37, 52, 59, and so on), and the language in the Gospel of John concerning the 'living bread' and suchlike has suggested to many scholars the Mandean teaching about a world of 'living,' that is, spiritual archetypes to which the initiate can be joined through a Mystery-rite.

2. To be 'raised up' in many of the Mysteries had a literal meaning. In Mithraism, the initiate was raised from a prone state (symbolically death and/or infancy) by the hierophant: the Christian Father Tertullian calls this a picture of (the) resurrection *(imaginem resurrectionis inducit)* — see M.J. Vermaseren 1963, pp.103 and 132; also R. Merkelbach 1984, Abbild 31 and commentary for the depiction of the scene in the Capua Mithraeum. Simon the Magus was called by the strange title of 'the Standing One' (see Chapter 4). Gnostic mythology often includes a scene of the primal Man or Adam being 'raised up' from the ground on which he lies inert by a divine messenger who imparts knowledge.

3. The Mandeans still call baptismal waters 'jordan' though they long ago left the Jordan region. Likewise every Mithraeum stands by a 'Euphrates,' so called even when it is only a tiny stream (Vermaseren 1963, p.37).

4. In Mithraism too the 'raising up' ceremony seems to have been intimately related to the sacred meal (Vermaseren loc. cit.).

5. The text switches confusingly between the ideas of climbing a mountain (cosmic ascension) and of entering the mountain (imprisonment in the underworld): both have a Babylonian background, shared by these several overlapping Mysteries. The Babylonian temple-ziggurat or step-pyramid represented the levels of the cosmic ascent: Marduk is shown striding up it to stand before his father Ea on cylinder seals, and in this sense the temple is an image of the world-mountain. A Mithraeum too, as is well known, represents an *imago mundi* and in it the initiates made a symbolic ascent through cosmic stages, led by the Pater (Father) who stands for the god. The other aspect concerns the overcoming of death or the fear of death. In Babylonian mythology and ritual, Marduk is temporarily defeated and held captive in the underworld or hollow interior of the world-mountain, but is rescued and restored to life/reborn. Mithraic temples took the form of underground 'caves': the god Mithras is said to be 'born from the rock' and this constitutes the model of the initiate's regeneration. Evidence of a direct link between this idea and Mysteries known in the Jewish environment is now furnished by the *Apocalypse of Adam* (see below p.217).

❊ The Mandean Mystery ❊

In the name of the Life![1]

"What did thy Father do for thee, Soul,
The great day on which thou wast raised up?"[2]

"He took me down to the jordan,[3] planted me,
And took me up and stood me upon its bank.
He broke and gave me bread,
Blessed the cup and gave me thereof to drink.[4]
He placed me between his knees
And pronounced over me the name of the Mighty Life.

"He passed into the mountain before me;[5]
He cried loudly that I might hear,
That I might hear he cried loudly,
    'If there is strength in thee, Soul, come!'
    'If I climb the mountain I shall fall;
I shall overturn and perish from the world!'
    I lifted mine eyes to heaven
And my soul waited upon the House of life.
    I climbed the mountain and fell not,
I came thither and found the life of my Self."

"What did thy Father do for thee, Soul,
The great day on which thou wast raised up?"

"He took me down to the jordan, planted me,
And took me up and stood me upon its bank.
He broke and gave me bread,
Blessed the cup and gave me thereof to drink.
He placed me between his knees
And pronounced over me the name of the Mighty Life.

6.   The theme of mastery over the elements is central to the Mysteries. Important
        here is the concept of the elements as forces both within us and as a larger
        reality in the 'great world.' The Mandean teachings include much about the
        'hidden fire,' that is, its inner aspect, and in this respect recalls much in
        Simon the Magus' *Great Annunciation* (see below p.163) and the mastery of
        the 'hidden forces' of the elements in the Essene writings (see Hymn 1 in
        Chapter 2 below). These forces can be creative or destructive: *gnosis* is the
        knowledge needed to control and make fruitful the energies within us which
        they represent by harmonizing them with the cosmos. Mithraism employed
        a very elaborate symbolism of the elements, assigned to various chambers in
        the temple, while the main space itself was designed 'for traversing the
        element of air by means of the seven planets ... He who passed through these
        ceremonies was, like the participant in the Isis mysteries, *vectus per omnia
        elementa* (transported through all the elements).' (C.W. Volgraff, cited in
        Vermaseren 1963, p.42).

7.   Lady Drower thus describes the Mandean rites: 'each is baptized singly, but
        the sacraments which must follow baptism are administered to a group. On
        the bank the baptized candidate makes a circuit of the fire and awaits in a
        crouching position the arrival of others who follow him into the baptismal
        waters. When these have joined him in their dripping white garments, they
        form a row facing the north ... A banner of white silk has been planted earlier
        in a spot to the right of the group, and before the ceremony began the brazier
        was kept supplied with a ritually-pure fuel. Into the brazier at certain
        moments incense is cast ... *Kushta* (the ritual handshake) is again performed
        with each communicant, and then the communicants return to the water's
        edge, immerse their right arms and hands, and return to the row. The priest
        passes along it with the sacred bread' (Drower 1956, p.230). He repeats the
        transit with wine in a bowl which, she notes, 'is of the same shape and size
        as the Parsi *fuliān*, and both resemble the Mithraic drinking-bowl as shown
        in bas-reliefs' (p.231).

8.   Here we have the water of the sea rather than the 'living water' of the river.
        In Babylonian myth the sea is in one aspect the chaos-monster Tiāmat who
        defeats Marduk in the initial encounter — whereas the other primordial being
        Apsu represents the 'sweet waters' which well up from the ground and are
        associated with Ea and Mystery-wisdom. In the structure of the ritual, the sea
        appears to stand for the dark, moist, feminine principle in contrast to the
        fiery, luminous, masculine principle, showing the influence of the dualism of
        ancient Iran. It is to be emphasised that both forces are necessary to existence,
        and rebirth. In Mithraism, Vermaseren discusses the pattern which shows
        Mithra as 'mediator' or Spiritus between Light and Darkness, and so
        'faithfully follows those Iranian conceptions which were incorporated into the
        mysteries of the Magi' (Vermaseren 1963, pp.106f).

"He passed into the fire before me;[6]
And cried aloud that I might hear,
That I might hear he cried aloud,
  'If there is strength in thee, Soul, come!'
  'If I go into fire I shall burn,
I shall scorch and perish from the world!'
To heaven I lifted mine eyes
And my soul waited upon the House of Life.
I went into fire and burned not,
I came, and found the life of my Self."

"What did thy Father do for thee, Soul,
The great day on which thou wast raised up?"

"He took me down to the jordan, planted me,
Took me up and stood me upon its bank.
He broke and gave me bread,[7]
Blessed the cup and gave me thereof to drink.
He placed me between his knees
And pronounced over me the name of the Mighty Life.

"He entered the sea before me;[8]
He cried aloud that I might hear,
That I might hear he cried aloud.
  'If there is strength in thee, Soul, come!'
  'If I go into the sea I shall sink,
I shall be overturned and perish from the world!'
To heaven I lifted mine eyes
And my soul waited upon the House of Life.
I went into the sea and was not drowned,
I came, the life of my Self I found,
Yea, Life! lo, Life! Life hath triumphed over this world
And Life is victorious."

2. The Essene Mysteries:
from the Dead Sea Scrolls

Until the discovery of the Dead Sea Scrolls at Qumran, it may be said that the Essenes were little more than a name to most theologians and scholars of the New Testament. All that changed with the extraordinary documents that emerged from the caves in the bleak hillside near the ancient 'monastic' settlement. Previously all that had been known about Essenism came from a few references in authors such as Josephus, Philo of Alexandria or the geographer Pliny. Now, the experts soon agreed, we possessed a whole library of works by Essene writers, lovingly copied along with the sacred books of the Bible in their *scriptorium* at Qumran.

There were many surprises. The public caught the mood and 'the Scrolls' became rather unexpectedly famous, a household word; later, a mood of caution set in which offset the initial infectious excitement. Today, some of the texts are still not made available to interested readers. Be that as it may, the writings from Qumran had long since upset the applecarts of scholarship. The hints in ancient authors concerning their remarkable doctrines had not prepared us for the striking inner world conjured up by the Scrolls. The fact that the Essenes were regarded, alongside the better-known Pharisees and Sadducees, as a third Jewish party, had made scholars think that they must be close in spirit to mainstream Judaism. It is easy to forget that the mainstream of Judaism only took its modern shape at a later date, after the Jewish wars. It turned out that in the centuries before Christ, the Jewish world had been open to a greater variety of ideas than anyone had expected — with an important exception to which I must return. What no-one had been able to predict from the written evidences was the fundamental difference which marks off the Essenes from most interpreters of the Jewish scripture: their orientation toward a cosmic religion.

The old prophets of Israel had led the discovery of the spiritual meaning of the 'I am.' They had identified the divine 'I AM' which

is at the root of Israel's destiny.* They had established on the basis
of it that powerful, direct relationship with God as a people which
shines through so much of the Old Testament. The relationship had
its struggles, its inner tensions. But the conviction that God would
be true to his people if they were faithful to him was unshakeable,
because he had given them their very identity. The history of the
relationship occupied the pages of the scriptures as the history of
the people of God. In its intensity it quite displaced the older Near
Eastern heritage from the cosmic religion of the Semites (such as the
Babylonians and the Phoenicians), the cyclic drama of seasonal
renewal. But now the recovery of the Essene writings brought a
novel twist into the story. Here, far on in the history of Judaism,
only a century or so before Christ, was an interpretation of the Bible
that said little about its sacred history. Though the Essenes searched
the Bible for spiritual meaning, they found it when it was set in the
context of their own cosmic revelations. Their Teacher of Righteousness (or Righteous Teacher) had shown them a new, hidden sense
in the scriptures. It was a meaning that spoke once more of a cosmic
struggle, of a Spirit of Light and a Spirit of Darkness who 'walk
with man' and are at war everywhere.

This cosmic meaning behind the surface of the scripture could
not be found by all. It could only be grasped by those who knew
the spiritual experiences, the inner light of divine 'knowledge'
which had come to the Teacher and would likewise come to those
who followed his path. But they must first be initiated. There
were long stages of preparation, or purification through study and
rite, described in the *Community Rule* of the Qumran Essenes — a
book which may well go back in its primary form to the Teacher
himself. Repeated baptisms formed an important part of the
community's life, and are characterized in terms which suggest John
the Baptist. John offered a hope to all Israel. But in the closed
community of the Essenes, the baptismal experience could be
intensified through repetition. The moral and intellectual 'new
beginning,' the 'change of mind' which is the deeper significance in
John's *metanoia* (traditionally rendered 'repentance'), deepened into
an inner rebirth. There was an 'illumination': the Essene became a
'son of Light.'

Only those who had undergone the inner process were allowed

* See Rudolf Steiner, *The Apocalypse of St John*, London 1977, pp.21ff.

to remain in the Community. Total commitment was then demanded, and all their worldly goods became communal property.
(A let-out clause for those who could not face the final step allowed
them to reclaim their property and leave after two years.) An Essene
became a member of the deliberative assembly, and attended the
cultic meals of the Community which were evidently experienced
as ritual occasions, anticipating the great cultic meal to be held in
the presence of the Messiah — an idea that seems to lie behind the
scene of the Last Supper especially in the version of the Gospel of
Matthew. Life in the Community was strictly ordered; any aberra-
tion was punishable by the authorities, under the Guardian or
Master. Care was provided for the sick and elderly in a sort of
communistic welfare system. Ritual and study of the sacred texts
bulked large in the curriculum of daily life. Through their illumination, the Essenes felt that they were already living in a new age-
about-to-begin. For their higher consciousness it was already made
manifest.

With its structure of insiders/outsiders, its 'illuminated' teachings, its psychological emphasis on transformation and the cosmic
dimension of Light and Darkness, Essenism has strikingly little in
common with the kind of Judaism scholars expected to find in
Palestine at the time of Jesus. It is nothing less than a Mystery in the
heart of the Jewish world. Its rites are all essentially rites of
initiation, which led its adepts to a deeper knowledge of the
'mysteries' of God's purpose. Evidence is increasingly coming to
light of the visionary nature of the experiences on which their
knowledge was based: we meet references to ascent into heaven, to
the vision of God's Throne-Chariot or of the 'work of creation' (both
subjects regarded as esoteric in Judaism).

Essenes were famous in antiquity for their powers of prophecy.
In the writings from Qumran there are fragmentary texts on
astrology and occult physiognomy, other sources refer to alchemy.
At the same time, the Essenes were devout worshippers of the
Jewish God. Theirs was not an alien religion but a higher wisdom
within the religion of the people. Until events forced a break, it
seems, Essenes were habitually present in the Temple and a special
quarter in Jerusalem continued to be associated with them. Their
history was bound up with that of their time, and their 'apocalyptic'
ideas of a new age beginning are reflected in more popular forms
in Jewish writings, often presented in a literal and catastrophic

manner as a miraculous overthrowing of Israel's enemies and an age of effortless peace and plenty. The Essenes knew the reality behind these apocalyptic images. They knew that the new beginning was visible only to those who were able to see it, that it would come about through spiritual and not only material change (though they expected that to come too).

The new age would belong to history, and not only to the inner world as in the pagan Mysteries. The older Mysteries, as we have seen, looked back to the origins of things and abolished history by recreating the time of creation. At the deepest level, in the heart of the initiate, the divine power was felt to be still active. The Essene Mystery too had a link with Paradise. It is hinted at in the *Community Rule*, the basic document of the Essene community at Qumran. As well as the rules for their way of life, the *Rule* contains a hymn or poem embodying the inner principle of their existence in a kind of shared affirmation of their experience:

> For from the source of His righteousness
>   is my justification,
> and from His marvellous mysteries
>   is the light in my heart.
> My eyes have gazed
>   on that which is eternal,
> on wisdom concealed from men,
> on knowledge and wise design
> (hidden) from the sons of men ...
> God has given them to His chosen ones
>   as an eternal possession,
> and has caused them to inherit
>   the lot of the Holy Ones.
> He has joined their assembly
>   to the Sons of Heaven
> to be a Council of the Community,
> a foundation of the Building of Holiness,
> an everlasting Plant throughout all ages to come.

The community is a 'plant' or 'tree,' not of the growing and withering kind but an 'everlasting' one such as flourished in Eden. It is a tree of knowledge, and for those with the inner vision it can still be seen. The Essene texts describe the initiatory process as the opening of the gates of Paradise and eating of the immortal fruit.

This is the blessing which has been given them by God, as another hymn asserts:

> For these hast Thou planted a Tree
> which blooms with flowers unfading,
> whose bough puts forth thick leaves,
> which stands firm-planted for ever,
> and gives shade to all things;
> whose branches tower to heaven,
> whose roots sink down to the abyss.
> All the rivers of Eden
> water its boughs ...

The paradisal Tree is also a cosmic symbol, linking the regions of heaven, earth and the depths of the abyss. It stands for the all-encompassing vision of the initiate, *gnosis*, and for the esoteric community — but it is also an active power, growing in the world and establishing a new order. Inner reality will transform outer reality. The gates of Paradise will be opened as an actual, historical event by the Messiah when he comes to fulfil the Essenes' prefiguration of the age-to-come. The Messiah himself is also a 'scion' or 'shoot' of David — a term which as we can see contains deeper significance than we usually perceive.

Thus the Essenes were evolving a kind of cosmic Mystery which could be translated into the consciousness of the Jewish people, with their understanding of history. The higher development which they have achieved through initiation brings knowledge and gifts which can gradually be made part of the awareness of humankind as a whole. History thereby gains a mysterious further dimension. The Essenes scrutinized the writings of the Old Testament for those deeper meanings. In the *Book of Jubilees*, a work from the Essene tradition which antedates the writings we now possess from the discovery at Qumran, the histories of the patriarchs, the stories of Abraham, of Jacob and Esau, and so forth, are viewed as episodes in a larger struggle, of God and Beliar (Satan), of Light and Darkness. The Essenes' references to their own community's history are shrouded in esoteric symbolism and hidden meanings: so much so that there is still no generally agreed reconstruction of events among scholars who have studied them.

All this is to say that the sources and origins of the Essene teachings lay only partly in the Old Testament, and in the symbols

such as the Tree in Paradise which it contained. To comprehend
them fully we must also look at the impact of spiritual teachings
from a different quarter: the ancient religion of the prophet
Zarathustra.

Zoroastrianism may without doubt lay claim to being the oldest
of the 'revealed religions' — those, that is to say, which originate
from the message of a specific teacher or prophet rather than
honouring universal and spiritual powers like those of the Greeks,
Romans or Hindus. The prophet himself is almost lost in grey
antiquity. Scholars used to incline toward the classical authors'
estimate of his date at around the sixth century BC; many would
now date him hundreds of years earlier, and some even thousands
of years before Christ. Many legends about him have survived, and
a core of historical fact. Most amazing among the survivals are
perhaps the *Gathas*, hymns attributed to Zarathustra himself which
were embedded in the Zoroastrian liturgy. They share some of the
characteristics we know from other prehistoric poetry, such as
that of the Norse Eddas, and are preserved in a form of Indo-
European language which is linguistically older than the Sanskrit
of the Vedas. Everything speaks in support of their immense age
and authenticity. But they are therefore difficult to translate and to
understand, even before we allow for their profound and indeed
esoteric character. Without the Zoroastrian tradition which grew up
on the basis of their teachings, it would be extremely hard to
interpret them at all.

Their evidence, together with the stories about his life, suggest
that Zarathustra was born in prehistoric times in eastern Iran. At
first his message had little response from the tribes to which he
belonged, but gradually his teaching spread. At some stage it won
over the powerful tribe of the Medes, one of the Iranian peoples
whose conquests brought them an extensive empire. One particular
caste among the Medes, called the Magi from the ancient word
magu, priest, were especially devoted to the 'good Religion,' as it
came to be called, and in historical times they alone were privileged
to perform the Zoroastrian rituals of worship and initiation. The
Magi became famous in the civilizations of the ancient world for
their mastery of the sacred element of fire, as well as for their
mysterious wisdom and strange powers. When the empire of the
Medes expanded, they went everywhere to serve as priests and
spread their spiritual influence. And when the empire of the Medes

was swallowed up in the still greater empire of another Iranian people, the Persians, they still acted in their priestly role across the world, from Ethiopia to India, from Babylon to Samarkand. Only when Alexander the Great seized the Persians' empire and added it to that of the Greeks did the world see a larger dominant power. With the rise of the great world-empires, communications were opened up between East and West; the movements of conquest were soon replaced by movements and meetings of ideas. The teachings of Zarathustra were a potent influence on the rise of Greek philosophy, and on the ethical and spiritual teachings of the religions of the ancient world, especially the Mysteries. During the 'Babylonian captivity,' the leaders of fallen Israel in their enforced exile would certainly have come across their ideas. It was under the Persian Cyrus that the rebuilding of the Temple in Jerusalem was authorized: a gesture which led to the flourishing of a new phase in Jewish history. Did it also lead to the opening up of spiritual contacts?

The orthodox handling of events in Jewish tradition would suggest not. The story told by the guardians of its spiritual history is of unswerving devotion to the religion of the Old Testament covenant. But on a more esoteric level, among those who saw that the consciousness of divine purpose in history and the cosmic wisdom of the Mysteries need not ultimately be in contradiction with each other, it is conceivable that more openness existed. Rudolf Steiner's spiritual investigations, his insights into the deeper history of consciousness, convinced him that a meeting between these complementary currents in the evolution of humanity did take place, and led to a new development in esoteric circles, among the Essenes. And the Dead Sea Scrolls have amply shown him to be right. The flowing together of these currents came to a head in the centuries immediately preceding the origins of Christianity and, as Steiner already pointed out, were the *sine qua non* of the Christian breakthrough — the new relationship between God and man achieved through Christ.

The ancient prophet Zarathustra had been transported in vision to the heavenly world of pure, immaterial light. He had known there the presence of the Wise Lord, Ahura Mazdah, who had revealed to him his creative power in its six aspects. But the Wise Lord had also revealed the existence of the Evil Spirit, Angra Mainyush, the power of darkness and destruction. Over the centuries or even millennia of transmission, the terms were contracted into the names familiarly given to the contrary powers in the classic Zoroastrian texts: Ohrmazd and Ahriman, the spirit of Light and the spirit of Darkness, ever at war. According to Zarathustra, theirs was an eternal duality to which we can see no beginning. However, because God or Ohrmazd has the standpoint of eternity from which to view these things, he is able to promise us (through his prophet) that Light will ultimately prevail and Darkness cease to be — but only in eternity, after the end of our temporal universe. Therefore we should choose the Light, the Good, the Truth rather than the Darkness, which is the Lie, the Unreal, the Transient; thus we will inherit eternal existence. Our destiny, in the profound vision of Zoroastrianism, is actually a part of the destiny of the universe, that wider mixture of Light and Dark. Indeed, our destiny is a part of the destiny of God as it is in all the cosmic Mysteries. At least seen from below, God himself is caught up in the life-and-death struggle with Ahriman which is the condition of the cosmos we know. From a higher perspective, from eternity, God transcends the struggle. Some forms of Zoroastrian teaching therefore speak of God as beyond the two spirits, calling him Zervan (Eternal Time). This was not so much a heresy as a deeper teaching within the Zoroastrian church, and indeed the term Zervan is already used in the so-called *Younger Avesta*, consisting of very ancient though not the oldest Zoroastrian texts. Later in the history of the 'good Religion,' it became the basis of a renewed form of the teaching in which (as we shall see) it exerted a fascinating if largely underground influence on many spiritual movements in the Mediterranean and ancient Near Eastern worlds.

And now imagine the surprise of the scholars who first deciphered and translated the *Community Rule* of the Essenes at Qumran when they came to a passage of cosmic instruction, teaching that the world is divided between the spirits of Light and Darkness:

> From the God of Knowledge comes all that is and
> happens ... He has created man to govern the world, and
> has appointed for him two Spirits in which to walk until
> the time of his visitation: the Spirit of Truth and the Spirit
> of Falsehood. Those born of Truth spring from a fountain
> of Light, but those born of Falsehood spring from a source
> of Darkness. All the children of righteousness are ruled by

the Prince of Light and walk in the ways of Light, but the
children of falsehood are ruled by the Angel of Darkness
and walk in the ways of Darkness.

One may without exaggeration call this passage the central statement of Essene theology. In it the God of Israel is honoured —
but not in the usual way, on the basis of biblical tradition and
the Temple cult. He is here 'the God of Knowledge,' the revealer
of wisdom to the Essene initiates. He is Lord of the cosmos — of
'all that is and happens' — rather than the God of the covenant
with a chosen people or their guide through history. He is the
power who determines the struggle of the two Spirits and its
outcome, the eventual triumph of Light at 'the time of his visitation.' Human beings are caught up in the struggle of Light and
Darkness, and what they are is dependent upon which side they
fight for. Man's relationship to the Prince of Light or to the Angel
of Darkness is an existential one. The worship of the Old Testament
God has been transformed to become a Mystery, and the thought-
forms which have made that possible are all drawn from the
Zoroastrian world of ideas and imaginations. The connection is so
strong that the author of the Essene passage must have known the
wonderful statement from the *Gathas* of Zarathustra preserved in
the liturgy (*Yasna* 30). 'There are so many parallels,' says one
modern authority, 'that this Iranian-Zoroastrian writing, which is
very much older, must have served as the foundation for the
Qumran text.'*

The inner confluence of spiritual traditions described by Steiner
can undoubtedly be seen in the case of the key Essene passage
incorporated in their *Community Rule*. As so often with the Qumran
texts, however, much remains inscrutably obscure about their
background. The only real evidence we have concerning the manner
in which the Mysteries made contact once more with the spirit of
Judaism comes from the repeated references in the 'Scrolls' to the
'covenant which was renewed in the land of Damascus.' It is true
that some who have studied the 'Scrolls' believe that 'Damascus'
is yet another code-word, a symbolic name for a place significant
in their own history rather than the city in Syria. But there is no
real reason to suspect the Essenes of such obscurantism, and there

---

* H. Burgmann, *Die essenischen Gemeinden von Qumran und Damascus*, Frankfurt am
Main 1988, p.22.

is also some corroborative evidence, e.g. that there continued to be
Essenes in the area of Damascus even after the community of
the writings we know had settled near the Dead Sea. Cardinal
Daniélou identified as Essene the religious settlement near Damascus with the interesting name Kokaba, the 'Star.' Later we hear of
further esoteric activities connected with the place. At any rate,
Damascus is an obvious meeting-point for people and ideas, since
it lies on the main route to the East, which necessarily skirts north
around the impassable deserts. Does the imaginative picture of the
Magi (Iranian priests) and their journey to Bethlehem, and the
mysterious star, have at least part of its inner meaning in the Essene
spirituality, absorbing into Judaism the teachings of the Mysteries
of Iran? One thing we know about Bethlehem is that, perhaps a
century and a half before the time of Jesus, it too was a centre of
Essene activity. Was it also the site of an enduring Essene community?

We have seen how the Gospel stories and the references in the
New Testament to the fulfilment of earlier, 'prophetic' ideas, may
presuppose more than just the Old Testament background preserved
by the Church. Some of the special, esoteric ideas connected with
the Essenes also have their fulfilment there. The expectations of
popular Judaism about the coming of the Messiah and his triumph
over Israel's enemies were modified by the profounder, more
spiritual idea of the cosmic triumph of the Light at the time of
God's visitation.

Long before Jesus, however, there arose among the Essenes a
great Teacher. He made no claim to be the Messiah, but he was a
prophet and one so deeply united with his work that his personal
name was no longer remembered. He features in the texts simply as
the *Moreh Zedek*, the Righteous Teacher (or Teacher of Righteousness). It is possible, and more than likely, that he is the one who
wrote or put together the *Community Rule*. He may also have
written the extraordinary work known rather innocuously as the
Temple Scroll, which is in fact one of the texts that would have
shocked any orthodox Jew beyond bearing: for it claims direct
vision of God and access to the very words he spoke to Moses,
presented in the biblical tradition as a unique and unrepeatable
revelation on Mount Sinai. 'Since then,' pointedly remarks Deuteronomy:

    no prophet has arisen in Israel like Moses, whom Yahweh

> knew face to face ... For no-one has ever shown the
> mighty power or performed the awesome deeds that
> Moses did in the sight of all Israel. (34:10-12)

The traditions of the Pharisees (later taken up by the Rabbis when they shaped Jewish orthodoxy) regarded prophecy therefore with suspicion. At most, a person might be granted the hearing of a divine voice *(bat kol)*. Even that, however, was to be subordinated to the written statements of the Bible and the Law. Yet the Righteous Teacher sets his own revelation on a par with that of the receiver of the Law himself; he makes himself equal in authority to the actual biblical revelation. The *Temple Scroll* is a creative reinterpretation of the Torah, the Law, different in spirit as well as in form from the interpretations advanced by other Jewish groups. There can be little doubt that it contains 'the "hidden Torah" of the Essenes.'*

Rudolf Steiner spoke frequently of a great Essene teacher in pre-Christian times, around 100 BC. According to Steiner, the Teacher was one of the great spiritual Masters, connected in particular with the power of speech, of the word. This figure seems identical with the *Moreh Zedek*, for among other things, the Scrolls contain some of the finest Hebrew poetry from ancient times. It has been strongly argued that some of these poems at least were written by the Teacher, and all of them deal with similar themes of the inner life of the community. The poems, which make up the so-called 'Thanksgiving Scroll,' may have been used for the purposes of meditation. They were almost certainly also used for liturgical purposes and as parts of the very process of initiation and illumination which was central to the Essene life. They are much more than pious hymns or imitations of the biblical psalms. They put into extraordinary language the deeper experiences of the Essene spiritual life, making great poetry which itself helped to produce the knowledge of their inner meaning among the meditants in the Order.

Before we come to the poems of initiation from the Dead Sea Scrolls, therefore, we can hardly put aside the question which has fascinated so many scholars of the Essene texts. Who was the poetic and religious genius of the Qumran community, and when did he live?

It is inevitably disappointing to those possessed of historical

* Y. Yadin, *The Temple Scroll*, Jerusalem 1984, p.229.

curiosity and those interested in the major personalities of religious
evolution that the Essenes expressed the events of their sect's past
in mystic and allusive terms, referring mainly to the fulfilment of
old prophecies, and that the imposing 'Teacher' is nowhere
mentioned by name. The lack of precise historical data has also led
to uncertainty over the dating of the Qumran texts; speculation has
ranged over several centuries. Here again, however, the writings
themselves in conjunction with the results of Rudolf Steiner's
researches can suggest an answer to the uncertainty. We must first
examine the riddling allusions of the texts more closely.

Let us start with the one solid factual identification. The *Commentary on Nahum* claims that a prophecy made in the Old Testament
book of Nahum has been realized in the person and actions of
'Demetrius king of Greece.' The situation described can readily be
identified. In the early first century BC, the Syrian-Greek king
Demetrius III tried to intervene in the affairs of Palestine and
overthrow the reigning Hasmonean priest-king Alexander Jannaeus
— unsuccessfully. The *Commentary* then refers to Alexander
Jannaeus under the image of a 'furious young lion who executes
revenge on those who seek smooth things and hangs men alive, a
thing never done formerly in Israel.' The 'seekers of smooth things'
seems to be the Essenes' way of indicating the Pharisees, who in
their eyes had compromised the true religious teaching. In fact,
according to Josephus, the prominent Jewish historian of the period,
eight hundred Pharisees were condemned to die on the   cross
following the disturbance. Such behaviour from a priest and a
divinely ordained ruler shocked all religious-minded men, and it is
highly likely therefore that Jannaeus is the figure who appears more
widely in the Qumran 'Scrolls' under the name of the Wicked Priest.
Some scholars have taken this as a starting-point for dating the
events described in the writings, and thus ascribe them to the reign
of Alexander Jannaeus, who ruled from 103 to 76 BC.*

'There is however,' writes A.R.C. Leaney, 'a difficulty in the
identification; the Wicked Priest is characterized largely by his
opposition to the Teacher of Righteousness, with whom he was
contemporary, so that the chronology must suit both.'† The

---

* Historical details have been worked out above all by M. Delcor and J. Carmignac.

† A.R.C. Leaney, *The Jewish and Christian World* (Cambridge 1984) p.178.

difficulty to which Leaney refers is that there is no obvious candidate in the reign of Alexander Jannaeus for the Teacher of Righteousness. A large number of scholars have therefore abandoned the identification of the Wicked Priest, and looked to the situation prevailing in Palestine c.170 for the setting of the Qumran scriptures.* Unfortunately, the same problem arises there: there is a good candidate for the Wicked Priest, but the various attempts to pin down the Teacher of Righteousness have failed to command wide assent, and some historians have abandoned the undertaking as hopeless.† This seems to be having the worst of both worlds, and throws away the only definite starting-point we have. The best solution is surely to stay with what factual evidence we have, i.e. for the period following 103 BC — especially as Steiner's descriptions cast a distinct light on an Essene teacher who flourished just at this time.

Steiner describes a great Essene prophet of around 100 BC:
> The task allotted to him was the spiritual guidance of
> the movement represented in the doctrines of the
> Therapeutae and Essenes and it was in these communities
> that his influence worked ... He is also known in Talmudic
> literature under the name of Jesus son of Pandira: Yeshu
> ben Pandira. He was a great and noble personality, about
> whom inferior Jewish literature has woven all kinds of
> fables that have been recently revived — and he is not to
> be confused, as some Talmudists have confused him, with
> Jesus of Nazareth. This herald of Christianity among the
> Essenes is known to us too as Jesus, the son of Pandira.
> And we know that he was accused of blasphemy and
> heresy by those to whom the teachings of the Essenes
> were anathema, and after being stoned was hanged on a
> tree, in order to add to his punishment the stigma of
> infamy.‡

---

* E.g. Geza Vermes and Martin Hengel. The dating is largely based on allusions in the *Damascus Rule*, where however it must be said that there is no such firm starting-point as in the *Nahum Commentary*.

† Vermes, *The Dead Sea Scrolls*, Cleveland, Ohio 1978, pp.154 and 160. Vermes also lists some of the many identifications that have been proposed.

‡ Steiner, *The Gospel of Matthew*, London 1965, pp.85-6.

It is surely remarkable that, long before the Dead Sea Scrolls came to light, Steiner described a great Essene leader during the reign of Alexander Jannaeus. It is moreover striking that the Qumran texts repeatedly hint at the martyrdom and 'crucifixion' of the Teacher. And if we once thoroughly free ourselves from the old assumption that the ben Pandira stories in the Talmud represent Jesus of Nazareth, we shall notice that they square much better with the Essene prophet and esotericist than with the man we meet in the Gospels.

For one thing, when the Talmudic passages have anything to say on the chronology of ben Pandira (which generally they do not), it is to place him firmly in the reign of — Alexander Jannaeus.* It must be admitted that the Rabbis rarely had any definite concept of the date of persons and events, but in so far as we have any indication of time we are directed to the period about a century before Christ. Then there is the nature of the charges brought against ben Pandira. We must remember that the Talmud is the literature of the Pharisees, and that after the Temple was destroyed (in 70 AD) the Pharisees became the sole authoritative voice of Judaism. To them the teachings of the Essenes were certainly anathema, and they would doubtless have remembered the 'Teacher of Righteousness,' if they did not choose rather to forget him as far as was possible, as a dangerous false prophet. A passage from the Talmudic tractate *Sanhedrin* concludes that ben Pandira had

> to be stoned because he practised magic and incited Jews
> to worship alien gods and as a false prophet led Israel
> astray.†

The charge of magic could now be justified from Qumran, where the more recent cave finds have brought us distinctly magical (astrological, physiognomical and other texts, some in cryptic letters). Other sections of the Talmud assert that magical healings were performed by dubious individuals in the name of Yeshu ben Pandira, and claim that the latter learnt his magic from the cele-

---

* Despite this, many take 'ben Pandira' to refer to Christ because he was the 'son of a virgin' *(parthenos):* an explanation which has rightly been criticized as far-fetched and improbable in itself, and never used by the Rabbis.

† Babylonian Talmud, tractate *Sanhedrin* 43a.

brated Babylonian Rabbi ben Perahya.* There may in fact have been nothing 'dubious' about these healings except that they were performed by Essenes; and we have seen that the Essenes and their Teacher did have connections with Syria and Babylonia — indeed their covenant was renewed 'in the land of Damascus.'

With the charge of magic goes the question of such foreign influence. The Essenes were open to currents of ideas and esoteric conceptions, especially from Iran, and in the eyes of the Pharisees admitting alien religious influences would clearly be seen as 'whoring after false gods' and 'leading Israel astray.' Here again, a date around the time of ben Pandira is more appropriate than the situation at the period around 180 BC: scholars who so situate the Essene Teacher are constrained to see the Essenes as conscious religious purists, violently rejecting the Hellenistic-oriental thought-world in favour of Israel's heritage in the aftermath of the 'crisis of Hellenism' and the Maccabean revolt. A scholar such as Martin Hengel is reduced to arguing that the Essenes were highly suscepti-ble to outside influences e.g. from Iran, but that they themselves were totally unaware of the fact and regarded their own role as conservative and opposed to all assimilation of foreign ideas. The structure of the argument certainly creaks a little.†

In conclusion, then, the charges brought by the Talmudic writers against Yeshu ben Pandira are appropriate to an Essene prophet who lived in the reign of Alexander Jannaeus. The charges are not likely to have been those remembered in connection with Jesus of Nazareth: it would be almost absurd of the Rabbis to remember and condemn Jesus for magical practices and for introducing foreign ideas and not mention the scandal that he had claimed to be the Messiah! Furthermore, the details of the prophet's martyrdom, stoning before crucifixion, do not fit any account of Jesus that has come down to us. On the other hand, a date for the Teacher of Righteousness around 100 BC is consistent with the historical allusions of the *Nahum Commentary* and the actions of the Wicked Priest. It is highly probable therefore that we should identify the

---

* Babylonian Talmud, tractate *Sotah* 47a; *Sanhedrin* 107b. Cf. Jerusalem Talmud, tractate *Hagigah* 77d; *Sanhedrin* 34a. For healings performed in the name of Yeshu ben Pandira, see Jerusalem Talmud, tractate *Avodah Zarah* 40d; *Shabbat* On ben Perahya's magic, see Neusner, *History of the Jews in Babylonia*, Leiden 1964-70, vol.5, pp.218-43.

† Hengel, *Judaism and Hellenism*, London 1974, I, pp.226-43.

Teacher of Righteousness with the Essene leader described by
Steiner, and see in the Talmudic stories of Yeshu ben Pandira the
refraction of his personality and role through the hostile lens of later
Pharisaism. Spiritual-scientific research thus inclines to place the
literary activity of the Essenes at Qumran somewhat later than the
date favoured by many scholars: specifically, in the reign of
Alexander Jannaeus (103-76 BC).* It is to that period that we must
likewise attribute the Teacher's compositions of the remarkable
Mystery-texts of the *Thanksgiving Scroll*.

The poems themselves form a collection of hitherto unknown
works. Although they are superficially 'biblical' in style, it would be
quite wrong to see them as mere imitations of the Old Testament
poetical books. Rather, they are connected directly with the inner
life of the community. They refer constantly to its special teachings,
e.g. in their recurring symbolism of light and dark, of spiritual
knowledge, etc. They have many affinities too with the poem incorporated into the *Community Rule* or basic document of Essenism
at Qumran, making it more than probable that the poems had a
liturgical role and may either have been declaimed or even chanted
collectively. At the same time, the poems have numerous points of
contact with each other, pointing to a single author or more likely
to a poet whose style was adopted and developed by his pupils and
successors. The original poet is certainly the *Moreh Zedek*. The exact
number of works attributable to him is disputed. On grounds of
stylistic analysis, numbers 5, 8 and 10 reproduced below are widely
supposed to be his compositions; but such methods characteristically make too little allowance for diversity and development in a
creative writer, and others too may come from his hand. Those
which do not nevertheless share many features of his writing,
because their authors have been through the trials and awakenings
of Essene initiation which are indicated in the poetic symbolism.
Indeed, it was clearly through poetry which could be repeated in

* A growing number of scholars have come to accept the 'Hasmonean' dating,
and the tendency is continuing despite the vociferous claims of such writers as
R. Eisenman and B. Thiering to have established definitive cases for their own ideas.
All new ideas merit attention – though even if they could be made to seem very
much more probable, these could not bear out the weight of speculation put upon the
merely possible by Thiering's theories in particular! Besides Delcor and Carmignac,
mentioned above, scholars who incline to the view that the Wicked Priest is
Alexander Jannaeus include such eminent figures as H. Segal, van der Ploeg and F.F.
Bruce.

liturgy and meditated intensively that Essene spiritual life achieved its inner depth. This should not be surprising when we recall the emphasis on books (and the Book) and the interpreting of the word in the organization of the movement at Qumran.

The poet has his own unusual way of beginning. He begins with a reference to God, which is not in itself unusual, since many Jewish hymns start with the formula 'Blessed be God ...'; the Teacher prefers something more personal, 'I thank you ...' This has given the title to the scroll which contains his work, the 'Thanksgiving Scroll.' It also indicates his influence in circles reaching outside Essenism in subsequent times. For the Gospel of Matthew has preserved a hymn composed by Jesus:

> I thank you, Father, Lord of heaven and earth,
> because you have hidden these things
>   from the wise and learned,
> and you have revealed them to little children.
> Yes, Father, for this was your good pleasure ...

The formula of address, points out David Flusser, is not the sole Essene feature here:

> Not only the opening of Jesus' hymn but also the free
> rhythm of the poem and its content show affinity with the
> Essene thanksgiving hymns ... Both Jesus and the author
> of the *Thanksgiving Scroll* proclaim that they reveal to the
> simple divine things hidden from others. Thus it seems
> evident that Jesus knew the Essene thanksgiving hymns
> and used their form in order to express his own place in
> the divine economy, though he introduced into his own
> hymn the motif of his divine sonship, which is naturally
> absent from the *Thanksgiving Scroll*.*

At the very least, Jesus knew these works and recognized the type of spiritual vision they convey, and was enabled to describe his own relationship to God partly in their terms.

The term 'Thanksgiving Hymns' *(Hodayot)* is however in one respect misleading. Whereas it might suggest the predominance of grateful thanks to God, the poems are actually full of terrible struggle and immense spiritual effort, phases of collapse and even physical breakdown. The granting of 'perfect light' and 'standing

---

* David Flusser in M.E. Stone (ed), *Jewish Writings of the Second Temple Period*, Assen and Philadelphia 1984, pp.566-67.

before God' to give thanks is reached only through an inner rebirth and the death of the old self. The pattern is the same as in the Greek Mysteries indicated by Plutarch:

> At first there are wanderings, and toilsome running about in circles, and journeys through the dark over uncertain roads and blind alleys; then, just before the end, there are all kinds of terrors, with shivering, trembling, sweating and utter amazement. After this, a strange and wonderful light meets the wanderer; he is admitted into clean and verdant meadows, where he discerns gentle voices, and choric dances, and the majesty of holy sounds and sacred visions. *(Fragment 168)*

The poet of the *Hodayot* has given these experiences unforgettable expression in Hebrew poetry.

There is no reason to suppose that the Teacher had any direct contact with the Greek Mysteries in particular (though there have been suggestions of a link to the Pythagoreans). The Mystery-experience rather has deep psycho-spiritual roots and forms a recurrent pattern of spiritual life. The historical contacts of Essenism with the Mysteries point more strongly to Babylonia and to Iran for particular influences. Furthermore, there is a new and unique quality which no influence from the older Mystery-cults is able to explain: the intensely individual spirit of the Teacher. In him the profound, universal patterns of the cosmic Mysteries are united for the first time to a sense of the 'I am.' The struggle of Light and darkness is internalized as the struggle of the two Spirits in Man. That is why it makes such magnificent poetry, and can still strike us as amazingly 'modern' in tone. The seer himself recognized that the real fulfilment of this union still lay in the future: hence the 'apocalyptic,' anticipatory nature of his vision. We still have much to learn from his words, for our own present and our own future.

Source: I QH I:5-39. Translated from the Hebrew by Theodor H. Gaster.

- 1 -

1. The poem which opens the collection of *Hodayot* is of a broad and rather comprehensive nature, and may have been placed at the beginning for that reason. It stresses many of the typical elements of Essene piety and thought, and includes thanks for the spirit of speech which God has placed in man. Poetry is a means 'that Thy glory may be made known/ and Thy wonders told forth.' All things are referred back to God, but there is much greater emphasis than in the Bible on the cosmic aspects of his power, expressed through the activities of the spiritual and angelic beings to sun, moon, stars and the elements. They keep the material forces of sea, storm and lightning within bounds, just as God assigns to each spirit a limited role in the cosmic order. When man is mentioned, he takes his place within a world organized by God and his angelic armies, and is likewise assigned his specific task. The feeling of human unworthiness for such exalted work, since man is a 'creature of clay' moulded from the substance of earth, leads to thanks for God's 'great loving kindness' in giving to him nevertheless the spirit of speech and the knowledge of 'God's deep Truth.' He gives this as 'the God of all knowledge,' but only to a few, whose spirits he has strengthened, presumably referring to Essene initiation. It is the strength needed by man to 'face his afflictions,' which must be accepted because God in his ultimate wisdom has foreseen and ordained them. The poet contrasts those who have knowledge with the worldly wise and those 'that are foolish at heart,' the characteristic dualism of insiders and outsiders in Mystery religion.

2. This passage has close relations to the *Book of Enoch* 69, which gives the divine oath 'before the creation of the world' which established order at the beginning 'and forever.' The sea 'at the time of its anger' is restrained by that oath. 'And by the same oath the stars complete their courses of travel,' and it controls the winds, thunder, lightning and so on, together with the 'reservoirs' of rain, hail, snow and mist. The *Book of Enoch* stresses the regularity of nature under the rule of the Lord of Spirits and the angels, 'the leaders of the chiefs of the thousands which are appointed over the whole creation and ... all the stars' (75), and provides the completely regular sun-calendar used by the Essenes in preference to the variable moon-calendar of mainstream Judaism. Fragments of the *Book of Enoch* in Aramaic have been found at Qumran, and these have been utilized by E. Isaac in his translation of the book, which otherwise survives complete only in an Ethiopic translation (E. Isaac in J.H. Charlesworth 1983). The *Book of Enoch* belongs to the Essene tradition at a stage prior to the writings of the 'Dead Sea Scrolls,' and certainly formed one of the major sources of Essene thought.

✳ Poems of Initiation ✳

- 1 -

Thou art the source of all might[1]
and the wellspring of all power;
yet art Thou also rich in wisdom
and great in counsel.
Thy fury is vented in the presence of ...;
yet are Thy mercies beyond number.

Thou art a God that visits wrongdoing;
yet also a God long-suffering in judgment.
In whatsoever Thou doest,
Thou hast ever done justly.
In Thy wisdom didst Thou call into being
spirits immortal,
and ere Thou didst create them,
didst foreknow their works for all time.

Apart from Thee can naught be done,
and naught apprehended save by Thy will.
Thou it is formed every spirit,
and set due rule and role for all their works.

When Thou didst stretch out the heavens for Thy glory,
and command all their host to do Thy will,
Thou didst also make potent spirits
to keep them in bounds.

Or ever spirits immortal
took on the form of holy angels,
Thou didst assign them to bear rule[2]
over divers domains:
over the sun and moon,
to govern their hidden powers;
over the stars,

3.   Cf. the 'central statement of Essene theology' in the *Community Rule* I QS
       III:18–IV:20. 'From the God of Knowledge comes all that is and happens ...
       He has created man to govern the world, and hast appointed for him two
       Spirits ... All the children of Light are ruled by the (angelic) Prince of Light
       and walk in the ways of Light.'

4.   This conception was carried into the organization of Essene life at the
       community in Qumran, where all aspects of life were strictly regulated and
       ordered by the Guardian and the statutes of the *Rule*. Evidently we are to
       understand their mode of life not just as religious discipline but as a
       reflection in society of God's cosmic decrees. The Mystery-idea of living-
       together with the cosmic order is given a Jewish meaning in its identification
       with the all-embracing Torah or Law.

to hold them to their courses;
over rain and snow,
to make them fulfil their functions;
over meteors and lightnings,
to make them discharge their tasks;
over the treasures of the deeps,
to make them serve their ends;
over fire and water,
to control their hidden force.

When, too, Thou didst create in Thy power
earth and seas and deeps,
in Thy wisdom didst Thou set in their depths
spirits immortal,
and thereby dispose to Thy will
all that therein is.

So too has Thou done
touching the spirit of man
which Thou hast created in the world
for all the days of time
and for ages infinite,
to bear rule over all his works.[3]

Thou hast assigned the tasks of men's spirits
duly, moment by moment,[4]
throughout their generations;
and Thou hast determined the mode
in which they shall wield their sway,
season by season;
yea, Thou hast prescribed their works,
age after age —
alike when men shall be visited with peace
and when they shall suffer affliction.

Thou hast ... man's spirit
and duly assigned its role

5.   Among the Essenes the giving of knowledge concerning the 'deep mysterious
        things' and God's foreordaining of destiny are closely linked. Devorah
        Dimant comments: 'The question remains what role is left for man. Man
        himself is incapable of deciphering that mystery, which embraces both his
        personal biography and history at large. His lot is to search all his life, by his
        own action, and by divine illuminating grace, in order to discover to which
        part he belongs, Light or Darkness. Thus, the emphasis is shifted from
        freedom of action to the mystery of knowledge. The freedom given to man
        is not to choose where to go but to discover where he is. This can be done
        only with the aid of divinely-inspired knowledge of the true meaning of the
        world, of man and of history. That is why the starting point of man is
        ignorance, while the final election is marked by a gift of knowledge' (D.
        Dimant in M.E. Stone 1984, p.538).

6.   Cf. Genesis 2:7: 'And Yahweh Elohim formed man from the dust of the
        ground and breathed into his nostrils the breath of life.'

7.   A visionary such as Enoch might claim to be raised up to God and see the
        vision of future events already laid out. See *Book of Enoch* 39. The vision
        might include his own destiny: 'Already my portion is there, for thus it has
        been reserved for me before the Lord of the Spirits.'

for all his offspring
throughout the generations of time;
and Thou hast ... it
for all years of eternity.
And in Thy knowing wisdom
Thou hast ordained men's fate,
or ever they came into being.

By Thy will all things exist,
and without Thee is nothing wrought.
These things have I come to know
through the insight wherewith
        Thou hast graced me,
for Thou hast opened mine ear
to deep mysterious things.[5]

Shapen of clay and kneaded with water,[6]
a bedrock of shame and a source of pollution,
a cauldron of iniquity and a fabric of sin,
a spirit errant, wayward and witless,
distraught by every just judgment -
what can I say that hath not been foreknown,
or what disclose that hath not been foretold?
All things are inscribed before Thee
in a recording script,
for every moment of time,
for the infinite cycles of years,
in their several appointed times.
No single thing is hidden,
naught missing from Thy presence.[7]

How can man say aught
to account for his sins?
How argue in excuse of his misdeeds?
How can he enter reply
to any just sentence upon him?

8.   'God of all knowledge': the 'God of Knowledge' is a frequent title of God in Essene literature. It is used in the Bible in 1 Samuel 2:3. However, the emphasis in these poems on God's pre-existence, his cosmic power, knowledge and justice strikingly recall the accounts of Ohrmazd, the supreme Iranian God 'whose body is Light and his spirit is Truth,' e.g. in the *Bundahishn* or Zoroastrian 'Book of Genesis' I,1: 'Thus it is revealed in the good Religion. Ohrmazd was on high, all-knowing and all-good. In infinite time he was ever in the Light ... Omniscience and goodness are the permanent disposition of Ohrmazd: some call them "Religion." The interpretation of both is the same, namely the permanent disposition of Eternal Time, for Ohrmazd and the Space, Religion and Time of Ohrmazd were and are and evermore shall be' (after Zaehner 1975, pp.34f).

9.   The recognition of our common misuse of God's gifts modulates rather suddenly into praise of the spirit of language. The idea that our faculties are God's creations yet it is for us to use or misuse them recalls concepts known from the *Testaments of the Twelve Patriarchs*. 'If the soul takes pleasure in the good inclination, all its actions are in righteousness ... But if it incline to the evil inclination, all its actions are in wickedness' — *Testament of Asher* I,6:8. On the *Testaments* and their relationship to the Essene writings from Qumran, see below.

10.   The 'strengthening' referred to must be the processes of Essene initiation. Like the baptism of 'transformation' given by John, the Essene baptismal rites and inner rebirth purge the spirit and cleanse it from the 'taint' of evil. Ideas like those from the *Testaments* suggest how this was possible. By changing the basic 'inclination' of man, the same gifts which were forces of evil now become powers of good. The dualism of the Scrolls refers to this often as a change from existential Darkness to Light. The change is brought about by knowledge, concerning the right use of the faculties which God has given.

The 'afflictions' are those of ordinary life, and not least those of life in the community which was obviously an extremely demanding one and called for the exercise of tolerance, charity and selflessness. The strain on personal resources in such a life figures in some of the most 'modern'-sounding of the poems! But the afflictions are especially the ordeals of initiation, frequently referred to below. Knowledge is the key to these also: knowledge shows them to be a part of God's ministration, leading 'to the end that Thy wonders may be shown forth' in the 'Son of Light,' the re-fashioned initiate. Cf. the words of Jesus in the Gospel of John 11:4: 'This sickness does not point to death, but to the revealing of God's glory' — referring to the 'dead' Lazarus who is about to be 'raised' to new life.

Thine, O God of all knowledge,[8]
are all works of righteousness
and the secret of truth;
while man's is but thraldom to wrongdoing,
and works of deceit.

That spirit that lies in man's speech,
Thou didst create.
Thou hast known all the words of man's tongue
and determined the fruit of his lips,
ere those lips themselves had being.
It is Thou that disposeth all words in due sequence[9]
and giveth to the spirit of the lips
ordered mode of expression;
that bringeth forth their secrets
in measured utterances,
and granteth unto spirits
means to express their thoughts,
that Thy glory may be made known,
and Thy wonders told forth
in all Thine unerring works,
and that Thy righteousness may be proclaimed,
and Thy name be praised in the mouth of all things,
and that all creatures may know Thee,
each to the meed of his insight,
and bless Thee alway.

But Thou in Thy mercy and Thy great loving-kindness
hast strengthened the spirit of man[10]
to face his afflictions,
and hast cleansed it of the taint
of multifarious wrongdoing,
to the end that Thy wonders may be shown forth
in the sight of all Thy works.

So, for mine own part,
I am braced against all the afflictions

11.   A characteristic contrast between the spiritual knowledge which changes the
        orientation of man's inner life, and the 'wisdom' of externally clever people
        who are really to be lumped together with the 'foolish at heart.' The passage
        exposes the hypocrisy of the self-styled righteous, perhaps the Essenes' arch-
        rivals, the Pharisees.

- 5 -

*Source: I QH III:3-18 translated from the Hebrew by Theodor H. Gaster. Attributed
by Jeremias on stylistic grounds to the Righteous Teacher (Jeremias 1963 pp.168ff).*

1.   After the Teacher's characteristic opening formula, the poem describes the
        Essene experience of death and rebirth in personal terms. The Teacher has
        been through a crisis of suffering which he compares, in classic Mystery
        language, to the throes of birth, the agonies of travail. The imagery of
        illumination, also typical of Mysteries, presents the positive side of his
        spiritual search. But it is not a simple process of repentance followed by
        blissful consciousness of divine grace: rather, the birth of the new self is an
        inner victory over the sources of affliction which continue to buffet the soul
        like a ship on stormy seas. The sources of suffering remain, for the Teacher's
        individual rebirth is part of a cosmic process, which will culminate in the
        birth of the Messiah 'long foretold.' This passage is based, as Theodor Gaster
        explains in his own commentary, 'on the concept that the world order is
        periodically dissolved and renewed, the renewal being signalled by the
        miraculous birth of a saviour' (Gaster 1957, p.204). The conception belongs
        not to the Old Testament religion but to pagan sources, including Zoroastrian
        and Hellenistic thought, which again seem to have inspired Essene ideas;
        however, it has been given a special meaning through being combined with
        the language of Isaiah and his famous prophecy of the birth of a miraculous
        man-child (Isaiah 9; etc). For the Essene, the spiritual rebirth has its reality in
        his own inner renewal, but inner reality will also become outer reality as
        history unfolds.

whereto I am condemned;
and will tell unto men all Thy wonders
wherein, through me, Thou hast shown Thy power.

Hearken, O ye wise,
ye, too, that are witless and rash,[11]
and be of sober mind.
Ye ..., sharpen your wits!
Ye righteous, have done with wrongdoing!
And all ye that are blameless of conduct,
hold fast to the ... of the meek!
Be slow to anger and spurn not ...!
For men that are foolish at heart
cannot understand these things, ...
and God's deep truth is hidden from them;
and men of unbridled temper
can but gnash their teeth.

- 5 -

I give thanks unto Thee, O Lord,[1]
for Thou hast illumined my face
with the vision of Thy truth;
wherefore I yet shall walk in glory everlasting
along with all the holy that hear the words of
      Thy mouth;
and Thou wilt deliver me from the pit and the slough.

Howbeit, at this hour,
my soul is sore dismayed.
Men deem me a worthless shard
and render my life like a ship stormtossed on the deep,
or like a bastion city beleaguered by the foe.

Yea, I am in distress
as a woman in travail
bringing forth her firstborn,
when, as her time draws near,

2. The language is modelled on Isaiah, where the woman symbolizes Jerusalem, and the birth symbolizes God's dealings with his chosen ones, as for instance in: 'Do I bring to the moment of birth and not give delivery? says Yahweh, Do I close up the womb when I bring salvation? says your God' (66:9. Cf. also 42:14). Isaiah is one of the biblical books found in the library at Qumran, and of all the prophets he was by far the most influential on the thought of the Essenes as on Jesus and on early Christianity. The imagery here cannot be explained simply in Isaian terms, however. Indeed it contrasts with the instant and miraculous birth ascribed to the children of Jerusalem, since it is concerned with the long-drawn-out sufferings of the initiatory ordeal which precedes rebirth. The pangs are those of 'hell,' for the initiate 'dies' and descends into the underworld. Thus the biblical language has been transformed once more by Mystery ideas. Like the figure in our New Testament Apocalypse (1:18) the initiate can say, 'I was dead, and behold I am alive for ever and ever.' The imagery of the 'man-child' and the struggle with the dragon is also taken up and developed in the Apocalypse (12:5 and elsewhere) perhaps pointing to an Essene background. Giving birth, becoming a child, and so forth, are widespread ways of describing the spiritual reintegration achieved by the initiated in the Mysteries.

3. The triumph of the forces of death and the underworld over the uninitiated is another typical Mystery theme. Cf. Sophocles' reference to those who have participated in the Mysteries:

    Thrice-blessed when they come to the realm of the shades who
    have seen these rites! They alone have life, for the rest there is
    only pain and toil. (fr.719)

the pangs come swiftly upon her
and all the grievous throes
that rack those heavy with child.

For now, amid throes of death,
new life is coming to birth,
and the pangs of travail set in,
as at last there enters the world
the man-child long conceived.[2]

Now, amid throes of death,
that man-child long foretold
is about to be brought forth.

Now, amid pangs of hell,
there will burst forth from the womb
that marvel of mind and might,
and that man-child will spring from the throes!

Delivery comes apace
for him that now lies in the womb;
as the hour of his birth draws near,
the pangs begin!

Come too the grievous throes,
the racking birth-pains come
upon all that bear in the womb
the seeds of the new life!

Yet, likewise unto them
that carry in their womb
the seeds of worthless things
are come the grievous throes,
the pangs of hell and the torment.[3]

For lo, the wall shall rock
unto its prime foundation,

4.   Plato says that the uninitiated 'sink in the mire' — cf. 'deliver me from the
        pit and the slough' at the opening of this poem. The Teacher translates the
        Mystery-ideas into historical terms. Rather than referring to the death of
        individuals, his imagery points to a turning-point in the ages of the world.
        The concept of world-ages came originally from Iran and was very well-
        known by the time of the Teacher. The *Book of Jubilees* which stands in the
        Essene tradition had already introduced a version of it, according to which
        history is divided into cosmic weeks or cycles of seven, into the interpretation
        of the Bible, beginning with the creation. The Teacher's Mystery-experience
        now shapes an apocalyptic vision of a life-and-death to ensue.

5.   Compare with the Teacher's vision that of Jesus: 'On the earth, nations will
        be in anguish and perplexity at the roaring and tossing of the sea. Men will
        faint from terror, in fear of what is coming on the world, for the heavenly
        bodies will be shaken ... When these things begin to take place, stand up and
        lift up your heads, because your redemption is drawing near' (Luke 21:25-28).
        We may suppose that Jesus' apocalypse arose out of similar spiritual
        experiences to those of the Essene initiates.

- 8 -

*Source: I QH IV,5-40. Translated from the Hebrew by Theodor H. Gaster. Ascribed
by Jeremias on stylistic grounds to the Teacher of Righteousness (Jeremias 1963,
pp.168ff).*

1.   The Teacher returns to his experience of illumination from another perspec-
        tive, that of his own personal destiny. In the first place, his experience sets
        him apart from the deluded teachers and 'prophets of lies' who do not
        possess knowledge yet set themselves up as leaders of the people — of God's
        holy people Israel. He sees in this contrast the reflection of the contrast
        between Light and Darkness, God and Belial. For the false teachers are not
        merely ignorant, they actively reject the 'vision of knowledge.' The Teacher
        trusts in God, however, and remains sure both of his own message and that
        the 'men of deceit' will wither away in the falseness of theirs. If Israel follows
        them, it will mean dispersal among the nations, that is, loss of their identity
        as God's holy ones. Against that he sets his own success in spreading illumi-
        nation upon 'the faces of full many,' his Essene followers. He recognizes that
        he has done this, not from his own power, but from the revelation to him of
        God's 'wondrous secret.' His initiation-experience brought home to him the
        struggle between weakness and spiritual strength, Darkness and Light, in his
        own person: he recalls the physical symptoms of his spiritual crisis in the
        time of his ordeal, trembling and quaking, his heart like melting wax. It was
        not in the strength of earthly human nature that he brought spiritual knowl-
        edge. It is God who through his secret or 'Mystery' is able to resolve the
        struggle of Light and Darkness and 'purify man from guilt.'

even as rocks a ship
storm-tossed on the waters.[4]

The heavens shall thunder loud,
and they that now do dwell
on the crumbling dust of the earth
be as sailors on the seas,
aghast at the roaring of the waters;
and all the wise men thereof
be as mariners on the deep
when all their skill is confounded
by the surging of the seas,
the seething of the depths,
the swirling of the tides.

High shall the billows surge,
loud the breakers roar;
and, even as they surge,
the gates of Hell shall be opened,
Perdition's shafts be loosed at their every step.

The deep shall resound with their cries,
and the gates of Hell shall open
upon all worthless things,
and the doors of Perdition shall close
on all the iniquity
which they would yet bring forth;
and the bars of eternity
on all unworthy intent.[5]

- 8 -

I give thanks unto Thee, O Lord,[1]
for Thou hast illumined my face
with the light of Thy covenant.

Day by day I seek Thee,

2.   The Teacher's destiny brought him into conflict both with the Temple
       authorities in Jerusalem, and with the lay religious movement of the
       Pharisees. It is the latter who seem to be referred to here as purveyors of
       'smooth words' instead of the arduous Essene path. In the Qumran
       Commentary on Hosea, there is a reference to the execution of the 'seekers of
       smooth things' by 'the furious young lion,' evidently meaning the hanging
       (or crucifixion) of eight hundred Pharisees by Alexander Jannaeus who ruled
       Judea from 103 to 76 BC and may well be the Spouter of Lies and the Wicked
       Priest, the enemy of the Teacher.

3.   Cf. the comment of Jesus: 'Woe to you, teachers of the Law, for you took
       away the key of knowledge; you did not enter in yourselves, and obstructed
       those who were entering' (Luke 11:52).

and ever Thou shinest upon me
bright as the perfect dawn.

But as for *them* —
they have dealt treacherously with Thee,
have made smooth their words.
Garblers of truth are they all,
witlessly stumbling along.
They have turned all their deeds to folly;
they have become abhorrent unto themselves.
Though Thou show Thy power through me,
they regard me not,
but thrust me forth from my land
like a sparrow from its nest;
all my friends and familiars
are thrust away from me,
and deem me a broken pot.

Preachers of lies are they,
prophets of deceit.
They have plotted mischief against me,
to make Thy people exchange for smooth words[2]
Thy teaching which Thou hast engraven on my heart.
They have kept the draught of knowledge
from them that are athirst,[3]
and given them in their thirst
vinegar to drink,
to feast their eyes upon them
as they are led astray,
make sport of them as they falter
and are caught in their snares.

But Thou, O God, wilt spurn
all the designs of Belial.
Thy counsel it is will prevail,
and the thought of Thy heart endure for ever.

4. The allusion to the stubbornness and active rejection of the Teacher's knowledge lends support to the view that the Pharisees and Essenes both originated from the spiritual movement of the 'Pious' (Hasidim, Asideans) in Maccabean times. The struggles of the Teacher were therefore not just against an uncomprehending external world, but against those within the wider movement who decided to reject his leadership and his claim to spiritual knowledge. They evidently manoeuvred to undermine his authority ('thrust me forth from my land/like a sparrow from its nest,') and certainly succeeded in becoming much more influential in outward terms than the Essenes. The latter clearly felt that the Pharisees were not only enemies, but traitors to their originally common cause. The reference to leaving 'my land' may point to the Teacher's departure for Damascus (cf. G. Vermes 1987, pp.26-27).

    The Teacher refers elsewhere to this period as one in which:

    > Thou hast sheltered me, O my God,
    > in the face of all mankind,
    > and hidden Thy teaching within me,
    > until it be shown unto me
    > that the hour of thy Triumph is come. (I QH V:11-12)

    From various references in the 'Scrolls' it seems likely that the Teacher did finally suffer martyrdom at the hands of the Wicked Priest. Cf. R. Steiner 1965, pp.85f.

5. The *Community Rule* contains an injunction to every Essene 'to love all the children of Light ... and to hate all the children of Darkness, each according to the measure of his guilt' (I QS I:9f). Since this is not said anywhere in the Old Testament but belongs to the dualism of Essene thought, it is generally accepted that Jesus must be referring to this commandment in the Gospel of Matthew 5:43f, and correcting it with his own injunction to 'Love your enemy.' It is worth noticing here that the Teacher does not take upon himself the judgment of the traitors, the 'sons of Darkness,' but leaves them to God who 'didst create/both the righteous and the wicked,' as he says later in the poem.

    It has recently been suggested by H. Burgmann (1988) that the Beatitudes (Matthew 5:3ff) and the whole framework of the Sermon on the Mount which follows them are based on Essene forms of thought (see his pp.459-502).

Crafty men are they;
they think base thoughts,
seek Thee with heart divided,
stand not firm in Thy truth.
In their every thought is a root
which blossoms to wormwood and gall.
In the stubbornness of their hearts
they wander astray[4]
and go seeking Thee through idols.
They make their iniquity
a stumbling-block before them,
and come to inquire of Thee
from the mouths of lying prophets,
men by error seduced.
Then, with stammering lips
and with barbarous tongue
they speak unto Thy people,
seeking guilefully
to turn their deeds to delusion.
They have paid no heed to Thy teaching,
nor given ear to Thy word,
but have said of the vision of knowledge,
    "It is not sure,"
and of the way Thou desirest,
    "There is no such thing."
But Thou, O God, wilt give them their answer,
judging them in Thy power
for all their idolatrous acts
and their manifold transgressions,
to the end that they shall be caught
in their own designs
who have turned away from Thy covenant.

Thou wilt sentence all men of deceit[5]
to be cut off,
and all the prophets of error
will be found no more.

6.   'Standing in Thy presence,' 'standing before Thee' as contrasts with the
       'erring' or 'wandering' or 'straying spirit' again recalls the language of
       Mysteries. We have quoted above Plutarch's mention of 'wanderings, and
       toilsome running about in circles'; the Mystery confers the direct vision of
       God, 'face to face.' Apuleius says *adoravi de proxumo,* 'I drew near and
       adored' *(Metamorphoses, or The Golden Ass* XI,23). *Epopteia* is the term in the
       Greek Mysteries for standing in the presence of the Mystery-god.
           Cf. also Paul, 1 Corinthians 13:10-12, where the context is spiritual
       maturation, the receiving of 'perfection.'

7.   The 'common accord' stresses the social nature of Essenism, which is evident
       in all the sources whether they concern the 'monastic' community at Qumran
       or the looser association of Essenes in the towns and villages of Judea. The
       influence of Judaism is paramount in this respect: the pagan Mystery-cults
       were much less exclusive (an initiate could belong to many other cults) and
       made fewer demands on the individual. Pagan Mysteries never became a
       'church' with a sense of unity binding together the scattered members.
       Essenism (and Christianity) brought the individual to a new level of
       commitment. Such intensity of social life was striking — and also brought
       unprecedented strains.

8.   Lit. 'in the council of the holy beings.' 'Since the Hebrew word here rendered
       "rallied" refers specifically to the marshalling of troops, and since the
       expression, "have hearkened unto me" may very well allude to the Roman
       practice of reciting the military oath to new recruits, it seems permissible to
       recognize a military metaphor, and for that reason the term "legion" has been
       used.' (Translator's Note)

For in all Thou doest there is no delusion,
and in all Thou thinkest no deceit.
And they that are pleasing to Thee
shall stand in Thy presence for ever,[6]
and they that walk in the way Thou desirest
rest firm for all time.

So, for mine own part,
because I have clung unto Thee,
I shall yet arise and stand upright
against them that revile me;
and my hand shall yet be upon all
that hold me in contempt.
Though Thou show Thy power through me,
they regard me not.
Howbeit, Thou in Thy might
hast shed upon me the Perfect Light,
and bedaubed not their faces with shame
that have let themselves be found
when that I sought them out,
who, in a common accord,[7]
have pledged themselves to Thee.

They that walked in the way Thou desirest
have hearkened unto me
and rallied to Thy cause
in the legion of the saints.[8]

And Thou wilt vindicate them
and plainly show forth the truth;
and suffer them not to stray
at the hand of froward men,
what time these plot against them.

Thou wilt yet cause Thy people
to stand in awe of them.
But for them that transgress Thy word

9.   The Teacher seems slightly surprised at the numbers who have in fact come
      forward to join the esoteric community. Archaeology confirms that the
      buildings at Qumran had to be expanded and rebuilt to accommodate larger
      numbers than had at first been expected. P.R. Davies points out that the
      redesigning of the refectory area meant that it had to be moved some sixty
      feet away from the kitchen — 'inconveniently distant' for catering purposes!
      (1982, p.48).

10.   Devorah Dimant points out: 'Peculiar to the *Hodayot* is the view that man is
      constituted of a duality of flesh and spirit; the flesh is base by nature, for it
      is susceptible to sin, while the spirit is capable of purification and repentance.
      This teaching is placed in the context of the general dualism and predestina-
      tion of the sect: God has created everything according to a pre-ordained plan
      which divides the world into two camps, Good and Evil, so that repentance
      from sin is the lot only of those who belong to the camp of Light' — in M.E.
      Stone 1984, p.524. There is a tension here which is radically extended in
      Gnosticism.

11.   A prominent Mystery-idea: ordinary mortals are incomplete, or have been
      born only as natural beings. To bring them to 'perfection' or full humanity,
      the second or spiritual birth of initiation is required. In ancient times such a
      rebirth through initiation would be enacted at the time of puberty, giving rise
      to the terminology of maturation, completeness or perfection in a biological
      sense. The Mysteries arose out of a similar sense of the incompleteness of
      man's ordinary existence. 'The starting-point of initiation,' Steiner points out,
      'was that a person came to feel that he was not a human being at all, but
      said: I must first become a human being' (Steiner 1968, p.34).

Thou shalt ordain dispersal
among all the peoples on earth,
passing sentence on them
that they be cut off.

Through me hast Thou illumined
the faces of full many,[9]
and countless by the times
Thou hast shown Thy power through me.
For Thou hast made known unto me
Thy deep, mysterious things,
hast shared Thy wondrous secret with me
and so shown forth Thy power;
and before the eyes of full many
this wonder stands revealed,
that Thy glory may be shown forth,
and all living know of Thy power.

Yet, never could flesh alone
attain unto this,[10]
nor that which is moulded of clay
do wonders so great
— steeped in sin from the womb
and in guilt of perfidy unto old age.

Verily I know
that righteousness lies not with man,
nor perfection of conduct with mortals.
Only with God on High
are all works of righteousness;
and ne'er can the way of man
be stablished save by the spirit
which God has fashioned for him,
to bring unto perfection
the life of mortal man;[11]
that all His works may know
how mighty is His power,

12.   The struggle between Light and Darkness is powerfully internalized in this and similar passages. Nevertheless it should be noted that it remains a struggle of cosmic and historical dimensions. The guilt which the Teacher feels that he carries is both his own and that of his forefathers. The uncertainty and sense of abandonment among the children of Darkness momentarily affects him too.

13.   The Teacher touches upon the physical aspects of the ordeals of initiation in ancient times. Close parallels are to be found especially in the Babylonian initiation-text 'I will praise the Lord of Wisdom,' a first-person narrative of spiritual and physical crisis. At one point its author declares:

> Sleep covers me like a net.
> My eyes stare straight ahead, but cannot see,
> My ears are open, but cannot hear.
> Feebleness has overcome my whole body,
> An attack of illness has fallen upon my flesh.
> Stiffness has taken over my arms,
> Weakness has come upon my knees,
> My feet forget their motion.
> A stroke has got me; I choke like someone prostrate.
> Death has approached and has covered my face.
> > (Translated from Akkadian [Babylonian] by R.D. Biggs,
> > in J.B. Pritchard 1975, p.153).

Although to us the text appears to be biographical, it concerns the man's relation to his god (Marduk, Lord of Wisdom) and has a ritual framework. On its themes of initiation in connection with Jewish and Christian traditions, cf. F.H. Borsch 1967, pp.177-81. Reading the Teacher's poem, we should also remember the context of its recital in the cultic life of the Essenes.

how plenteous His love
to all who do His will.

When I called to mind
all my guilty deeds
and the perfidy of my sires[12]
— when wicked men
opposed Thy covenant,
and froward men Thy word —
trembling seized hold on me and quaking,
all my bones were a-quiver;
my heart became like wax
melting before a fire,
my knees were like to water
pouring over a steep;[13]
and I said: "Because of my transgressions
I have been abandoned,
that Thy covenant holds not with me."

But then, when I remembered
the strength of Thy hand
and Thy multitudinous mercies,
I rose again and stood upright,
and my spirit was fortified
to stand against affliction;
for I was stayed by Thy grace
and by Thine abundant love.

For Thou wilt wipe out all sin,
and in Thy bounty it lies
to purify man from guilt.
Man alone cannot do
as Thou hast done;
for Thou it is didst create
both the righteous and the wicked.

- **10** -

Source: I QH V:20–VI:35. Translated from the Hebrew by Theodor H. Gaster. Ascribed by Jeremias on stylistic grounds to the Teacher of Righteousness (Jeremias 1963, pp.168ff). According to Vermes, the manuscript originally had at the opening of the poem the words 'I thank Thee,' which have been corrected to the more usual Jewish hymn style 'Blessed art Thou' (Vermes 1987, p.179).

1.   The Teacher combines into a wide-ranging whole elements of his personal vision, community life with its struggles, physical symptoms and an apocalyptic vision stretching to the resurrection of those 'that lie in the dust.' He begins with a contrast between God, with his infinite power and glory, ministered to by the ranks of angels, and man the fatherless orphan. The terms contain a mystic special sense, however, for the 'poor' are the *ebionim*, beggars not in a material but in a spiritual sense, cf. Gospel of Matthew 5:3. The term is used in the *Hodayot* and in other Qumran writings such as the *Commentary on Habbakuk* (I Q p.Hab XII,3,6,10) to designate the Essene Community itself, which appears in several symbolic guises in the course of the poem (e.g. the Tree of knowledge, the stronghold founded on the rock, etc.). The poet then turns to the internal struggles of the Community. He recalls his own difficult destiny once more, and the terribly demanding life asked of those whom God has chosen to follow consciously the 'way' of spiritual development. As the account proceeds, however, we become aware that it is really characterizing the crisis in the Teacher's view of that life, and the struggles are sometimes expressive even of a kind of paranoia. The poem in fact traces the psychic process of breakdown and renewal which belongs to the pattern of initiation here among the Essenes as in other Mysteries, working itself out on the social level. God has established this pattern, so that it may lead through knowledge to purification from guilt and 'communion' with God himself. Thus renewed, man stands among the ranks and shares the 'estate' of the angels, the cosmic powers who are actively part of the divine-cosmic order. The regeneration is represented under the symbol of the immortal and unfading Tree of Paradise, presently known only to the initiates but destined to bring about wider change in the apocalyptic future. The Teacher contrasts his former state of being buffeted like a sailor on the stormy seas, with the firm centre in himself and in the esoteric Community, the fortress in which he awaits in inner certainty the time of God's visitation. The imagery of warfare with which he characterizes the apocalyptic struggle is probably not to be taken literally, but stands for the 'victory' of God and the Light over the Darkness in each individual. The outward expression of the victory is rather the resurrection of the dead, corresponding to the death and rebirth already experienced by the Essene initiates.

And I said: "Through Thy covenant
I shall go strengthened for ever,

*

and on Thy grace be stayed.
   For Thou Thyself art truth,
and all Thy works are righteousness."

- 10 -

Blessed art Thou, O Lord,[1]
for Thou hast never abandoned the orphan
neither despised the poor.
   Unbounded is Thy power,
and Thy glory hath no measure.

Angels of wondrous strength
minister unto Thee,
and they walk at the side of the meek
and of them that are fearful of right-doing,
and of all the lost and lorn
that stand in need of mercy,
lifting them out of the slough
when that their feet are mired.

So, for mine own part,
to them that were my familiars
I had become a thing of contention;
a symbol of strife and discord
unto my friends;
an occasion of fury and anger
unto my fellows;
of murmuring and complaint
to all mine acquaintances.
All that ate of my bread
lifted their heels against me;
all that shared my board
mouthed distortions about me;
and they with whom I consorted

2.   The poet emphasises again the actual physical symptoms of a psycho-somatic
      nature which attend the crisis of initiation. In many Mysteries, the neophyte
      entered a state of death-like collapse and was ritually buried. Though this
      had obvious 'symbolic' connotations, we should not neglect the overwhelm-
      ing reality of the experience among those who 'drew near the gates of death.'

3.   Although these passages may have a basis in the career of the Teacher when
      he attempted to win over the existing body of Hasidim (the 'Pious') to his
      vision, it soon becomes evident that he is describing predominantly inner
      experiences: the light turns to darkness, he feels 'confusion and panic,'
      everyone seems to be against him, even inanimate things seemed to be hostile
      toward him. Such 'anxiety' images point to the inner process of breakdown
      and renewal. Close parallels can be found once more in the Babylonian
      initiation-text: 'I will praise the Lord of Wisdom':

              I, who used to walk like a proud man, have learned
                   to slip by unnoticed.
              Though I was a respectable man, I have become a slave.
              To my many relations I have become like a recluse.
              If I walk the street, fingers are pointed at me;
              If I enter the palace, eyes blink.
              My own town looks on me as an enemy;
              Even my land is savage and hostile.
              My friend has become a stranger,
              My companion has become an evil person and a demon.
              In his rage my comrade denounces me,
              Constantly my associate furbishes his weapons.
              My close friend has brought my life into danger;
              My slave has publicly cursed me in the assembly ...
              ... the crowd has defamed me.
              When someone who knows me sees me, he passes by
              on the other side.
                   (Translated from Akkadian [Babylonian] by R.D. Biggs,
                   in J.B. Pritchard 1975, p.150).

      All Mysteries included a stage of alienation, of wandering or of inner
      estrangement from the living order of society and the cosmos. In some
      primitive societies, the neophytes are treated like ghosts, shunned and feared,
      until they are ritually purified by the completion of their initiation and
      welcomed as newly born beings.

turned their backs upon me
and defamed me up and down.

By reason of the secret
which Thou hast hidden within me
they went spreading slander against me
to men that were bent on mischief.

Because they hemmed in my way,
and because of their infamy,
the fount of understanding was hidden
and the secret of truth,
while they — they went on contriving
the mischief of their heart,
opening their shameless mouths,
unleashing their lying tongues
which were like the venom of adders
fitfully spurting forth;
like reptiles they shot forth their hissing
— vipers that could not be charmed.

It was a constant pain,
a fretting wound
in the body of Thy servant,[2]
causing his spirit to droop,
wearing down his strength,
until he could not withstand.
    They overtook me between the straits,
where there was no escape.

*

They thundered abuse of me
to the tune of the harp,
and in jingles chorused their jeers.

Confusion and panic beset me,
horrendous anguish and pain,[3]
like to the throes of travail.

4.   A stage at which bodily existence is experienced as constriction and
       'imprisonment' is general in Mysteries. On one level it is the further
       extension of the death-and alienation-symbolism just noted: the initiate's own
       body becomes strange and hostile to him, trapping him rather than
       expressing his living presence. In Gnosticism these aspects are carried to still
       further extremes. It is already found in our Babylonian text, however:

   My arms are powerless — my own flesh is a manacle,
   My feet are fallen flat — my own person is a fetter.
           (Pritchard, p.154)

My heart was distraught within me;
I clothed me in mourning garb;
my tongue cleaved to the roof of my mouth.
In their hearts they reviled me,
and openly vented their spleen.
The light of my face turned to darkness,
my radiance to gloom.

Thou, O my God,
hadst enlarged my heart,
but ever they sought to constrict it.
They hedged me about with thick darkness.
I ate my bread amid sighs,
and my drink was mingled with tears
which had none end.
Mine eyes were dimmed with anguish,
and with all that beclouds the daylight
my soul was overcast.
Sorrow was all about me,
and the pall of shame o'er my face.
The very bread that I ate
seemed to be quarrelling with me,
the very drink that I drank
to be at odds with me.

They purposed to trammel my spirit,
to wear down all my strength
with blasphemous mystic lore,
converting the works of God
into that which they guiltily imagined.

I was bound with unbreakable cords,
with fetters that could not be sundered.[4]
A strong wall was upreared against me;
bars of iron restrained me
and doors of brass.

*

5.   The water-symbolism employed in interestingly varied ways in the Essene
poems is 'unhistorical,' that is, floods are not an actual threat in the deserts
of Syria and Judea; nor is the sea-storm imagery derived from the actual
experience of sea-faring, but has its origins in the Mystery-language of Egypt
and Babylonia. 'Death by drowning' has a Mystery-significance in the Adonis
cult too. On similar elements in the biblical tradition, especially the Psalms
of royal initiation, see F.H. Borsch 1967, pp.123-25. The waters which threaten
to close over the head of the initiate are not literal waters but the powers of
unconsciousness, overwhelming his mind.

He is rescued from them by the intervention of the god. In the Bible we
find the symbolism especially in Psalm 69:

> Save me, O God: for the waters have come up to my neck,
> I sink in deep mire, where there is no foothold;
> I have come into deep waters, and the flood sweeps over me ...
> Let not the flood sweep over me, or the deep swallow me up,
> or the pit close its mouth over me. (Psalm 69:1f, 15).

We may understand it as an extension of the 'anxiety-symbolism,' the
pressing in upon the soul of a world perceived as hostile and alien. Now it
actually threatens consciousness altogether. The initiate, however, has to let
his old identity be overwhelmed. The waters are symbolic also of the 'abyss'
from which the world was created (the conscious world arising from the
unconscious powers of the soul). By trusting in the god or in Yahweh, he will
be reborn from the deep. The waters of flood and of raging sea in this poem
of the Teacher will reappear shortly as the feeding waters in the depths,
nourishing the Tree: the rivers of Eden.

The accounts of early Christian and Gnostic baptism preserve much of the
initiatory symbolism of water in its several aspects. Sometimes the river of
the baptizer is said to become a raging whirlpool! Through baptism-initiation,
the unconscious energies are harmonized, however. See my *Beginnings of
Christianity*, Edinburgh 1991, pp.92ff.

Over my soul swirled the torrents of hell.[5]

*

My heart was sore distraught
because of their obloquy
which they did heap upon me.

*

Ruin encompassed me,
disaster which knew no bound,
destruction which had no end.

*

But Thou, O my God,
didst open mine ear,
didst vindicate my cause
against all them that traduced me.
Yea, Thou didst deliver me
from the company of the vain,
from fellowship with crime,
and bring me into communion
with all the holy and pure,
purging my soul of guilt.

So am I come to know
that in Thy loving-kindness
lies hope for them that repent
and for them that abandon sin,
and confidence for him
who walks in the way of Thy heart
without perversity.

Therefore, though peoples roar,
though kingdoms rage,
I shall go comforted.
When that they gather together,
I shall not be dismayed,
knowing that in a space
Thou wilt raise a reviving for Thy people

6.   The poet seems to envisage a kind of missionary activity. Despite the closed
        character of the Essene sect, some sort of active search for disciples must
        have been organized, and we should remember the existence of the scattered
        Essene communities up and down the country alongside the Community at
        Qumran. A commissioning to preach is by no means incompatible with the
        Mystery-character of Essenism. Cf. the 'sending forth' of the prophet in the
        Hermetic *Poimandres* 27 (see below p.204).

7.   The Essenes have direct knowledge of divine things through their initiation.
        Their consciousness enables them to live already in the still-to-be-manifested
        age, and in their rituals they are in the company of the divine beings (angels).
        They need no intermediaries such as prophets, the priests of the Jerusalem
        Temple, etc. The idea of partaking in the life of the Angels who stand before
        God and perform a liturgy is known in the Jewish esoteric tradition: see
        especially the work known as *III* or *Hebrew Book of Enoch* 39-40. The latter
        work represents the same tradition as the *Merkavah* mystics, the 'descenders
        to the Chariot,' that is, the esoteric teaching of the Pharisees and their
        successors. That Essenes and Pharisees had common roots is again suggested,
        for at Qumran has been found an 'Angelic Liturgy' (4Q 400-407, 11Q 5f: in
        Vermes 1987, pp.221-30).

and grant to Thine inheritance a remnant,
and refine them, to purge them of guilt.

Whenas in all their deeds
they have done as Thy truth enjoined,
Thou wilt judge them with loving-kindness,
with plenteous compassion
and abundance of forgiveness,
guiding them according to Thy word,
stablishing them by Thy counsel,
by Thine unswerving truth.

Thou hast acted for Thyself and for Thy glory,
that the Law may come to fruition,
and has sent among mankind
men that be schooled in Thy counsel
to tell forth Thy wonders through the ages,[6]
world without end,
to rehearse Thy deeds of power
without surcease,
that all nations may know Thy truth,
and all peoples Thy glory.

All these men hast Thou brought
into communion with Thee,
and hast given them common estate
with the Angels of Thy Presence.
There stands no intermediary among them
to approach Thee in their behalf
and bring them back Thy word
filtered through his mind;[7]
for they themselves are answered
from out of Thy glorious mouth.
They are Thy courtiers,
sharing the estate
of all the heavenly beings.

8.   The Tree fuses many aspects of esoteric symbolism. Its different aspects are well surveyed in Eliade 1958, pp.265ff. The present Tree is already discussed in the introductory section of this chapter: it combines above all the aspect of the cosmic Tree, linking the three regions of the universe (heaven, earth, abyss) and so standing for cosmic knowledge, and the paradisal Tree, which gives life and immortality. Among the Essenes, the traditional symbolism is given a special emphasis, however. Pre-Qumranian works in the Essene tradition, such as the *Testaments of the Patriarchs*, already mention the idea that the Messiah will re-open the Gates of Paradise and give the chosen fruit from the Tree of Life (see below, pp.138f). From the poem of the Teacher, it appears that the initiates already partake in the unfading life of the Tree, which in one sense becomes therefore an image of the Community and its dynamic role, growing and burgeoning as the 'new age' becomes reality both inwardly and in outer events. The 'rivers of Eden' connect it with Paradise, but the 'fountain' next becomes a source of light and heat pointing to the Last Days.

The fiery judgment reflects Iranian ideas again, and particularly the characterization of its different impact upon the righteous and the sinners. In Iranian thought the 'fountain' is imaged as pouring molten metal. 'The ordeal causes no discomfort to those who are already saved,' explains R.C. Zaehner, 'for the surging metal seems to them like warm milk; but the damned must experience the full rigour and reality of the torment' (Zaehner 1975, p.142). The apocalyptic 'river of fire' is more fully described in another poem from the 'Thanksgiving Scroll' (number 6 in Gaster's numeration):

> when the rivers of Belial
> burst their high banks
> — rivers that are like fire
> devouring all that draw their waters,
> rivers whose runnels destroy
> green tree and dry tree alike
> rivers that are like fire
> which sweeps with flaming sparks
> devouring all that drink their waters
> — a fire which consumes
> all foundations of clay,
> every solid bedrock;
> when the foundations of the mountains
> become a raging blaze,
> when granite roots are turned
> to streams of pitch,
> when the flame devours
> down to the great abyss,
> when the floods of Belial burst forth
> unto hell itself ...
>   (I QH III:27-32).

The Essene initiate experiences this too by anticipation. For he is already involved in the 'warfare of the angels' (Light against Darkness) in his higher

For these hast Thou planted a tree[8]
which blooms with flowers unfading,
whose boughs put forth thick leaves,
which stands firm-planted for ever,
and gives shade to all things;
whose branches tower to heaven,
whose roots sink down to the abyss.
All the rivers of Eden
water its boughs;
it thrives beyond all bounds,
burgeons beyond all measure.
Its branches stretch across the world,
beyond all bounds,
and its roots sink deep into hell.

For them, too, shall the Fountain of Light
    well forth,
a perpetual spring unfailing.
Howbeit in its fiery sparks all infamous men shall
    be burned;
it shall be as a flame devouring the guilty,
until they be destroyed.

These men were mine own familiars,
who shared the same fortune as I,
but they let themselves be seduced
by garblers of truth,
that they no longer wished to do right.

Thou hadst given them commandments, O God,
that they might have profit of their lives
by walking Thy holy way,
whereon the uncircumcised and unclean
and profane may not pass.
But they wavered from the way of Thy heart
and ensnared themselves in their lusts.
Belial counselled their hearts

consciousness, though it becomes outwardly visible only at the Judgment. Individual death may have been another moment of such judgment for the Essenes: signs of burning on many of the remains in the cemetery at Qumran suggest a special rite which some have represented as a 'baptism by fire.'

9.   Another imagery of the Essene Community, an esoteric stronghold until the 'time of God's visitation.'

10.   The Teacher applies to the Community the language traditionally applied to God's Temple. Since his activity led to a rupture with the authorities of the actual Temple at Jerusalem, we may take this passage as evidence of an 'internalizing' of the whole concept of a Temple in which divine presence is manifested. The tendency was taken much further in early Christianity. Among the Essenes, there may have been an expectation (following their usual pattern) that the inner reality would become outward too when history unrolled to the new age: the *Temple Scroll*, which may be by the Teacher, may describe the Law of the age-to-come and likewise the grandiose Temple and environs which God will then establish. But the interpretation of the *Temple Scroll* in this visionary or 'eschatological' way remains uncertain.

and, through their wicked devisings,
they tainted themselves with guilt.

Even I aforetime
was as a sailor in a ship
when the seas do froth and foam.
All the breakers thereof
kept pounding against me,
and the whirlwind blew about me,
and there was no moment of calm
wherein to catch my breath,
neither could I steer
a course upon the waters.
The deeps echoed my groaning,
and I came near to the gates of death.

But now I am as one
that has entered a stronghold,[9]
taken refuge behind a high wall
until deliverance come.
For I have stayed myself on Thy truth, O my God,
knowing full well
that Thou foundest Thy structure on a rock,
that its rafters are truly poised
and its stones well laid,[10]
that of tested stone are its walls
and unbreakably strong its bars,
that all who repair unto it
shall never be moved,
for there shall no stranger invade it.
Its doors are a sheet of protection
which none may force,
and its bars are strong bars
which cannot be broken.
No armed band can storm it,
neither all the war-hosts of wickedness together.

11.   The stage of the Judgment also described in poem 6:

> when the depths of the abyss are in turmoil,
> cast up mire in abundance,
> when the earth cries out in anguish,
> for the havoc wrought in the world,
> when all its depths are aquake,
> and all that is on it quails
> and quivers in mighty havoc;
> when with his mighty roar
> God thunders forth,
> and his holy welkin trembles,
> as his glorious truth is revealed,
> and the hosts of heaven give forth their voice,
> and the world's foundations rock and reel;
> when warfare waged by the soldiers of heaven
> sweeps through the world
> and turns not back until final doom
> — warfare the like of which
> has never been.
>   (I QH III:33-36).

Note that the 'warfare' in these documents is not a war among men, but a spiritual and cosmic one.

12.   That the Essenes believed in bodily resurrection is asserted by the Church Father, Hippolytus, whose knowledge was accurate in other respects:

> For they confess that the flesh also will rise and be immortal as the soul is already immortal, which they now say, when separated from the body, enters a place of fragrant air and light, to rest until the judgment ... For they say there will be a judgment and a conflagration of everything, and that the wicked will be eternally punished. (Hippolytus, *Refutation of All Heresies* IX, 22).

It is most likely therefore that the end of the poem should be interpreted as a reference to resurrection. Vermes takes the verbs in the passage as imperatives:

> Hoist a banner,
> O you who lie in the dust!
> O bodies gnawed by worms,
> raise up an ensign for the destruction of wickedness!
> The sinful shall be destroyed
> in the battles against the ungodly.

Hippolytus' comment that the body shall become immortal 'as the soul is already immortal' shows a good grasp of the real meaning of the Essene doctrine (which was also taken up by the Pharisees). Resurrection is not an arbitrary miracle, but inner reality becoming outer reality, as in all Essene thinking. The death and regeneration of the initiate in their Mysteries is an anticipation of what will one day become historical actuality.

For when at the last they so essay,
the sword of God will be swift
to wreak a final judgment,[11]
and all who acknowledge His truth
will rouse themselves to do battle
against the forces of wickedness,
and all the sons of guilt
will be no more.

The Warrior will bend his bow,
and lift the siege for ever,
and open the gates everlasting
to bring forth His weapons of war;
and His legions shall go marching
from end to end of the earth,
and there shall be no escape
for the guilty impulse of men.
They shall trample it to destruction,
that naught remain thereof.
There shall be no hope for it
in weapons never so many,
neither any escape
for all that fight in its cause.
   For the victory shall belong
unto God on High,

*

and though they that lie in the dust[12]
will have raised their flag,
and though this worm which is man
will have lifted up his banner
to do battle against the truth,
yet shall they be cut off
when battle is joined with the presumptuous;
and he that sought to bring
the scourge of a flood overflowing
will never reach that stronghold.

- 12 -

Source: I QH VII:26-33. Translated from the Hebrew by Theodor H. Gaster.

1. The poet uses the specifically Essene opening formula, and this short poem summarizes the Essene attitude to the gift of knowledge: wisdom is a heavenly mystery, God's secret. Man's knowledge of it cannot be ascribed to his own attainment, nor does he have any right to it. Not even the angels can claim so much, but must stand humbled before God. God is utterly unique and transcendent, and alone has the eternal vision which he chooses to share with his creatures.

    In the moment of insight, therefore, the Essene initiates felt exalted but at the same time held to the biblical view of man's unworthiness (cf. Psalm 8:4: 'What is man that Thou art mindful of him, or the son of man that Thou dost care for him?') Knowledge came from outside. There is a clear contrast here with the interpretation of such moments by the Gnostics whom we shall meet below. They identify themselves, not with the mortal vessel which receives divine knowledge, but with the exalted, knowing spirit. It is true that in the Gnostic understanding knowledge still comes from without; but they interpreted that to mean that man's true self lies in the 'beyond,' making his earthly identity only an illusion or state of alienation from his real being. It is as though Essenes and Gnostics share many of the same religious experiences, centrally that of *gnosis* (knowledge of the divine mysteries), but develop their understanding of them in polar opposite ways. Looking at them historically, we should not forget how much they had in common or that the visionary tendencies within Essenism sometimes threatened to disrupt the biblical framework and that 'the sect was mystical and dangerously near to gnosticism in some of its ideas' (John Pryke's comment in his 'Eschatology and the Dead Sea Scrolls,' in Pryke 1969, p.56).

- 19 -

Source: I QH XI,27–XII,35. Translated from the Hebrew by Theodor H. Gaster.

1. The poet's emphasis now falls on the achieving of knowledge and the 'inner vision.' This comes about, however, only through God's grace. Just as in the time of 'travail' and inner ordeal the initiand had to rely on the support of God's mercy, so now he has God to thank for the revelation and the joy it brings. Even the power to sing praise to him is itself given by God. The initiated soul stands or abides in the presence of God: Mystery-language recalling the *epopteia*, the *adoravi de proxumo* of the pagan cults, but also looking forward to the 'abiding' in the presence of the Christ described in the Gospel of John. The symbolism here also includes a reference to the 'tent' (or 'tabernacle') of the divine presence, which likewise figures importantly in the background to John. The inner vision has a cosmic meaning, for it is next related to the cycles of day and night, the seasons and 'all the birthdays of time.' The attainment of vision is similarly a 'birthday,' and is reached at a 'turning-point' analogous to those of the cosmic rhythms, which as in the

- 12 -

I give thanks unto Thee, O Lord,[1]
for Thou hast given me insight into Thy truth
and knowledge of Thy wondrous secrets.
    In loving-kindness to lowly man,
in abundance of mercy to wayward hearts,
who is like Thee among the gods, O Lord,
and what truth is like Thine?

Who can prove righteous in Thy sight
when Thou bringest him unto judgment?
Not even a spirit can answer Thy charge,
and none can withstand Thy wrath.

Yet, all that are children of Thy truth
Thou bringest before Thee with forgiveness,
cleansing them of their transgressions
through Thine abundant goodness,
and, through Thy plenteous mercies,
causing them to stand in Thy presence for ever.

For Thou art a God everlasting,
and all Thy ways hold firm for all time;
and there is none else beside Thee.
    But what is man — vain, empty man,
that he should understand Thy great wondrous works?

- 19 -

Blessed art Thou, O Lord,[1]
Who hast given unto man the insight of knowledge,
to understand Thy wonders,
discern Thy truth,
tell forth Thine abundant mercies.

Blessed art Thou, O God of compassion and grace,
for the greatness of Thy power,
the abundance of Thy truth,

Book of Enoch are said to be 'decreed by the mouth of God' (cf. above, Poem 1, note 2). Imagery of water recalls the rituals of baptism (already associated with the 'holy spirit' of God) and the 'flood'-symbolism of the overwhelming of consciousness; but all is now harmonized, brought back from darkness into light: 'a light everlasting.' No man can grasp this by his own strength. To attempt to do so is to commit the sin of 'overhaste,' instead of waiting for the inner ripening brought about by God and loses the sense of harmony. The initiate must learn to wait for the reward of his discipline, which comes suddenly — it 'bursts upon them, they shall rejoice' — rather than in a consciously expected way. With the vision of the contrast between the merely human and the infinite glory of God, the poet touches the limits of conscious utterance altogether and ends, not on a note of affirmation, but in passionate questions.

2.   'Standing in the presence of the god' was the climax of the pagan Mysteries, the *epopteia*. The terminology here also anticipates the Gospel of John, however, with its language of 'abiding' or 'remaining' in the presence of Christ: see especially John 15:4ff. Connections with the Gospel of John and its background are notably frequent in this poem.

3.   The 'tent' as the 'holy abode' of God is the tent or tabernacle which preceded the Temple as the place of worship for the wandering Israelites. The *Trimorphic Protennoia* XIII 47: 14f, uses the symbolism in its reference to the 'revelation in their tents,' and once again stands in close relation to the Prologue of the Gospel of John, which at 1:14 reads literally 'he pitched his tent among us,' with a play on words suggesting the Hebrew word for 'divine presence' (cf. Welburn 1991, p.260).

   The Essenes at Qumran, of course, did not live in tents, but the underlying external reality is suggested by a passage in Philo, *On the Contemplative Life* about the Therapeutae. The latter were an order among the Alexandrian Jews which was very similar, if not identical to the Essenes of Palestinian Judaism. They have their settlement, near the Mareotic Lake as the Essenes were near the Dead Sea. 'In each house there is a sacred chamber, which is called a sanctuary or *monasterion* in which in isolation they are initiated into the Mysteries of the holy life. They take nothing into it, neither drink nor food nor anything else necessary for bodily needs, but laws and oracles delivered through the prophets, and psalms and the other books through which knowledge and piety are increased and perfected' (*De Vita Contemplativa* 26).

the profusion of Thy mercies
over all Thy works.

Rejoice the soul of Thy servant in Thy truth,
and in Thy righteousness make me clean,
even as when aforetime I waited on Thy bounty
and hoped on Thy mercies and forgiveness,
Thou didst bring release to my travail,
and even as when I leaned on Thy compassion,
and Thou didst comfort me in my sorrow.

Blessed art Thou, O Lord,
for Thou it is hath wrought these things,
and placed in the mouth of Thy servant
power to pray and to win Thy grace,
and all readiness of tongue;
and hast prepared for me the guerdon of righteousness
and the reward of devotion,
that I may attain to stand in Thy presence.

... my soul will exult
because it hath come to abide in Thy presence[2]
and to dwell secure in Thy holy abode,
in calm and quietude.

In my tent I will chant[3]
songs of joy and salvation,
and in the midst of them that fear Thee
tell forth the praise of Thy name
to all ages to come;
pouring forth prayer and supplication
always, at all times and seasons;
when daylight comes forth from its abode;
when, in its ordered course,
day reaches its turning-point,
in accordance with the rules of the sun;
and again at the turn of the evening,

4.   The phrase recalls the 'Aion'-mysticism of the Mysteries: at the completion of a cycle, time is 'reborn' as the new day or year. The death-birth of the Aion was celebrated in the yearly cycle on 6 January, the day adopted by the early Christians as that of the 'epiphany' or 'manifestation' of Christ at his baptism in the Jordan. Important to the Mystery-idea is the idea of 'crisis' or turning-point (cf. the Gospel of John again: the *'krisis* of the world,' only partly rendered by our modern term 'judgment,' as we see from 3:19: 'and this is the *krisis*, that the light has come into the world.') A turning-point offers us the possibility of a new 'beginning,' or of rejecting the light and remaining behind — which is what merely continuing actually amounts to.

5.   The conveying of God's 'holy spirit' and the water-imagery that accompanies it alludes to the baptismal rites of the Essenes. An exciting new source has been brought forward by R. Eisenman and J. Wise (1992) in the 'Admonitions to the Sons of Dawn' (4Q298). Baptism evidently follows an all-night vigil (hence the title) at a turning-point of light. Adding this evidence to that of column iii in the *Community Rule*, they comment: 'The *Maskil* (Guardian) is "to make known to and teach the sons of Light ... the Ways of Light" and how to "be reckoned among the Perfect ..." In particular, he is to instruct them in baptismal procedures, which include being "purified by the Holy Spirit," "looking upon the Living Light ..." and "walking in Perfection in all the Ways of God, which he commanded concerning his appointed times ...".' (p.163). Eisenman and Wise point repeatedly to connections between the Scrolls and the early Christian literature in the name of James, brother of the Lord and leader of the Jewish Christians. Some traditions in his name assert that through baptism one becomes a 'son of the Holy Spirit' just as the Essenes became 'sons of Light.' Links with Christian baptism are further evident in the references to the 'spring of knowledge,' and so on. The closest analogy is again the Gospel of John, for instance 4:14 where Jesus imparts 'a spring of water welling up to eternal life' in contrast to the water which leaves one to be thirsty again. Similar language is to be found however in the *Gospel of Thomas* 13 where Jesus tells Thomas, 'Thou hast become drunk from the bubbling spring which I have measured out,' and immediately afterwards gives him secret instruction. See also the *Gospel of Thomas* 108: 'Jesus said: He who shall drink from my mouth shall become like me; I myself will become he, and the hidden things shall be revealed to him.' Drinking the water forms a part of the ritual of baptism among the Mandeans, and may have done so among other esoteric baptizing sects.

when daylight departs,
as the rule of darkness begins;
and again in the season of night,
when it reaches its turning-point,
and when the morning breaks;
and when, in the presence of the daylight,
night withdraws to its abode;
when night departs and day comes in,
alway, at all the birthdays of time,[4]
at the moments when seasons begin;
when they reach their turning-points;
when they come in order due
according to their several signs,
as these have dominion in due order assured,
decreed by the mouth of God
and by the laws of existence.

*

Behold, for mine own part,
I have reached the inner vision,
and through the spirit Thou hast placed within me,
come to know Thee, my God.

I have heard Thy wondrous secret,
nor heard it amiss.
Through Thy holy spirit,[5]
through Thy mystic insight,
Thou hast caused a spring of knowledge to well up
     within me,
a fountain of strength,
pouring forth waters unstinted,
a floodtide of loving-kindness and of all-consuming zeal.
Thou hast put an end to my darkness,
and the splendour of Thy glory has become unto me as
     a light everlasting.

Wickedness hath been consumed altogether,
and deceit existeth no more.

6.   The poet stresses the surprise and suddenness of the awakening to knowl-
        edge. This knowledge cannot be acquired step by step: however much effort
        a man makes, he must still wait for God to ripen the knowledge within him,
        to unloose the spring which then wells up to his joy and wonder.

7.   Visionary knowledge is never absolute, but is given by God and accommo-
        dated to each individual's capacity. This is a principle of the Essene
        community which ought to have helped the members work together. The
        different knowledge given to each corresponds in the human world of the
        spiritual Community to the divinely ordained limits set to the spirits and
        powers of nature, who may not transgress the bounds established by the
        divine word (see Poem 1, note 2 above, and the references to these ideas in
        the *Book of Enoch* there).

8.   These passages in the Essene *Hodayot* repeatedly suggest Paul and his concept
        of the 'old Adam,' who was 'of the earth, earthy' and who is put off, like an
        old garment, at baptism. See particularly 1 Corinthians 15:47-50 which leads
        Paul to reveal 'a mystery' (15:51). The contrast of old and new Man, together
        with Mystery-instruction, with its setting in the rite of baptism, is thus part
        of the common heritage of Christianity and was obviously influenced directly
        by esoteric Jewish practices like those of the Essenes. In Christianity they
        were taken up in rather strikingly different ways. Moreover, there were also
        types of baptism which had no connection with the giving of the 'Holy
        Spirit,' but rather suggest Gnostic practices and ideas (see Acts 18:24–19:7,
        probably all referring to Alexandrian practice).

Perverseness is gone down to perdition,
for ... existeth no more ...
insolent fury is at an end,
for it cannot withstand thine anger.

The sins which I committed aforetime
I committed in overhaste;
for now am I come to know that no man is righteous
    with Thee.
For there is none can understand all Thy hidden things,
nor answer Thy charge against him;
but all must needs wait upon Thy goodness,
for Thou, in Thy loving-kindness wilt reveal to them
    Thy truth,
that they may come to know Thee;
and when Thy glory bursts upon them, they shall
    rejoice.[6]

According to each man's knowledge,
and the meed of his understanding[7]
hast Thou drawn them nigh unto Thee,
that they may serve Thee in their several domains,
as Thou hast assigned their roles,
... transgressing not Thy word.

Behold, I was taken from dust,
nipped out of clay,
and I am become but a source of filth
and of shameful nakedness,
a heap of dust,
a thing kneaded with water,
a dwelling-place of darkness.

That which is moulded of clay must needs return to dust
at the end of its term,[8]
and lie again in the dust
whence it was taken.

9. The poet has reached the bounds of poetic expression, and his questions do not attempt to contain the infinite, but rather to hold him open to God's inspiration. It is a characteristic Essene mixture of absolute commitment and selfless abandonment to God.

- Additional hymn -
Source: I QH XIV:1-27. Translated from the Hebrew by Theodor H. Gaster.

1. In a somewhat fragmentary hymn, the poet identifies the Essene Community of initiates with the promised 'faithful remnant' who are to inherit the biblical rewards forfeited by sinful Israel. The esotericism of the sect is thus given a historical role and related to the Old Testament. It makes the Community into the 'true Israel,' since the 'kingdom of priests and an holy nation' is the phrase in Exodus 19:6 for God's chosen people, as God himself described them to Moses. Here however the title can be applied only to those who have 'had vision' of God, and who have 'discernment,' that is, the ability to distinguish the cosmic principles of Light and Dark, who participate directly in the 'holy spirit' and 'draw near' to God through the stages of Essene initiation. The cosmic dimension points way from history, claiming validity for 'all generations of time' and 'for all ages to come.' (Ideas of a 'remnant,' and a similar tension between earthly-historical and cosmic meaning, are crucial to early Christian thought — see for instance Paul's Letter to the Romans 11:5 — and especially to the thought of Jesus). The keeping of God's Law is thus not merely a precondition of spiritual enlightenment: it makes the Essenes a 'proof' of God's truth and a manifestation of his proffered love.

How can mere dust and clay give answer to its Maker,
or how understand His works,
or how stand before its Accuser?
    Even the holy angels,
the everlasting spirits,
the reservoirs of glory,
the wellsprings of knowledge and power,
— even they cannot tell forth all Thy glory,
nor stand against Thine anger,
nor answer Thy charge.
For Thou art ever righteous,
and none can gainsay Thee.
How much less, then, he who returns to his dust?

Lo, I am stricken dumb.[9]
What can I say against this?
I have spoken but according to my knowledge
and only with such sense of right
as a creature of clay may possess.
But how can I speak except Thou open my mouth,
and how understand, if Thou give me not insight;
or how contend, save Thou open my heart;
or how walk straight save Thou guide my feet?
How can my foot stand,
how can I be strong in power,
how can I endure save by thy grace?

- **Additional Hymn** -
I give thanks unto Thee, O Lord,[1]
for Thou hast granted a remnant
unto Thy people
and a revival
unto Thine inheritance.
    Thou hast raised up among them
men of truth
and sons of light,

*

2.   The participation in the 'holy spirit' referred to takes place specifically through the ritual purifications of Essene baptism (see especially the previous poem and notes), and 'drawing close' to God, evidently in stages ('The nearer I draw') rightly suggested to Gaster that this passage must be understood in a strictly sectarian sense (1957, p.215 and his cross-reference to p.201 n32). Josephus says in his account of the Essenes that a member who had successfully weathered the first probationary year was regarded as 'one who comes nearer' — probably a technical term (*Jewish War* II,7,7).

men of abundant compassion
men of stalwart spirit,
men of tempered soul,
men steeled to sustain Thy judgments.

Through them hast Thou kept Thy covenant
and confirmed Thy pledge,
to render us unto Thee
a kingdom of priests and an holy nation
for all generations of time
and for all the ages to come.
   Verily, O Lord, Thou dost sustain
them that have vision of Thee.

Blessed art Thou, O Lord,
Who puttest the sense of discernment
into the heart of Thy servants,
that they may walk blamelessly before Thee,
and be steeled against all the devices of wickedness,
and that they may bless Thy name,
loving all that Thou lovest
and abhorring all that Thou hatest,
and stray not in the waywardness of men,
but, through the spirit of discernment
      which is theirs,
distinguish the good from the wicked
and keep all their deeds undefiled.

Behold, for mine own part,
through that discernment which Thou hast bestowed
I indeed have attained to such knowledge,
for by virtue of Thy good pleasure
I have been granted a share in Thy holy spirit,[2]
and Thou hast brought me close
to an understanding of Thee.
The nearer I draw to Thee,
the more am I filled with zeal

3. The strict enforcement of the Law in the Qumran Community was the task of the Guardian, and adherence to the divine Law was what made the esoteric Community an image of the divine law in the cosmos. Recently published materials from the fragmentary Scrolls include a Conclusion to the *Damascus Rule*, of which several copies are known. Many of its themes overlap with our poem: the priestly nature of the Community and its leaders, again with reference back to Moses, expulsion of those who refuse to keep the Law, the destiny of the Nations and the inheritance. The sons of Levi are instructed to bless those within the fold, and to curse those outside. The 'nationalism' here should be understood, however, in terms of the 'remnant' or 'true Israel' idea, which represents an intensification and spiritualizing of the Jewish ideal, rather than as a jingoistic 'orgy of nationalistic "cursing",' as Eisenman and Wise assert (1992 p.10; for their further comments and the text, pp.212-19). We have to do here with a literary form going back to Deuteronomy.

4. Josephus stresses that the Essene 'must swear terrible oaths, first that he will revere the Godhead, secondly that he will deal justly with men, will injure no-one either of his own accord or at another's bidding, will ever hate the wicked and co-operate with the good, will keep faith at all times and with all men — especially with rulers, since all power is conferred by God' (*Jewish War* II,7,8). His account again confirms the sectarian reference of our hymn. Oaths are a feature of esoteric and Mystery cults, and feature strongly in earlier references to Christianity.

against all that do wickedness
and against all men of deceit.
For they that draw near to Thee
cannot see Thy commandments defied,
and they that have knowledge of Thee
can brook no change of Thy words,[3]
seeing that Thou art the essence of right,
and all Thine elect are the proof of Thy truth.

Thou wilt bring eternal doom
on all frowardness and transgression,
and Thy righteousness will stand revealed
in the sight of all Thou hast made.

Lo, through Thy great goodness
I have come to know these things,
and committed myself by oath[4]
never to sin against Thee
nor do aught that is evil in Thy sight;
and I have been granted admittance
to this community.

So, for mine own part,
I will admit no comrade
into fellowship with me
save by the measure of his understanding,
and only by the measure
of his share in this common lot
will I show friendship to him.
I will not countenance evil,
neither recognize fraud.
I will not barter Thy truth for wealth,
nor all Thy judgments for a bribe.
Only as Thou drawest a man unto Thee
will I draw him unto myself,
and as Thou keepest him afar,
so too will I abhor him;

5.   The 'new' ending to the *Damascus Rule* states explicitly that 'he who was
      expelled' (that is, for non-obedience of the Law 'must leave, and whosoever
      eats with him or asks after the welfare of the man who was excommunicated
      or keeps company with him, that fact should be recorded by the Overseer
      according to established practice and his judgment will be completed'
      (Eisenman and Wise, p.219).
          Such an undertaking was probably implicit in the 'oath' mentioned by
      Josephus. The curse on those who 'barter Thy truth for wealth' also often
      forms part of such initiatory oaths: cf. the *Secret Book of John* which says
      'Cursed be everyone who will exchange these things for a gift or for food or
      for drink or for clothing or for any other such thing' (II 31:34-37). Compare
      too the Hermetic oath (p.24).

6.   With an emphasis unusual among the Essene writings, which so stress the
      themes of wisdom and morality, the poet now views the existence of the
      esoteric Community, the 'faithful remnant' as less a human achievement than
      a sign of God's love and the fulfilment of his promise. To offset our
      impression — our quite correct impression — of moral severity, we are here
      shown that the whole organization was at the same time regarded as
      dependent on God's love, and the response at the highest level should be the
      poet's: 'I in turn will love thee freely.'
          The extraordinary individualism which Essenism united with the cosmic
      content of the Mysteries meant intense struggles, both against one's own
      lower nature and within the Community. It is necessary to be reminded,
      therefore, that the individual attains his goal not just in sheer individuation
      (rebirth) but in that mutual love given and received by God. At the juncture
      of history at which Essenism flourished, the achieving of individuality still
      had to be the predominant aspect of the struggle. Christianity was certainly
      continuing and bringing to a higher level the love-aspect of the struggle
      which the Essenes are able to touch upon only at moments. Without the
      strivings of these highly committed and strongly motivated individuals in
      their Community of the 'age to come,' that further step might well have been
      inconceivable.

and I will enter not into communion
with them that turn their back upon Thy covenant.[5]

Blessed art Thou, O Lord,[6]
Who, in the greatness of Thy power,
in Thy manifold, infinite wonders
and in the greatness of Thy forbearance
forgivest them that repent their transgression,
but visitest the iniquity of the wicked.

Verily, on the righteous
Thou bestowest freely Thy love,
but perversity Thou hatest for ever.
So hast Thou graced me, Thy servant,
with the spirit of knowledge and truth,

                              *

and made me abominate
all ways of perversity.

So, for mine own part,
I in turn will love Thee freely
and with all my heart
I will ... Thy ...
For by Thy hand has this thing been wrought,
and without Thy will can naught be done.

3. The two Messiahs:
from *The Testaments of the Patriarchs*

The work which goes under the title *Testaments of the Twelve Patriarchs* was known long before the discovery of the Dead Sea Scrolls. It was extant in Greek and in a range of other languages such as Armenian, Slavonic and (in parts) Hebrew and Aramaic. Subsequently, fragments especially of the section called the *Testament of Levi* were discovered at Qumran, although they do not always agree very closely with the earlier-known versions, and the history of the document has been reconstructed in different ways by almost every scholar working on its problems. In its present form, the complete *Testaments* is undoubtedly a Christian writing, and the text includes unequivocal references to Jesus, Mary and the crucifixion. But the general nature of the work, and now the discovery that it was used by the pre-Christian Essenes at Qumran, prove that its substance goes back to a Jewish writing of Maccabean period. In fact, agreements between the *Testaments* and the 'Scrolls' on the teaching of the 'Two Ways,' the angelic forces of Light and Darkness, the apocalyptic tone and the references to the 'age to come,' the strong ethical content, etc. has convinced such scholars as Dupont-Sommer and Philonenko that we have to do with an Essene document. Their view is greatly made more plausible by the light shed from Qumran on the riddling expressions in the *Testaments* about 'the Two Messiahs,' who have both been identified with Jesus by the subsequent Christian editor or re-writer of the text. For it is only in the 'Scrolls' that we find revealed the esoteric doctrine of a Priestly and a Kingly Messiah expected by the Essenes.

One of the earliest references in the Dead Sea Scrolls to this teaching may be the passage in the *Community Rule* which specifies the way of 'the men of holiness':

> They shall depart from none of the counsels of the Law to
> walk in the stubbornness of their hearts, but shall be ruled
> by the original precepts in which the men of the
> Community were first instructed, until there shall come
> the Prophet and the Messiahs of Aaron and Israel.

Several things are striking here. In the first place, the ordinance identifies the Essene Community as essentially Messianic. The precepts of the founding fathers are presented as valid for the period up to the coming of the Messiahs, who are to be proclaimed by the Prophet — normally identified with Elijah in Jewish expectation. The whole *raison d'être* of Qumran will then have been fulfilled. We should certainly not suppose, however, that the Law will then come to an end in a new dispensation. That is not the Essene idea. If many Essenes became Christians, it was by taking a radical step beyond the framework of the Law which had served them as their previous all-embracing guide, their ladder of spiritual ascent. The concept here is rather the one we have met repeatedly in the *Hodayot:* the Essenes are a Community already living, consciously, in the 'age to come,' whose outward advent will be signalled by the fulfilling of the prophecies, the Messianic prophecies above all. When that time comes, the Essenes will no longer be a closed, esoteric Community such as is constituted by the 'original precepts.' Inner reality will have become outer reality. Poem 5 (above) from the *Hodayot* made it clear that the birth of the wondrous child is an inner reality for the Essene initiate. The appearance of the prophesied *Wunderkind* in historical fact is not an arbitrary intervention by God, but expresses the fact that all of humankind may now experience that reality.

The second striking fact is the mention of two Messiahs, from Aaron and Israel. Israel, the name of God's chosen people and the name given to their forefather Jacob after he had wrestled with an angel, indicates the more traditional Messianic hope of Judaism. The Messiah was expected to be a royal figure, from the House of David to which God had promised rule without end. And that is what we find in a short *Messianic Rule* from Qumran, where 'the Messiah of Israel' is pictured in the age-to-come sitting as a prince at the head of all the tribes:

> And then the Messiah of Israel shall come, and the chiefs
> of the clans of Israel shall sit before him, each in the order
> of his dignity ... And before them shall sit all the heads of
> family of the congregation, and the wise men of the holy
> congregation, each in the order of his dignity.

He will preside over a meal, consisting of first-fruits: bread and wine. 'Thereafter, the Messiah of Israel shall extend his hand over the bread' — but interestingly it is not to bless it for the congregation. Rather 'all the congregation of the Community shall utter a blessing, each man in the order of his dignity.' Everything remains strictly hierarchical, subjected to the prince at the head of Israel, but nonetheless every man has the power of blessing in his own degree. Holiness has become the quality of every man. Moreover, the prophetic vision forms the basis for an Essene rule, and 'It is according to this statute that they shall proceed at every meal at which at least ten men are gathered together' — i.e. at the Essene cultic meals of the initiates. Once again, the Qumran Community is itself revealed to have been Messianic; the historical event prophesied will make outwardly real the communion of initiates in their esoteric rites.

At the meal is also present, says the prophecy, another figure — 'the Priest,' who does give the meal a special blessing and is first at the feast. He is almost certainly the one termed elsewhere 'the Messiah of Aaron,' since Aaron is the brother of Moses and an archetypal priestly figure who stands alongside the representative of the Law. This idea of a priestly Messiah has few roots in the Bible or in the popular expectations of a Messiah among the Jews of pre-Christian times. There are traces of it only in the latest parts of the Old Testament, such as Malachi 3:1. The spiritual reality behind the Essene Messiah of Aaron, however, lies more in the deepened, spiritualized interpretation of the Messianic prophecies in their esoteric teachings. Whereas the Messiah of Israel fulfils the popular hopes and the traditional role of the Davidic prince in restoring Israel, the priest expresses the special wisdom of the 'sons of Light' and has a more universal meaning. In all the Qumran documents he ranks higher than the traditional Messiah of Israel. This reflects, of course, the claim of the Essenes to be the true priesthood, the Jerusalem Temple having been defiled by the Wicked Priest and the common festivals being celebrated on the wrong days because the authorities use the moon-calendar, not the esoteric Enochian sun-calendar. Many of the Essenes undoubtedly came from the priestly tribe of Levi, and some were Zadokites, forming a special priestly élite. If the Messiah of Israel is to affirm the traditional ideas of Judaism, it is the priestly Messiah of Aaron who will give the events of the age-to-come their spiritual further dimension, fulfilling the deeper esoteric vision of the Essenes.

Their vision stemmed not just from the Old Testament but from the Mysteries of Zoroastrian Iran. The idea of the age-to-come arising out of the inevitable movement of the cycles of time, bringing to outer manifestation the reality of the spirit, and the polarity of King and Priest as dynamic powers in the cosmic struggle are further instances. For Zarathustra had prophesied the coming of a 'world Saviour,' the Saoshyant. Some of the legends among his followers referred to three such figures, later to six or even twelve Saoshyants who would be born at crucial moments in the cycles of history. Wondrous predictions about them were made: they would be born of virgin mothers, for instance; or others said they would be born when a star fell to earth. Other stories related them to the mythical beginnings of time and the first man, Jamshid. It was said that Ohrmazd, the God of Light, had approached Jamshid and offered him the total revelation of the divine, including the knowledge that was later revealed in the form of the 'Good Religion' by Zarathustra. But Jamshid refused the revelation of the Religion and accepted from Ohrmazd only that part relating to the sacred Kingship. Ohrmazd in his omniscience had of course known this in advance, together with the fact that this unfortunate dividing of the forces of good meant that the struggle against Ahriman, the dark power, would be very much more protracted:

> For if the highest power of the dignity of Kingship had
> been joined to the highest power of the dignity of the
> Good Religion in Jamshid, or if the highest power of the
> dignity of Kingship as it existed in Jamshid had been
> joined to the highest dignity of the Good Religion in
> Zarathustra, then the Destructive Spirit would have met
> with swift destruction, creation would have escaped from
> the Aggressor, and the desired Transfiguration (of the
> Earth) would have been brought about ...

As it is, however, the defeat of the powers of darkness could only be predicted. The Zoroastrian seers knew that it would come about when the two trajectories, of the Kingship and the Religion, finally met:

> When these two dignities meet in one man, then will the
> Aggressor be completely vanquished and creation saved
> and purged; from this the final Transfiguration proceeds.
> The Good Religion reveals that these two dignities will
> meet together in the Saoshyant.

Thus it is in the Zoroastrian 'Saviour' that the unity of Priesthood and Kingship will be accomplished.

These Zoroastrian ideas certainly help to explain how among the Essenes both the Priest and the King attain to Messianic dignity, and are woven into the vision of the cosmic struggle and its temporal phases. They help unlock the riddle, too, of those further passages in the Essene writings from Qumran which hint that the 'two Messiahs' will after all become one: 'the Messiah of Aaron and Israel.' Such a single yet clearly compound figure is foretold in the *Damascus Document*, and is referred to in several of the biblical interpretations from Qumran, notably those of the Psalms. The *Damascus Document* may well come from those Essenes who belonged to the 'Community of the Star' near Damascus, rather than having settled in Qumran. Did they also have a hand in the *Testaments of the Twelve Patriarchs*, which recent studies have connected with northern Israel or Syria?

At any rate we can now return to the teachings of the *Testaments* and recognize in them a stage on the way to the esoteric doctrines spelled out in the writings from Qumran. If we find very little in them to remind us of the strict legalism of the Community by the Dead Sea we should remember that they are attributed to the patriarchs who were supposed to live before the advent of the Law. On the other hand, the teaching of 'the Two Ways' is already fully developed in terms of strong general moral principles, and we should not forget the tradition that all the patriarchs before Moses already, out of sheer goodness, as it were, obeyed all the injunctions of the Law even though God had not yet made them obligatory. We should be wary, therefore, of assuming that the Community which produced the *Testaments* was in practice less legalistic than the one at Qumran. As for the Christians who have modified or re-drafted the texts to show the fulfilment of the prophecies, they were presumably among the ranks of the *Ebionim*, or Jewish Christians with an Essene esoteric background who played such an important part in organizing the movement in its earliest stages.

We can trace the impact of their teaching in early Christianity, for example in the writings of Hippolytus, best known for his book on *The Apostolic Tradition* and his work against heretics. In his commentary *On the Benedictions of Isaac, Jacob and Moses* he asserts that he has read prophecies to the effect:

> that the Christ would be born, according to his bodily
> descent, from the tribe of Levi, from the priestly order,
> from the house of Aaron ...

Of course he knows the other prophecies too, concerning a royal, Davidic figure. In fact, the prophecies on which he bases himself make sense of the whole picture:

>   For we have found it written that the Christ must also
>   appear from the tribe of Levi, as a priest of the Father,
>   from a commingling of the tribe of Judah with the tribe of
>   Levi, so that the Son of God should be made known from
>   both as King and as Priest.

This is exactly the Essene teaching, and the derivation of the dual promise from the blessings uttered by Moses (in the book of Deuteronomy) agrees with the *Messianic Anthology* found among the Dead Sea Scrolls. Hippolytus uses the esoteric doctrine to make sense of the two quite different genealogies of Jesus, prefixed to the Gospels of Matthew and Luke. But although the idea was taken up by Ambrose, who was certainly an influential figure in the Christian tradition, the meaning of the genealogies of the 'two Messiahs' and their flowing together into one was scarcely understood by the Church when it cut its links with the Essene esoteric background of its beginnings. An understanding of their significance was limited to those like Rudolf Steiner who reached it by quite independent means — at least until the discoveries of the twentieth century brought their remarkable confirmation.

Can we infer anything about the spiritual setting of the *Testaments* in their primal state? They did not come from a closed initiatory Community like Qumran. Those scholars may well be correct who see in them the spiritual background for the Hasmonean dynasty of priest-kings who governed in Jerusalem after the time of the Maccabean victories. In so far as they were trying to bring closer the dignities of Priest and King and unite them into one ideal, the Hasmoneans would obviously have attracted the support of the Essenes and others among the Hasidim. Later, when the political reality of the Hasmoneans became only too unpleasantly clear, there was a split which led to the final confrontation between the Essene leader and the 'Wicked Priest.' But that evidently lies in the future at the stage represented by the *Testaments*. The themes of initiation, the priestly and royal rites so prominent in their content, most likely relate therefore to the practices of the reigning dynasty. Parallels with later Christian ritual, as well as with the Mandean Mystery and the ordinances of Qumran, are abundant. Some of them will be pointed out in the notes. Our selection includes major portions of *The Testament of Levi* and *The Testament of Judah*.

The genre 'Testament' is itself an important and interesting one. Several religious writings have come down to us alongside *The Testaments of the Twelve Patriarchs* which likewise take the form of 'last words' of an ancient sage or father of the race. There is also, for example, a *Testament of Abraham* and a *Testament of Isaac* which again have many points of contact with Essene and apocalyptic literature. Attributing a work to such a figure from the revered past is not just a literary device. It evidently corresponds to a real imaginative experience: it indicates the living intensity of a tradition, where an individual's own experiences are felt to be less important, even less real than the hallowed values which go back to Abraham or Jacob (also called Israel). The initiates of the Essenes deepened the sense of identification with a founder-figure to the stage of mystical identification, and by 'remembering back' to the beginning are able to survey the meaning of history from that time down to the present. And then, following the momentum of the cycles of time, they are carried even beyond their actual present into an apocalyptic vision of the future.

We see this pattern in the *Testaments of the Twelve Patriarchs*, and notably in that of *Levi*. There is some information about the patriarch's life, but more prominent are mystical visions (whose type obviously reflects those of the seer who actually wrote it) and visions of the events leading up to the Last Days and the coming of the Priest Messiah, i.e. things still in the future when the book was written down. The 'Testament' is thus really a special kind of apocalypse: a revelation of 'heavenly secrets' concerning the past and the future. Its theory of cosmic cycles has particular similarities to the *Book of Jubilees*, and may share an oral tradition standing behind both these and related written documents which overlap in substance but not in such a way as to suggest literary dependence. In its present form, as we have noted, it includes Christian alterations and additions to show the fulfilment of the original prophecies.

Source: Testaments of the Patriarchs, *translated from the Greek by Robert Sinker. His version is based on the manuscript in the University Library, Cambridge, sometimes referred to in modern times as the b manuscript: it has recently been argued by H.J. de Jonge that this version has preserved the oldest stage of the existing Greek text. All subtitles are of course editorial. The selection consists of Chapters 1-8 and 16-19.*

Fragments of the Aramaic version of the Testament of Levi are now translated in Eisenman and Wise 1992, pp.136-45.

1.   The writer assumes in his readers familiarity with the biblical accounts of the patriarchs and events, and does not attempt to retell them. See Genesis 34.

2.   The biblical Abel-Meholah: see Judges 7:22.

3.   Levi here becomes the type of the visionary, in whom the seer who wrote the *Testament of Levi* finds his own mystical experience prefigured. The 'spirit of understanding' reminds us of the 'Angel of Truth' in the Qumran *Community Rule*, which also asserts that God 'will shed the spirit of truth' upon the initiate (I QS IV:20-22): 'to the end that, being made upright, men may have understanding of transcendental knowledge and of the lore of the sons of heaven' (that is, the angels). The vision conveys 'understanding' in the sense that it reveals the spirits of Light and Darkness at work in the world, as here the predominance of 'iniquity' and the longing for salvation.

4.   The dream-vision and ascent into heaven starting from a high mountain are widespread features of experience in the Mysteries: cf. the Mandean Mystery of 'climbing the mountain' and entering into the forces of water and fire by being 'raised up.' The background is especially that of the Mysteries of Babylonia and of Iran. Parallels in other pagan Mysteries are manifold, e.g. the *per omnia vectus elementa remeavi* ('I was caught rapt through all the elements') in Apuleius' account of his Isis-initiation. In the centuries before Christian origins the Mysteries came together in a new synthesis with Judaism: from a stage prior to the Essene writings from Qumran special mention should be made of these themes in the *Book of Enoch* 14.

5.   Cf. the introductory account of the vision granted to Hermes in *Poimandres* 1: 'a being of vast, immeasurable size drew near, and called me by name and said ...' (see below p.193). As Hermes becomes the founder of the Mystery, so Levi is commissioned to 'stand near the Lord' as a priest and to 'declare His mysteries to men.' The 'angel' or 'being' who interprets the vision is a messenger of higher truth, cf. the Qumran 'Angel of Truth' who is equivalent to the 'spirit of understanding' — or conversely, for the Essene higher knowledge puts the initiate already among the ranks of the 'sons of heaven,' so that the 'angel' is virtually his higher self. The personal address 'by name' leads to the same association of one's own identity with the content of the vision. This higher self or angelic interpreter appears in many apocalyptic

* From The Testament of Levi *

The Words of Levi. His Ascent into Heaven

1. The copy of the words of Levi, what things he appointed to his sons, according to all that they should do, and what things should befall them until the day of judgment. He was in sound health when he called them to him, for it had been shown to him that he should die. And when they were gathered together he said to them:

2. I Levi was conceived in Haran and born there, and after that I came with my father to Shechem. And I was young, about twenty years of age, when with Simeon I wrought the vengeance on Hamor for our sister Dinah.[(1)] And when we were feeding our flocks in Abel-Maul,[(2)] a spirit of understanding of the Lord came upon me,[(3)] and I saw all men corrupting their way, and that unrighteousness had built to itself walls, and iniquity sat upon towers; and I grieved for the race of men, and I prayed to the Lord that I might be saved. Then there fell upon me a sleep, and I beheld a high mountain:[(4)] this is the mountain of Aspis in Abel-Maul. And behold, the heavens were opened, and an angel of God said to me, Levi,[(5)] enter. And I entered from the first heaven into the second, and I saw there water hanging between the one and the other. And I saw a third heaven far brighter than those two, for there was in it a height without bounds. And I said to the angel, Wherefore is this? And the angel said to me, Marvel not at these, for thou shalt see four other heavens, brighter than these, and without comparison, when thou shalt have ascended thither: because thou shalt stand near the Lord, and shalt be His minister, and shalt declare His mysteries to men, and shalt proclaim concerning Him who shall redeem Israel; and by thee and Judah shall the Lord appear among men, saving in them every race of men; and of the portion of the Lord shall be thy life, and He shall be thy field and vineyard, fruits, gold, silver.

3. Hear, then, concerning the seven heavens. The lowest is for this cause more gloomy, in that it is near all the iniquities of

and visionary works of Judaism and Christianity, but is lacking in the older pagan visions, in which the adept had to be trained beforehand to understand and interpret what he saw, and often to reply with the correct magical formula. The Jewish feature thus represents a greater individualization of the visionary experience. For the place of the Hermetic Mysteries in this development, see below (p.189f).

6.   Visions of the heavenly liturgy performed by the angels are important at Qumran and in some of the Jewish apocalypses. See among the 'Dead Sea Scrolls' especially 'The Words of the Heavenly Lights' (IVQ504) and 'Songs for the Holocaust of the Sabbath' (otherwise known as 'The Angelic Liturgy' (IVQ400-407). Few direct accounts of heavenly ascension-experiences have been found at Qumran. In fact, as Morton Smith has shown, they are usually replaced there by an emphasis on the coming down of heavenly realities to the Community: see 'Ascent into Heaven' in L.H. Schiffman 1990. We may see this once more in terms of the growing individualization of spiritual experience among the Essenes and of their principle that inner reality becomes outer reality. It is not a denial of the cosmic experience, but its fulfilment when the historical appearance of the Messiah(s) brings about the enactment of the cultic meal on earth.

7.   The 'knowledge' given to Levi becomes a version of the myth of Light and Dark, leading to an apocalyptic vision: the imagery is strikingly like that in the *Hodayot* (see Poem 10, notes 8 and 11).

8.   The 'son' here is clearly Levi, but the Christian who reworked the *Testaments* seems to conflate this 'son' with the 'Son of God' who is the Christian fulfilment of the Priestly archetype. In the 'Dead Sea Scrolls' oracles of 'sonship' are applied sometimes to the Community, which included a large priestly or Levitical contingent. It is only since the Qumran writings revealed to us the full doctrine of the 'Priestly Messiah' alongside the Kingly or Davidic Messiah that the meaning of such passages has become clear.

9.   An evident Christian insertion.

men. The second hath fire, snow, ice, ready for the day of the ordinance of the Lord, in the righteous judgment of God: in it are all the spirits of the retributions for vengeance on the wicked. In the third are the hosts of the armies which are ordained for the day of judgment, to work vengeance on the spirits of deceit and of Beliar. And the heavens up to the fourth above these are holy, for in the highest of all dwelleth the Great Glory, in the holy of holies, far above all holiness. In the heaven next to it are the angels of the presence of the Lord, who minister and make propitiation to the Lord for all the ignorances of the righteous; and they offer to the Lord a reasonable sweet-smelling savour, and a bloodless offering.[6] And in the heaven below this are the angels who bear the answers to the angels of the presence of the Lord. And in the heaven next to this are thrones, dominions, in which hymns are ever offered to God. Therefore, whenever the Lord looketh upon us, all of us are shaken; yea, the heavens, and the earth, and the abysses, are shaken at the presence of His majesty; but the sons of men, regarding not these things, sin, and provoke the Most High.

4. Now, therefore, know that the Lord will execute judgment upon the sons of men; because when the rocks are rent, and the sun quenched, and the waters dried up, and the fire trembling, and all creation troubled, and the invisible spirits melting away, and the grave spoiled in the suffering of the Most High, men unbelieving will abide in their iniquity,[7] therefore with punishment shall they be judged. Therefore the Most High hath heard thy prayer, to separate thee from iniquity, and that thou shouldest become to Him a son,[8] and a servant, and a minister of His presence. A shining light of knowledge shalt thou shine in Jacob, and as the sun shalt thou be to all the seed of Israel. And a blessing shall be given to thee, and to all thy seed, until the Lord shall visit all the heathen in the tender mercies of His Son, even for ever. Nevertheless thy sons shall lay hands upon Him to crucify Him;[9] and therefore have counsel and understanding been given thee, that thou mightest instruct thy sons concerning Him, because he that blesseth Him shall be blessed, but they that curse Him shall perish.

10.   Another feature common to many Jewish esoteric visions, going back to Ezekiel's description of the *merkavah* or Throne-Chariot of God (Ezekiel 1) which was regarded as esoteric by the tradition of the Pharisees and rabbis as well as the Essenes. The *Book of Enoch* 14 also culminates in a vision of the temple and the throne, with the Great Glory seated upon it.

11.   The records of the divine decrees: the visionary who has projected himself back into Levi sees history as if it is simply the reading of the already ordained decisions of God, the working out in time of something existing already in God's mind (and the visionary's).

12.   The angel is Michael. In Daniel 10:13 and 10:21 we have a parallel to the 'heavenly tablets' in the 'Book of Truth' and Michael is named as the angel who fights for Israel so that it does not perish utterly. Other angels stand for the spirits of the other nations: see D.S. Russell 1964, pp.244ff. For an important text involving Michael, his ascent into 'the highest heaven' and his reading there a visionary book, see Eisenman and Wise 1992, pp.37-39. The book contains the decree concerning the building of Jerusalem and the temple where God's name will dwell.

13.   The place names are unknown and hard to relate to non-Greek forms (e.g. *aspis* = shield in Greek) to which the writer of the Greek text has assimilated them and offered his own interpretation of their meaning.

14.   The point of the text is not to re-tell the biblical story but to interpret it. It is regarded as wrong to have taken vengeance on those who have been circumcised and so are under the same religious covenant.

The Battle against Shechem

5. And the angel opened to me the gates of Heaven, and I saw the holy temple, and the Most High upon a throne of glory.[10] And He said to me, Levi, I have given thee the blessings of the priesthood until that I shall come and sojourn in the midst of Israel. Then the angel brought me to the earth, and gave me a shield and a sword, and said, Work vengeance on Shechem because of Dinah, and I will be with thee, because the Lord hath sent me. And I destroyed at that time the sons of Hamor, as it is written in the heavenly tablets.[11] And I said to Him, I pray Thee, O Lord, tell my Thy name, that I may call upon Thee in a day of tribulation.[12] And He said, I am the angel who intercedeth for the race of Israel, that He smite them not utterly, because every evil spirit attacketh it. And after these things I was as it were awaked, and blessed the Most High, and the angel that intercedeth for the race of Israel, and for all the righteous.

6. And when I came to my father I found a brazen shield; wherefore also the name of the mountain is Aspis, which is near Gebal, on the right side of Abila;[13] and I kept these words in my heart. I took counsel with my father, and with Reuben my brother, that he should bid the sons of Hamor that they should be circumcised; for I was jealous because of the abomination which they had wrought in Israel. And I slew Shechem at the first, and Simeon slew Hamor. And after this our brethren came and smote the city with the edge of the sword; and our father heard it and was wroth, and he was grieved in that they had received the circumcision,[14] and after that had been put to death, and in his blessings he dealt otherwise with us. For we sinned because we had done this thing against his will, and he was sick upon that day. But I knew that the sentence of God was for evil upon Shechem; for they sought to do to Sarah as they did to Dinah our sister, and the Lord hindered them. And so they persecuted Abraham our father when he was a stranger, and they harried his flocks when they were multiplied upon him; and Jeblae his servant, born in his house, they shamefully handled. And thus they did do to all

15.   Again we see the 'prophetic' perspective. The visionary adopts the identity
        of Levi in order to grasp the whole pattern of events which start in his time
        and looks forward to their fulfilment and to the apocalyptic future. The linear
        model gives way to a 'spatial' one in the visionary consciousness. Rudolf
        Steiner has described the 'transformation of memory' that takes place in
        spiritual development. 'Whenever the pupil is in a state of consciousness in
        which he is investigating the spiritual world through a faculty analogous to
        that of memory, what he observes in that world presents itself not in time but
        spatially. Memory is completely transformed': see the full treatment in
        Macrocosm and Microcosm, London 1968, pp.168ff.

16.   In many ancient royal initiations and Mystery-rites seven such figures appear.
        The initiate-king in Babylon received attributes corresponding to the seven
        planets, the forces of cosmic rule. The objects here mentioned in the first list
        are those required for a priest according to Exodus 28; strikingly different,
        however, are those given in the second listing. F.H. Borsch comments: 'There
        is now a girdle of purple, the royal colour. Levi holds a staff as do kings. He
        is given a branch from an olive tree, derivatively a symbol of his lordship
        over the garden (of Paradise). The anointing, purification with water and the
        sacred meal (in this case bread and wine) stand in long association with kings
        or priest-kings. Because of such details, their apparent intrusion and
        otherwise unnecessary and incongruous presence, both Widengren and
        Jansen believe that the author is basing himself upon a cult pattern and not
        merely upon literary sources. If they are right, the author is dealing with
        materials and ideas which are *alive* to him and not just indulging a spirit of
        archaism' (Borsch 1967, p.165). In other words, we catch our visionary in the
        very act of projecting back onto Levi, the traditional first priest, the
        framework of his own initiation and adding its details to those given in
        Exodus 28. The 'cult pattern' is obviously close to that in the *Community Rule*
        which we have repeatedly mentioned: baptism and the cult meal of bread
        and wine. One should note however that the analogy to the Mandean
        Mystery is also far-reaching: as among the Mandeans, anointing accompanies
        baptism, though not in the same order. Reference to the 'planting' connects
        the initiate with Paradise and its garden; there is a meal of bread and wine;
        each Mandean initiate becomes a 'king' and receives the 'crown of light.' The
        expression used in the *Testament of Levi* ('a new name shall be called over
        him') recalls the Mandean formula 'And pronounced over me the name' (see
        above p.39). It is likely that the rites evoked in the *Testaments* belong to the
        practices of the Hasmonean priest-kings. If so, it appears that things were
        done much 'after the fashion of the Gentiles,' and the cult among the Essenes
        who withdrew to Qumran may be 'toned down' from the days when they
        were able to sway the leaders of the nation in Jerusalem.

strangers, taking away their wives by force, and the men themselves driving into exile. But the wrath of the Lord came suddenly upon them to the uttermost.

7. And I said to my father, Be not angry, sir, because by thee will the Lord bring to nought the Canaanites, and will give their land to thee, and to thy seed after thee.[15] For from this day forward shall Shechem be called a city of them that are without understanding; for as a man mocketh at a fool, so did we mock them, because they wrought folly in Israel to defile our sister. And we took our sister from thence, and departed, and came to Bethel.

Priestly Initiation
8. And there I saw a thing again even as the former, after we had passed seventy days. And I saw seven men[16] in white raiment saying to me, Arise, put on the robe of the priesthood, and the crown of righteousness, and the breastplate of understanding, and the garment of truth, and the diadem of faith, and the tiara of miracle, and the ephod of prophecy. And each one of them bearing each of these things put them on me, and said, From henceforth become a priest of the Lord, thou and thy seed for ever. And the first anointed me with holy oil, and gave to me the rod of judgment. The second washed me with pure water, and fed me with bread and wine, the most holy things, and clad me with a holy and glorious robe. The third clothed me with a linen vestment like to an ephod. The fourth put round me a girdle like unto purple. The fifth gave to me a branch of rich olive. The sixth placed a crown on my head. The seventh placed on my head a diadem of priesthood, and filled my hands with incense, so that I served as a priest to the Lord. And they said to me, Levi, thy seed shall be divided into three branches, for a sign of the glory of the Lord who is to come; and first shall he be that hath been faithful; no portion shall be greater than his. The second shall be in the priesthood. The third — a new name shall be called over Him, because He shall arise as King from Judah, and shall establish a new priesthood, after the fashion of the Gentiles, to all the Gentiles. And His

17.   As a prototype of the visionary, the initiate, Levi is shown as in possession
       of esoteric knowledge not to be revealed.

18.   The cycles of time are schematized as cosmic 'weeks' or series of sevens: see
       1 *Enoch* 91-93, the so-called 'Apocalypse of Weeks' which culminates in a
       vision of the Last Days:
           An apostate generation shall arise; its deeds shall be many, and all
           of them criminal. At its completion, there shall be elected the elect
           ones of righteousness from the eternal plant of righteousness, to
           whom shall be given sevenfold instruction ... (93:9).
       The contents of the prophecy have been reworked in the light of the Gospels
       and the destruction of Jerusalem (70 AD) by the Christian editor-writer of the
       Testaments. The 'plant of righteousness' as a symbol of the esoteric Commu-
       nity is used repeatedly by the Essenes. The Christianity which developed on
       their foundations saw in Jesus 'the man who reneweth the law' and remains
       basically legalistic despite the allusion to Christian 'faith and water.'

19.   A 'jubilee' is a cycle of seven times seven. The prophecy of Levi is a
       'foreseeing' of the history (decline) of Israel from its original closeness to God
       through the stages of its history, including the Captivity and the return to
       Judea. The descent reaches a 'crisis-point' of divine judgment. The *Testaments
       of the Twelve Patriarchs* has many points of contact with the *Book of Jubilees*,
       with which it shares in all probability an oral tradition prior to the forming
       of the literary works. *Jubilees* covers the period of Genesis and the patriarchs,
       and is available in J.H. Charlesworth 1985, pp.35ff. Prominent in its
       interpretation is the struggle of Light and Darkness, cycles of time (sevens),
       etc. One should compare all these ideas with the Gospel of Matthew 1:1-17
       and Rudolf Steiner 1965, pp.66ff.

appearing shall be unutterable, as of an exalted prophet of the
seed of Abraham our father. Every desirable thing in Israel shall
be for thee and for thy seed, and everything fair to look upon
shall ye eat, and the table of the Lord shall thy seed apportion,
and some of them shall be high priests, and judges, and scribes;
for by their mouth shall the holy place be guarded. And when
I awoke, I understood that this thing was like unto the former.
And I hid this also in my heart, and told it not to any man
upon the earth.[17]

The Ages of the World
16. And now I have learnt in the book of Enoch that for seventy
weeks will ye go astray, and will profane the priesthood, and
pollute the sacrifices, and corrupt the law, and set at nought the
words of the prophets. In perverseness ye will persecute
righteous men, and hate the godly; the words of the faithful
will ye abhor, and the man who reneweth the law in the power
of the Most High will ye call a deceiver; and at last, as ye
suppose, ye will slay Him, not understanding His resurrection,
wickedly taking upon your own heads the innocent blood.
Because of Him shall your holy places be desolate, polluted
even to the ground, and ye shall have no place that is clean; but
ye shall be among the Gentiles a curse and a dispersion, until
He shall again look upon you, and in pity shall take you to
Himself through faith and water.[18]

17. And because ye have heard concerning the seventy weeks,
hear also concerning the priesthood; for in each jubilee there
shall be a priesthood. In the first jubilee,[19] the first who is
anointed into the priesthood shall be great, and shall speak to
God as to a Father; and his priesthood shall be filled with the
fear of the Lord, and in the day of his gladness shall he arise
for the salvation of the world. In the second jubilee, he that is
anointed shall be conceived in the sorrow of beloved ones; and
his priesthood shall be honoured, and shall be glorified among
all. And the third priest shall be held fast in sorrow; and the
fourth shall be in grief, because unrighteousness shall be laid
upon him exceedingly, and all Israel shall hate each one his

20.   Since the fifth week of cosmic time-reckoning lies a fair way behind the
       author of the *Testaments* — he is writing in the second century BC, and Ezra
       had restored the Temple around 450 BC — it is evident that he regards
       himself as standing in the last of the seven ages. Perhaps, however, the worst
       of the corruptions of the priesthood are regarded as still to come. The
       structure of the *Testament of Levi* is thus typical of the 'apocalyptic' conscious-
       ness. Mirrored back from an archaic figure such as a patriarch, a pattern or
       'grand design' of history emerges which is almost completed, but lacks the
       corner-stone, the fulfiment that lies still in the future for the seer. He lives in
       the intense moment of anticipation, seeing already in inner vision what has
       not yet been actualized in the outside world. Here, the fulfilment is to be the
       advent of the priestly type in Messianic completeness.

21.   The fulfilment comes when the 'trajectories' of King and Priest cross or
       coincide. As well as the reference to 'king' here, the whole imagery of this
       poetic section points to the union of the two roles — while simultaneously
       the Priest Messiah is a separate figure with his own prophetic symbolism and
       tradition, quite different from the 'Messiah of Israel' or Judah (see below).
       The *Damascus Rule* from the 'Dead Sea Scrolls' likewise interprets Numbers
       24:17 ('A star shall come forth out of Jacob and a sceptre shall rise out of
       Israel') in a Messianic sense (see CD VII,18). And there too the Star is the
       Priest-Messiah, 'the Interpreter of the Law.'

22.   Cf. 1 *Enoch* 49:1 and 51:4. This Messiah is the fulfiller of the esoteric,
       Enochian tradition.

23.   Usually taken as an addition in the light of the Gospels, this passage
       nevertheless has parallels in the formula of the pre-Christian *Apocalypse of
       Adam* (see below p.227): 'He received glory and power. And thus he came on
       the water.'

neighbour. The fifth shall be held fast in darkness, likewise also the sixth and the seventh. And in the seventh there shall be such pollution as I am not able to express, before the Lord and men, for they shall know it who do these things. Therefore shall they be in captivity and for a prey, and their land and their substance shall be destroyed. And in the fifth week they shall return into their desolate country, and shall renew the house of the Lord.[20] And in the seventh week shall come the priests, worshippers of idols, contentious, lovers of money, proud, lawless, lascivious, abusers of children and beasts.

The Priestly Messiah. The Two Ways

And after their punishment shall have come from the Lord, then will the Lord raise up to the priesthood a new Priest, to whom all the words of the Lord shall be revealed; and He shall execute a judgment of truth upon the earth, in the fulness of days. And His star shall arise in heaven, as a king[21] shedding forth the light of knowledge in the sunshine of day, and He shall be magnified in the world until His ascension. He shall shine forth as the sun in the earth, and shall drive away all darkness from the world under heaven, and there shall be peace in all the earth. The heavens shall rejoice in His days, and the earth shall be glad, and the clouds shall be joyful, and the knowledge of the Lord shall be poured forth upon the earth, as the water of seas; and the angels of the glory of the presence of the Lord shall be glad in Him.[22] The heavens shall be opened, and from the temple of glory shall the sanctification come upon Him with the Father's voice, as from Abraham the father of Isaac. And the glory of the Most High shall be uttered over Him, and the spirit of understanding and of sanctification shall rest upon Him in the water.[23] He shall give the majesty of the Lord to His sons in truth for evermore; and there shall none succeed Him for all generations, even for ever. And in His priesthood shall all sin come to an end, and the lawless shall rest from evil and the just shall rest in Him. And He shall open the gates of Paradise, and shall remove the threatening sword against Adam; and He shall give to His saints to eat from the

24. The themes of the 'tree' or 'plant' which sprouted from Paradise and forms the symbol of the Community with its ritual meal points to the Essene tradition (see our discussion above, pp.46ff) once more. The Priest Messiah is to fulfil in actual event what is already possible in the anticipatory consciousness of the initiate, born 'before his time': the regaining of Paradise in the 'new age.'

25. The result of the visionary experience is to pose the initiate a choice — the choice described in the Essene *Community Rule* as between Light and Darkness, and here God or Beliar (Satan). Note that this choice only exists for those with the 'inner vision.'

   As evidence that many of the early Christians came from Essene and similar circles, and recognized Jesus as the Messiah of the more esoteric tradition, we may mention the striking similarity of the Christian Rule-book called the *Didache* in its teaching on 'The Two Ways':

   > There are two Ways of teaching, and two wielders of power; one
   > of light and the other of darkness. Between those two Ways there
   > is a vast difference, because over the one are posted the light-
   > bearing angels of God, and over the other the angels of Satan; and
   > one of these two is the Lord from All eternity to all eternity, while
   > the other stands paramount over this present age of iniquity ...
   > (*Didache* 18)

   Other formulations of a similar type are to be found both in the *Testaments* and other early Christian literature such as the *Letter of Barnabas*.

   The fullest version of the teaching in the *Testaments* themselves is the following:

   > Two Ways hath God given to the sons of men, and two minds,
   > and two doings, and two places, and two ends. Therefore all
   > things are by twos, one corresponding to the other. There are two
   > ways of good and evil, with which are the two minds in our
   > breasts distinguishing them. Therefore if the soul take pleasure in
   > good, all its actions are in righteousness ... But if his mind turn
   > aside in evil, all his doings are in maliciousness, and he driveth
   > away the good, and taketh unto him the evil and is ruled by
   > Beliar; and even though he work what is good, he perverteth it to
   > evil.
   > (*Testament of Asher* 1:3-9)

tree of life, and the spirit of holiness shall be on them.[24] And Beliar shall be bound by Him, and He shall give power to His children to tread upon the evil spirits. And the Lord shall rejoice in His children, and the Lord shall be well pleased in His beloved for ever. Then shall Abraham and Isaac and Jacob be joyful, and I will be glad, and all the saints shall put on gladness.

19. And now, my children, ye have heard all; choose therefore for yourselves either the darkness or the light, either the law of the Lord or the works of Beliar.[25] And we answered our father, saying, Before the Lord will we walk according to His law. And our father said, The Lord is witness, and His angels are witnesses, concerning the word of your mouth. And we said, We are witnesses. And thus Levi ceased giving charge to his sons; and he stretched out his feet, and was gathered to his fathers, after he had lived a hundred and thirty seven years. And they laid him in a coffin, and afterwards they buried him in Hebron, by the side of Abraham, and Isaac, and Jacob.

The Testament of Judah

Another of the *Testaments* — the *Testament of Naphtali* — contains a dream involving prophetic revelations. Its meaning is again connected with the two Messiahs:

> In the fortieth year of my life, I saw on the Mount of
> Olives east of Jerusalem that the sun and the moon stood
> still. And behold, Isaac, my father's father, was saying to
> us, 'Run forth, seize them, each according to his capacity;
> to the one who grasps them will the sun and moon
> belong.' All of them ran, but Levi seized the sun and
> Judah, outstripping the others, grasped the moon. Thus
> they were exalted above the others. When Levi became
> like the sun, a certain young man gave him twelve date
> palms. And Judah became luminous like the moon, and
> twelve rays were under his feet. *(Test. of Naphtali* 5:1-5)

The dream-vision is partly modelled on Joseph's dream in Genesis 37 and like it points to the future greatness of certain tribes of Israel rather than others. In this case, however, the historical interest is all but eclipsed by the cosmic dimension. Levi and Judah are preeminent by joining themselves to the heavenly forces of sun and moon, and are transfigured by their light. The twelve palms and rays suggest the zodiac; later Naphtali interprets them within his dream to refer to the twelve nations which surround Israel and share in the redemption-process through their contact with the Chosen People, even though this was often hostile. Thus we have a heavenly 'totality,' and an earthly reflection in history about to be 'fulfilled.' The fulfilment or completion of the pattern on earth will be the coming of the Messiahs: in them the cosmic forces will be manifested on earth, therefore, as in the vision which seer has projected back to the time of the patriarchs in order to see the pattern whole.

We have already seen that Levi's solar transfiguration points to a Priestly Messiah, of higher significance spiritually than the usual Kingly Messiah. The sun-calendar belongs to the Enochian tradition and was followed at Qumran, necessitating the rejection of the traditional moon-calendar of the Jerusalem Temple and more orthodox Judaism; the Essenes have a higher priesthood serving the spiritual sun. But the Kingly Messiah himself attains to cosmic significance in this visionary scheme of things. In the *Testament of Judah* we have a 'foreseeing,' mirrored back from the founder of the royal tribe of David, of the Kingly Messiah's role. As the moon-force embodied in a living person, he reflects the light of the spiritual sun back to earth. Hence the esoteric spirituality of the Essenes is not divorced from ordinary history, from the hopes and expectations of ordinary Jews based on the Bible. Or at most the separation is temporary. The Essene consciousness is ahead of its time; but when God's 'Visitation' happens at the turn of the cycles of apocalyptic time, inner reality will become outer reality and the breach will be healed. In the *Testaments* of *Dan* 5:10 and *Gad* 8:1 we already find the teaching that the two figures will actually appear in one man 'from Levi and Judah' (cf. the 'Messiah of Aaron and Israel' from the Dead Sea Scrolls.)

The selection comprises Chapters 20-26. For the source of the text and the translation, see the notes to the extracts from the Testament of Levi.

1. Another version of the Essene teaching. By mentioning the 'spirit of understanding' which moves between 'truth' and 'error,' the author of the *Testament* stresses the centrality of man's own mind in the struggle. The cosmic dimension is present; but there is much more emphasis on the individual moral agent here, than in the Zoroastrian prototype.

2. Note that moral judgment is self-judgment: God does not condemn, but 'he who sinneth is burnt up by his own heart.' Something similar is shown in the Gospels, where Jesus does not condemn his opponents: 'But for John,' as the noted scholar R.E. Brown remarks, 'the presence of Jesus in the world as the light separates men into those who are sons of darkness, hating the light, and those who come to the light. All through the Gospel Jesus provokes self-judgment as men line up for or against him; truly his coming is a *crisis* in the root sense of that word, where it reflects the Gr. *krisis* or "judgment"' (R.E. Brown 1971, p.cxvii, and see further p.345). The popular notion of a 'Day of Judgment' is thus understood by the Essenes, and later by the writer of the Fourth Gospel, as an inner reality not an external one. Or better, the popular religious images have their reality in the inner experience of the initiates, or 'sons of light.'

3. As at Qumran, the Priest Messiah is regarded as definitely superior to the traditional King Messiah, 'as the heaven is higher than the earth.'

❋ From The Testament of Judah ❋

The Words of Judah. The Two Ways

20. Learn therefore, my children, that two spirits wait upon man
— the spirit of truth and the spirit of error; and in the midst is
the spirit of the understanding of the mind, to which it belong-
eth to turn whithersoever it will.[1] And the works of truth and
the works of error are written upon the breast of men, and each
one of them the Lord knoweth. And there is no time at which
the works of men can be hid from Him; for on the bones of his
breast hath he been written down before the Lord. And the
spirit of truth testifieth all things, and accuseth all; and he who
sinneth is burnt up by his own heart, and cannot raise his face
unto the Judge.[2]

The King and the Priest

21. And now, my children, love Levi, that ye may abide, and
exalt not yourselves against him, lest ye be utterly destroyed.
For to me the Lord gave the kingdom, and to him the priesthood, and He set the kingdom beneath the priesthood. To me
He gave the things upon the earth; to him the things in the
heavens. As the heaven is higher than the earth, so is the
priesthood of God higher than the kingdom upon the earth.[3]
For the Lord chose him above thee, to draw near to Him, and
to eat of His table and first-fruits, even the choice things of the
sons of Israel, and thou shalt be to them as a sea. For as, on the
sea, just and unjust are tossed about, some taken into captivity
while others are enriched, so also shall every race of men be in
thee, some are in jeopardy and taken captive, and others shall
grow rich by means of plunder. For they who rule will be as
great sea-monsters, swallowing up men like fishes: free sons
and daughters do they enslave; houses, lands, flocks, money,
will they plunder; and with the flesh of many will they
wrongfully feed the ravens and the cranes; and they will go on
further in evil, advancing on still in covetousness. And there

4.   The restoration of the kingly rites by the Hasmoneans, who combined them
        with the priesthood, may be interpreted as a sign of the imminent coming of
        Israel's salvation. It seems that according to Judah's prophecy there was to be
        no kingship until the manifestation of the King Messiah.

5.   At several places in the *Testaments,* the coming of the Messiahs is associated
        with a manifestation of the divine presence. Cf. above, *Testament of Levi* 4:4.
            This is not yet the Christian doctrine of the Incarnation of God, which has
        no place in Jewish thought and required a complete readjustment of the
        framework of ideas concerning God and his relation to the world. The Essene
        tradition anticipates something spiritual, not an incarnation. The 'God of
        righteousness,' in accordance with the moral idea of self-judgment, will be
        manifested when men judge themselves and become 'sons of light,' that is,
        when the Essene initiation-consciousness becomes general in the 'age to
        come.' The Messiah's 'kingship' will thus be present to all men, indeed within
        all men: perhaps that is the meaning of Judah's being blessed by the Angel
        of the Divine Presence in Chapter 25. The other aspect concerns Levi, or the
        Priest Messiah. In his day the whole earth will become a Temple precinct,
        and the 'light' of the Lord will shine out to all the nations. The experience of
        the ritual is thus the other model for the awareness of the divine in the 'time
        of God's Visitation.' In all cases, the Gentiles as well as the Jews participate
        in salvation. The special role of the Jewish people is part of universal (even
        cosmic) history, just as the special role of the Essenes within Judaism, and the
        deeper wisdom of the Priest Messiah, is to be reunited with the stream of
        esoteric religion and the King Messiah.

shall be false prophets like tempests, and they shall persecute all righteous men.

22. And the Lord shall bring upon them divisions one against another, and there shall be continual wars in Israel; and among men of other race shall my kingdom be brought to an end, until the salvation of Israel shall come,[4] until the appearing of the God of righteousness,[5] that Jacob and all the Gentiles may rest in peace. And he shall guard the might of my kingdom for ever: for the Lord sware to me with an oath that the kingdom should never fail from me, and from my seed for all days, even for ever.

23. Now I have much grief, my children, because of your lewdness, and witchcrafts, and idolatries, which ye will work against the kingdom following them that have familiar spirits; ye will make your daughters singing-girls and harlots for divinations and demons of error, and ye will be mingled in the pollutions of the Gentiles: for which things' sake the Lord shall bring upon you famine and pestilence, death and the sword, avenging siege, and dogs for the rending in pieces of enemies, and revilings of friends, destruction and blighting of eyes, children slaughtered, wives carried off, possessions plundered, temple of God in flames, your land desolated, your own selves enslaved among the Gentiles, and they shall make some of you eunuchs for their wives; and whenever ye will return to the Lord with humility of heart, repenting and walking in all the commandments of God, then will the Lord visit you in mercy and in love, bringing you from out of the bondage of your enemies.

The Royal Messiah

24. And after these things shall a Star arise to you from Jacob in peace, and a Man shall rise from my seed, like the Sun of righteousness, walking with the sons of men in meekness and righteousness, and no sin shall be found in Him. And the heavens shall be opened above Him, to shed forth the blessing of the Spirit from the Holy Father; and He shall shed forth a spirit of grace upon you, and ye shall be unto Him sons in

6.   Heavily reworked in the light of the Gospels and Christian baptism.

7.   Messianic symbolism related to the 'plant' or 'tree' in Paradise. The reference
       to the Messiah as 'a Man' also conceals Mystery-symbolism, and derives from
       'the picture of the ruler representing the god in the garden of paradise. It is
       clear, for instance, that several Near Eastern temples had in their precincts a
       garden (the garden of the gods) in which there were located the tree and
       waters of life. This idea is carried right on into the Book of Revelation and
       has influenced earlier Israelite beliefs. The king is the gardener, possessing
       the *plant* and water of life ... He is so closely associated with these that he can
       even be *identified* with them and himself be seen as the tree under which his
       people find protection and as the source of the life-giving water. The sceptre
       of the king, the sceptre which is often said to bud, is derived from the tree
       of life ideogram. Widengren holds that this is behind the tradition of Moses'
       rod and points to Israelite legend in which it is maintained that this rod has
       been passed on from Adam to Seth and through his descendants to Moses ...
       So, too, in Israel as elsewhere, the description of the ruler as a *shoot* or *branch*
       ultimately depends upon this symbolism ... the king is obviously, in this
       whole portrayal, being considered as the First Man' (Borsch 1967, pp.98f); see
       also G. Widengren 1951). We have seen repeatedly that the Essene initiates
       experienced the condition of paradise, and looked forward to its restoration.
       Initiation is the process of becoming fully human, the Man as he was made
       by God. The King Messiah restores the condition of earthly Man, universal
       humanity, as the Priest Messiah restores man's relation to God.

8.   Cf. the pattern of Jesus' sayings in the 'Beatitudes' — Matthew 5:3ff. It has
       recently been argued by H. Burgmann that these and much else in the
       'Sermon on the Mount' derive from Essene forms and meditative patterns:
       see Burgmann 1988, pp.459ff.

truth, and ye shall walk in His commandments, the first and the last.[6] This is the Branch of God Most High, and this the Wellspring unto life for all flesh. Then shall the sceptre of my kingdom shine forth, and from your root shall arise a stem; and in it shall arise a rod of righteousness to the Gentiles, to judge and to save all that call upon the Lord.[7]

25. And after these things shall Abraham and Isaac and Jacob arise unto life, and I and my brethren will be chiefs, even your sceptre in Israel: Levi first, I the second, Joseph the third, Benjamin fourth, Simeon fifth, Issachar sixth, and so all in order. And the Lord blessed Levi; the Angel of the Presence, me; the powers of glory, Simeon; the heaven, Reuben; the earth, Issachar; the sea, Zebulun; the mountains, Joseph; the tabernacle, Benjamin; the lights of heaven, Dan; the fatness of earth, Naphtali; the sun, Gad; the olive, Asher: and there shall be one people of the Lord, and one tongue; and there shall no more be a spirit of deceit of Beliar, for he shall be cast into the fire for ever. And they who have died in grief shall arise in joy,[8] and they who have lived in poverty for the Lord's sake shall be made rich, and they who have been in want shall be filled, and they who have been weak shall be made strong, and they who have been put to death for the Lord's sake shall awake in life. And the harts of Jacob shall run in joyfulness, and the eagles of Israel shall fly in gladness; but the ungodly shall lament, and sinners shall weep, and all the people shall glorify the Lord for ever.

26. Observe, therefore, my children, all the law of the Lord, for there is hope for all them who follow His way aright. And he said to them: I die before your eyes this day, a hundred and nineteen years old. Let no one bury me in costly apparel, nor tear open my bowels, for this shall they who are kings do: and carry me up to Hebron with you. And Judah, when he had said these things, fell asleep; and his sons did according to all whatsoever he commanded them, and they buried him in Hebron with his fathers.

4. The *Great Annunciation* of Simon the Magus

From Essenes to Gnostics

Among the Essenes we see the Mystery-rites in a new form. There are many similarities to the practices of Mandeans, Mithraists and others influenced by the same Near Eastern milieu, with its ideas reaching back to origins in Babylon and archaic Iran; but there is at the same time a new direction in evolution. Instead of the old loose association of the initiates, the Essenes developed a highly cohesive social structure; in place of the old sense of becoming one with a cosmic whole, the Essenes stressed the responsibility of the individual who is 'ahead of his time.' Instead of being a force of stability and harmony, the Mysteries thereby acquire the potential of becoming a force in history, and the visions of the Essene seers adopt the perspective of imminent transformation. The pattern of the past is beheld, but not as a completed whole, expressing the divine wisdom, as in the ancient myths. For the Essene it is incomplete, but thrilling on the verge of realization in the 'age to come,' when it will be 'fulfilled.' The change in direction which we see in the Essene Mystery is of enormous significance — part of the discovery of our modern, forward-looking consciousness. The Jewish culture contributed the moral individual, in his social and spiritual dimension. It contributed the Law, the framework within which individuals can work together. It contributed the prophecy of the Messiah, the pivot around whom the events of God's 'Visitation' revolve. All these were in turn deepened, transfigured in the light of the Mystery-experience.

Yet it was clear that the Mysteries could not be contained in any single direction of evolution. Their spirituality could not be brought down to earth and channelled into history without a certain loss as well as enrichment. Individuality appears in the Essenes in the guise of total commitment: but individuality also opens the way to

exhilarating freedom. To work within a framework is a basic
achievement of social life: but there is also value in the search for
insights that challenge the framework, which draw our attention to
what we have overlooked or failed to value aright. There is a proper
humility which enables us to learn from a righteous teacher: but
there are also things that we can never learn unless we find them
for ourselves and in ourselves. To wait for the ripening of conditions around us when the hoped-for goal may be 'fulfilled' is
essential to wise living: but it is also true that there are things we
can never receive from outside, and must set ourselves up in
opposition to all external powers if we are to break through to the
'fulfilment' which we bear solely in ourselves. All these aspects
come to the fore in another extraordinary development of the
Mysteries, generally identified by the term Gnosticism.

Gnosis — spiritual knowledge — is the goal of all initiation, and
lies at the root of all Mysteries. In the Dead Sea Scrolls we find
many references to the 'knowledge' vouchsafed by God enabling the
initiate to recognize the Light and distinguish it from the Darkness.
There, however, *gnosis* is an attribute of the Community and a grace
from above: it enables an individual to share his experience, to
describe it in a common language of symbols, to give it a meaning
beyond himself by relating it to the traditions and forms of life
derived from the Bible and the Community's history. *Gnosis*
generates a quite different spirituality when it is pursued as an end
in itself, assumes central place in the religious mind and challenges
the existing traditions and received ideas, on the basis that: *He who
knows himself knows all things in himself.* What then results is best
called Gnosticism. It does not produce a tight community, but rather
a loose and scattered organization often imaged as sparks of light
strewn through the world. The Gnostic adepts do not find themselves at home within a single framework, such as the Bible, but
work within any framework and 'recognize' another Gnostic by
imaginative sympathy that overleaps bounds of culture and faith.
And whatever the framework in which the Gnostic must work, he
does so as an 'alien,' an outsider in spirit. No-one can 'teach' the
Gnostic what he needs to know — except the divine Messenger who
speaks within. If there are nevertheless teachers or Masters it is only
in the capacity of helpers on the way to the incommunicable
authentic moment. The teaching cannot convey it; but then, as one
Gnostic manual remarkably expresses it: *It is not necessary to have*

that which you give. In the *Gospel of Thomas* we have a portrait of
Jesus understood in Hermetic and Gnostic terms. When asked what
Jesus is like, various of his disciples attempt to compare him to a
wise teacher or a righteous angel, but Thomas refuses to play this
game and will not try to fit him into any framework. Upon which
Jesus says:

> I am not thy master. Because thou hast drunk, thou hast
> become intoxicated from the bubbling spring which I have
> measured out.

He takes him aside and gives him esoteric teaching, which needs
few words and cannot be conveyed to the others — it would be
dangerous even to try.

It is obvious that the Gnostic can therefore find nothing to his
purpose in outer events or history. The 'awakening' which he seeks
cannot be awaited from the working-out of God's providence on the
model of the Essene vision of an 'age to come.' External nature and
the actions which take place there are foreign to the inmost essence
of human spirit, grasped only in *gnosis.* The Creator of biblical
thought, therefore, who makes the world and so sets the stage for
history and the developing relationship between God and his
people, cannot show the way to the divine. The maker of the
Ultimate Framework, the ordered world, can be for the Gnostic only
the Ultimate Obstacle to his liberation, which is essentially liberation
from all frameworks. Again in the *Gospel of Thomas* Jesus says:

> Teach me concerning this stone which the builders
> rejected. It is the corner-stone.

In the Gnostic tradition Jesus is presented as the one who sets us
free from the Law, from enslavement to outward customs and fixed
roles in the community. 'To be "children of the living Father",' says
Helmut Koester in summary of the *Gospel of Thomas*, 'is to be free
from the society and not to be bound to the world and its values.
"Blessedness" does not depend upon the marks of success in this
world. One's identity should not be determined by whatever is
valuable for personal status in the social fabric of the world:
householder, family member, religious leader, successful business
person.'[*] The Gnostic must reject all that is presupposed as 'reality'
by the community, which accordingly figures in Gnosticism not
as a divinely ordained creation but as the botched work of a blind,

---

[*] H. Koester, *Ancient Christian Gospels*, London and Philadelphia 1990, p.128.

deluded Demiurge — a strange mixture of God and devil. The creation is a trap, a snare for the soul in which it is trapped by its own 'ignorance,' its mistaken notion of its own being and the interpretation imposed upon it from outside, which can never give it its true identity.

The *Gospel of Thomas* occupies a complex place in the development of these ideas and in our picture of their history from our vantage-point today. It was not originally a Gnostic Gospel — at least in the sense of a Gospel used by a special Gnostic group — but is rather a very early tradition of the words of Jesus, with many claims to give his sayings and especially the parables in an earlier, more authentic form than the Gospels of the New Testament. Its version of his message gives a more coherent account of the coming of the Kingdom, the criticism of the Law, etc. than much in the Church's version preserved in our Bible, and also shows up certain links between the three 'synoptic' Gospels of Matthew, Mark and Luke and the more esoteric Gospel of John since materials in *Thomas* overlap with both. That would suggest that it tells us of an earlier phase of development when Christian doctrine was still close to its esoteric roots. But at some stage *Thomas* was drawn into a line of Gnostic evolution that led its users to split with the mainstream, and there are small but tell-tale signs of alterations in the text to make it more unambiguously Gnostic than it was at first. It was caught up, in other words, in that great polarization which split the Church in the second century, dividing it into a Gnostic and an ecclesiastical wing. Tensions and differences which had been contained in the Christian movement from the outset pulled apart, divisions hardened, choices narrowed: we can be certain that many of the more subtle and interesting positions disappeared at precisely this time. A valuable early witness like the *Gospel of Thomas* was lost to the Church because it did not fit into either camp; the Gospel of John is another case where the Church came perilously close to rejecting a work which likewise bridged the supposedly irreconcilable, and the knowledge that it came from the Beloved Disciple, occupying a unique place in the tradition of Jesus' work and teaching, was forgotten. Accidents of history have had to restore to us the more subtle picture which was then reduced to a stark black and white.

Most of the evidence for Gnostic ideas comes from that wing of Christian evolution which went its own way in the second century amid furious doctrinal arguments which crystallized the concept of 'heresy' for the medieval Church. However, it is also clear that the polarization which split Christianity had wider ramifications and earlier roots. Just as we can see behind the Essenes a meeting of Judaism with the Mysteries, so we can see signs of a 'Gnostic reaction' already in the esoteric schools of Samaria, in the Hermetic Mysteries of pagan Alexandria, in the retelling of the Bible history in the *Apocalypse of Adam* and in the related traditions of the *Book of the Blessed* which mingle a sort of proto-kabbala with exotic myths. In these obscure documents we see the other side of the same picture. All the elements familiar from Essenism are here encountered in alien guise: the background in the Mysteries of Babylon and the cosmic cycles from ancient Iran, the Two Ways or equivalent versions of Light and Darkness, and from Judaism the idea of a 'Coming One' or Messianic incarnation. These mingle now with features from other sources — the Egyptian cult of Thoth-Hermes, the lore of the Samaritans and Mysteries of other regions of the ancient world. But the encounter with Judaism again plays a crucial role: not this time in a synthesis but in a dual vision. The unfolding of Old Testament history from creation through exile to the 'age to come' is replaced by a sense of estrangement in an alien, anti-divine universe; the part which the individual is called upon to play in society becomes a disguise, so successful that he forgets all else, including his divine, illimitable origin; the earthly messenger is to be contrasted, rather than identified with the true or heavenly messenger. The Judaic emphasis on the individual and the unique, unrepeatable events of history is rejected in favour of cosmic myth, where the individual loses himself in retelling the primordial, ever-repeated story, of which no telling is ever final, and shares in the creative power of the Beginning, which the Jewish God claims for himself alone. The Creator's establishing of the Ultimate Framework, which the Essenes felt to be a 'gift from above' and a discipline of the spirit, leads in the Gnostic reaction to a flight into the limitless possibilities of the mythological consciousness. The new world of history and self-consciousness cannot be conjured away, however. The myths of eternal return cannot quite dissolve the obstinate historical reality brought into focus by the spiritual tradition of Judaism.

All the Mysteries which show the 'Gnostic reaction' belong to areas on the fringes of Judaism — Syria, Samaria, Alexandria with its strong Jewish presence. They indicate that the conflicts in values and even in the sense of what constitutes reality was happening on a wider scale, and that Christianity was indeed part of a broader development. The Gnostic crisis in Christianity in the second century AD was an expression of a clash between history and myth, individual experience and cosmic experience, which was precipitated earlier and left its mark also in the pagan Mysteries.

I have chosen documents which show the early stages of this process. All of them have connections with Christian themes and currents which emerged within Christianity; but they are not yet touched by Christianity, or in the case of the *Book of the Blessed* (see Cahpeter 7) the groundwork is older and different from that which became the orthodox theology. They show collectively a response from the Mystery-side which was just as important, I believe, as the Essene synthesis for the Christian vision. The Essene Messiah would have been a 'renewer of the Law,' showing man his allotted place in the divine economy: not the one who revealed the truth and said that 'the truth will set you free.' We must not ourselves fly to Bultmann's extreme of presenting Christianity as an offshoot of the Gnostic-Mandean myth about a Messenger. But without its mythical-Gnostic dimension Christianity would not have been the rich, complex spiritual phenomenon that it is — and it is time that we rediscovered those aspects of its richness which point to its heritage from the Mysteries with greater understanding.

The Gnostics' burden of alienation, their sense of working within a framework of values and truths that is not quite their own, finds an echo in many minds today. It is not exactly analogous to the alienation of secular civilization, being rooted in the feeling of the 'other-worldly,' unlimited being of man in the mythical universe, crowded with angels, gods and sharing the drama of the divine life. Yet it may have much to tell us for that very reason, and teach us the truth behind those sustaining myths in the inner experience of the Gnostic which we can give new form and power for today. We may start with the Gnostic origins of a figure who for many has come to express one central strand of modern man's striving: the figure of Faust.

Faust in Samaria

How did Faust come to be in Samaria? Readers of Marlowe's *Faustus*, or Goethe's *Faust*, may be forgiven for thinking that there must be an episode in the legend they have missed. Faust's voyage to Rome, or through time to ancient Greece: these are familiar from the great literary treatments which have done so much to establish the Faust-figure as a representative of modern man in his 'endless striving' to realize the truth about himself and the world, the human spirit and the spirit of God, or the Devil. Relatively few readers of these modern masterpieces of the imagination are aware that the origins of the figure of Faust can be traced back, behind the picture of the Renaissance sage and magician, as far as New Testament times, to an obscure village in Samaria, or that the prototype of later Fausts himself appears in the New Testament, in the Book of Acts.

Simon, called Simon Magus, was reputedly born in Gitta, a small township in the central hilly part of Palestine called Samaria, a contemporary of Jesus. The Samaritans had a bad name among Jews (so bad, in fact, that the parable plays on the evident contradiction of a 'good Samaritan' to make us see that black-and-white assumptions may blind us to inherent human qualities in the people around us). The Jews regarded them as having betrayed the covenant of God's people because after the crisis of the Exile and the return, they had refused to take part in the great reform and rebuilding guided by Ezra the Scribe which effectively created Judaism as we still know it. The Samaritans still clung to the traditions of Moses, but they held back from the reorganization programme centred on Jerusalem and the New Temple; they worshipped God on Mount Gerizim, as indeed the remaining Samaritans do today. There are nowadays only a handful of Samaritans left. But in New Testament times they far outnumbered the Jews, and when the Romans turned Palestine into a province of the Empire it was natural that they made their administrative centre in Samaria, not in Jerusalem, the small and troublesome Temple-state to the south.

Much of Simon's life is impenetrably shrouded in obscurity and legend, both sensational and hostile. But many reports connect him with the esoteric teacher within Samaritanism called Dositheus. Some scholars believe that he also made contact with the Magi, the priestly followers of the ancient Iranian prophet Zarathustra, and learnt many of their secrets. Perhaps it was also from his association with them that he came to acquire the title 'Magus' himself. However that may be, he soon established himself as a teacher of a kind of *gnosis*, a secret wisdom capable of transforming his pupils, giving 'magical' powers. He himself was regarded as a wonder-worker, capable of miracles such as the creation of an *homunculus* (a man-made man) out of air and water, dying and returning to life, and shamanic feats such as levitation or flight through the air. The popular legends which thrived on such information were based on vulgar misrepresentation of spiritual achievements and teachings: the Gospel of John also taught, for example, that it is possible to 'make a new man' out of water and air (spirit), through the mystery of baptism. Every initiate must die to his old self and be reborn, 'returning to life and light' as was said in the ancient Mystery religions. Simon's followers certainly regarded him as a great spiritual teacher; and it was for that reason that they honoured him with the name of 'Favoured One,' *Faustus*.

Simon did not give out his teaching in the modern way, under his own authority. He spoke in the name of the 'Great Power,' which is in fact a circumlocution for 'God.' He believed that the divine Power manifested in the world was essentially Fire: there were 'manifest' aspects of the primal energy, and other aspects of it which were 'occult,' and the manifest and occult aspects totalled six. There also existed, however, latently within each human being, the Seventh Power. If man could awaken this Seventh Power, actualize it within himself, he could realize his own identity with the Divine, the hidden source. It was in this sense that he himself spoke as one who had realized his divine potentiality. Only later was his claim misunderstood, and the Christian heresy specialists of the early Church thought that he had set himself up as a rival of Christ. In reality, Simon was making no special claim to be a unique embodiment of divine Power; he spoke in the name of a Power which he regarded as existing in all men, if they were only made aware of it and learnt how to unleash it in themselves. His universalist teaching is contained in an extraordinary work called the *Great Annunciation*, probably written in his name quite early on by his pupils, and surviving at least in extensive summary and quotations.

From the *Great Annunciation* we learn in addition the nature of the faculty by which man can awaken the Seventh Power. It must be awakened by the use of *imagination*. What exists unformed and latent in the unconscious depths of the soul must be 'formed as an image.' Man must create his own ideal self, project his own higher nature by the effort of his imagination, giving form to his dim apprehensions of the 'hidden' truth, and can finally forge his projected self into actual identity with the occult source, the divine Power within. Here we have the aspect of *gnosis* which appears again most strongly in the Renaissance and Romantic visions of Faust, the confidence in the ability of man to transform himself and recreate his moral being through imagination, rather than by submitting to a code of rules. In the case of Simon, imagination is still experienced, however, as a cosmic force: it is a divine energy hidden in man which can overwhelm and sweep away his 'illusory' sense of individuality, his separate identity. Later, when we come to the Faust figures of modern times, imagination will have come more within the control of man's ego, giving to his aspiration and imaginative struggle an individual pathos lacking in the wisdom of the ancient Magus of Samaria.

A female Emanation, a being who reflected the Thought *(Ennoia)* of God, succumbed and was sucked into the vortex of deaths and births, the downward spiral of incarnations. She appeared in life after life as an embodiment of the divine beauty which men half remembered from before the Fall, and drove men mad with the loveliness of the unattainable. As Helen of Troy she provoked the senseless destruction which followed for both sides, Greeks and Trojans alike. Trapped within the web of rebirths she herself grew spiteful and, when the Greek poet Stesichorus denigrated her beauty, struck him blind, though she later restored his sight when he repented and worshipped her. Lower and lower she sank, until she became a whore in the Phoenician city of Tyre, her last and most degraded incarnation. It was there that she was recognized by Simon, in whom the Seventh Power had come to know itself once more as the original unity of the Divine. He saw in her the lost *Ennoia*, God's primal thought, and took her as his companion, restoring her to the knowledge of her origin and spiritual self.

Such at any rate is the teaching in legendary form which has come down to us. The legend lived on in the quest of Faust for the 'Eternal Feminine,' whom he finds partly through mortal beauties but also partly in the mysterious Helen of Troy (a woman or a phantom?) whom he journeys to ancient Greece to find. She represents for Goethe, as Rudolf Steiner pointed out, his own ideal self. In fact, the myth probably expresses in a popular form the essential teaching of Simon about man's imagination and his ability to vision forth his higher nature. Again, it was only later that literal-mindedness prevailed and a romance blossomed in ever more extravagant guises. Yet it is a testimony to the power of the myth that the truth behind it lived on too, and could still be used by a great modern poet to express essential insights into man's imaginative potentiality.

Within the Christian tradition, on the other hand, misunderstanding and hostility became ever more firmly established. Esoteric wisdom or *gnosis* like that of Simon formed part of the background to Christianity itself, but in order to absorb the radical truth of Christianity such wisdom had also to be the transformed. Those teachers who clung to ancient ways constituted a danger to the Christian way, and among these one has to include the followers of Simon's Faustian doctrine. Already in the writings of Luke (the Gospel and the Book of Acts) a clear distinction is drawn, and Simon himself is presented in a thoroughly bad light. Luke evidently wrote for the educated Greek-speaking culture of his time, and doctrines like those of Simon's *gnosis* were certainly known there. Acts (Chapter 8) describes Simon, and his claim to speak in the person of 'what is called the great Power' of God. A particular misunderstanding arose because Simon offered money to the disciples in exchange for esoteric knowledge and power. This episode, scandalous as it seemed to the early Christians, and out of keeping with the Christian spirit as it was, constituted a normal practice which carried no stigma of offence in ancient times. It continues to be normal practice among Masons and similar organizations of today, where charters to perform rites and confer grades are bought by those who require them and are instructed in their use. The first Christians, however, looked at matters in a different light, and the term 'simony' came into existence. Later Christian legend presents Simon as the arch-enemy of St Peter, dogging the apostle's steps as he travels the world evangelizing, until finally, at one of Simon's sorcery demonstrations, Peter prays beneath the levitating magician who falls to the ground and is killed. But here we enter the domain of the pious and fanciful romance-writers of the Church.

Modern analysis suggests, however, that the legends and the 'philosophical' teachings of the *Great Annunciation* are indeed twin lines of development from the same source — Simon's original teaching. The one version is popular and imaginative, the other more esoteric and doctrinal. In its present form the *Great Annunciation* is a Christian document and quotes Paul's letter to Corinth; parallels with other Gnostics and the reference to 'holy Homer' show that it received its final polish in Alexandria. Walter Schmithals showed that its teachings are based essentially on the mythological content shared with other accounts of Simon, however, and that it is in all essentials a document of Jewish-Samaritan *gnosis*, contemporary with Christian beginnings but owing little or nothing to Christian influence. Hippolytus, the Church Father who preserves it, is fundamentally correct in attributing its ideas to Simon himself and the words in the quotations are probably traditions of Simon's actual language.

Modern analysis has also suggested some striking conclusions of a different kind! In the once famous book *The Myth of God Incarnate*, Michael Goulder argued ingeniously that Simon was not so much the father of all heretics as the father of Christian orthodoxy. The pattern of Simon's thought includes a cosmic divinity, who then speaks through a human representative on earth, before resuming his cosmic glory: Goulder saw in the earthly representative a model for the Christian concept of the 'Incarnation' of a heavenly redeemer on earth. In reality, though, the similarities are not very far-reaching. Simon's divinity is never actually embodied in a redeemer-figure, but is rather the 'One who Stood, Stands and Will Stand,' who exists eternally. Everyone, according to Simon, can come to knowledge of this being through an inner awakening of the Seventh Power. Such knowledge (*gnosis*) confers liberation from the fall into matter and individual existence, rather than incarnating the Power in a physical form. What the analogy that there is with Christianity shows us is, perhaps, more subtle and more interesting.

Schmithals examines the heresy-hunters' accusations against Simon that he claimed to be the Christ. He finds that this accusation cannot be upheld, if by it we mean the Church's conception of Christ: a redeemer in the shape of an individual man on earth. Simon made no such claim. Yet behind the 'Standing One,' in whose name Simon speaks, Schmithals too recognizes that it is the Christ who is spoken of. This Christ or Messiah is however a heavenly being, or Primal Man, not incarnate on earth but a reality in the world above. *Gnosis* brings about union with him — and so with God, whose image he is. And that 'image' can take on reality within us at the turning-point of the cosmic process. Following the pattern of the ancient Mysteries, the god is not present on earth but transcends the earthly and restores us to our spiritual origin. But the Mystery-god is now recognized as the Christ, the Messiah of Jewish prophecy in his archetypal reality.

The Essene apprehension of the Messianic trajectory into the future, when inner reality would become a truth on the external plane, is perfectly complemented by the Gnostic teaching. The same elements are fused together, and contact between the Essenes and Dositheus, Simon's teacher, has been thought likely. But the Gnostics are not interested in the temporal future — only in eternal truth. They grasped the Christ in his present reality, above the earth.

Goulder's insight may therefore have an application more subtle than the one he intended. Simon's Mystery-teaching may indeed show the very kinds of ideas that were being developed at the time of Jesus about the Christ, and the Christ's place in a divine drama which could involve the soul of everyman. In Jesus the drama took a further step into earthly actualization. Redemption for the first time became a force in history. Simon may not himself have been able to comprehend the full extent of the transform-ation this required of the ancient ideas. Though the Acts of the Apostles records his baptism, his followers continued to hold the Gnostic, supra-earthly view of the Christ. Or at least many of them did. Perhaps some of them, on the other hand, helped formulate that original harmony of history and cosmic myth which is the unique Christian fusion. Goulder's claim that Paul appro-priated the idea of Jesus' incarnation in the course of dialectic with the Samaritan missionaries in Corinth and Ephesus between 50 and 55 AD remains purely speculative. But the Gnostic pattern of ideas does show us the cosmic Christ and a universal dynamic of salvation in a form that could have flowed into Christianity at its beginnings.

One last link — not with Paul, but with Jesus himself. The *Gospel of Thomas* stands in intimate connection with the Gnostic traditions in Christianity, and with Jesus' sayings in the New Testament

Gospels. It is a very early and authentic account of his teachings. And is it not striking that in it Jesus teaches something oddly like Simon's version of 'becoming an image'?

> Jesus said: When you see your likeness, you rejoice. But when you see your images which came into being before you, and which neither die nor become manifest, how much will you have to bear! (Saying 84).

Source: report on the teachings of Simon the Magus in Hippolytus, Refutation of All Heresies *VI,9:4–18:7. Translated from Greek by J.M. MacMahon.*

1.   Hippolytus identifies the author of the *Great Annunciation* with the Simon mentioned in the Acts of the Apostles 8:9ff as practising *magia* and speaking under the authority of 'the Great Power' — a well-known circumlocution for God. He is said to have come from the village of Gitta in Samaria, and Hippolytus accuses him of making himself a God or Christ, but the *Great Annunciation* makes it clear that the Great Power is not himself but the source and subject of his revelations, the God whom he proclaims. The quotation — one of only three direct quotes in Hippolytus' summary — announces his basic message: that the creative power which is the root of the universe exists also, in hidden form, within man. It can be actualized by an act of 'intellectual apprehension,' *gnosis.*

2.   That is, irreducible: the Greek theory of 'elements.' Simon's teaching does not derive from a theory of physical substances.

3.   In her discussion of parallels between Simonian and Mandean ideas, Lady Drower points out that 'in the Mandean books we get constant references to two kinds of fire, *'kilta* and *haita,* "consuming" and "living"' (Oxford 1960, p.90). She may be correct in seeing a direct influence of Zoroastrian thought on Simon: fire for the Magi is the metaphorical 'son' or manifestation of Ahura Mazda in the visible world. Daniélou noted that Simon's teacher Dositheus or Dostai is said to have come from 'Kokaba near Damascus, the site of an Essene community,' and it was there, he thinks, 'that Simon, a disciple of Dositheus, was converted to dualism by Zoroastrian magi (hence Simon is "Magus")' — cited by S.J. Isser 1976, p.198.

4.   Part of Hipploytus' sustained attempt to derive all 'heresy' from the ideas of Greek philosophy; here as almost everywhere it is a misguided effort.

✳ On the Teachings of Simon the Magus ✳

The Unlimited Power

9:4. Simon denominates the originating principle of the universe an unlimited power, expressing himself thus: "This is the treatise of a revelation of the voice and name recognizable by means of intellectual apprehension of the Great Unlimited Power. Wherefore it will be sealed, and kept secret, and hid, and will repose in the habitation, at the foundation of which lies the root of all things."[1] And he asserts that this man who is born of blood is the aforesaid habitation, and that in him resides an unlimited power, which he affirms to be the root of the universe.

Now the unlimited power which is fire, constitutes, according to Simon, not any uncompounded essence, in conformity with the opinion of those who assert that the four elements are simple, and who have therefore likewise imagined that fire, which is one of the four, is simple.[2] But this is far from being the case: for there is, he maintains, a certain twofold nature of fire; and of this twofold nature he denominates one part a something secret, and another a something manifest, and that the secret are hidden in the manifest portions of the fire, and that the manifest portions of the fire derive their being from its secret portions.[3] This, however, is what Aristotle denominates by the expressions "potentiality" and "energy," or what Plato styles "intelligible" and "sensible."[4] And the manifest portion of the fire comprises all things in itself, whatsoever any one might discern, or even whatever objects of the visible creation he may happen to overlook. But the entire secret portion of the fire which one may discern is cognized by intellect, and evades the power of the senses; or one fails to observe it, from want of a capacity for that particular sort of perception. In general, however, inasmuch as all existing things fall under the categories, namely, of what are objects of Sense, and what are objects of Intellect, and as for the denomination of these Simon

5.   Or 'occult.'

6.   Another version of the cosmic Tree, such as we find among the Essenes
        (above pp.46ff) from whose fruit the initiated (or redeemed humanity) are
        said to eat — related also to the imagery of 'planting,' the Messiah as a
        'shoot,' etc. which we find developed among the Mandeans as well as in the
        Bible. The reference to the dream of Nabuchodonosor (Nebuchadnezzar) in
        Daniel 4:7ff is less the source of the image than an attempt of Simon or his
        followers to relate their secret doctrines to the well-known text of the Bible
        or, elsewhere, to Homer, etc.

        Among the Mandeans, the 'planting' which happens in initiation is a link
        with the beginning of time (Paradise). The Essenes add to this a sense that
        the Tree will 'put forth a shoot' in the 'age to come,' when the Messiah will
        open the gates of Paradise once more and give humanity the fruit of the Tree
        of Life. The Simonians give the image a more Gnostic interpretation: the
        visible-material substance which is produced, as bark is formed around the
        living wood of a tree, from the hidden energy will be 'burned up,' and the
        'fruit' that is harvested has its reality in the spiritual world. When we attain
        gnosis, the material world will fall away from us like chaff being committed
        to the fire, and serve no further purpose. Behind this again lies the Iranian
        idea of the eventual spiritualization of the world at the Transfiguration, when
        matter will be 'burned up'; the Essenes too expected this in the future. But
        in *gnosis* it happens already in the seer, as part of a cosmic process of the
        awakening of individual 'sparks' of light, who are thereby set free from their
        entanglement in matter.

7.   On how the spirit ('fruit') receives form, see further below, p.171. The
        analogy of spiritual development to ripening or to the 'fully grown' wheat is
        rooted in ancient Mystery-language. Cf. also *Gospel of Philip* 115.

8.   Isaiah 5:7.

9.   W. Schmithals sees in Simon's system a case of 'the transferral of the Jewish
        title of Christ (Messiah) to the Gnostic primal man' and the 'introduction of
        the Jewish figure of the Messiah into the Gnostic mythology' (1971, p.49). In
        the encounter between the Mysteries and Judaism, the Messiah ('the man of
        Judah ... the beloved plant') must be understood in a cosmic way. Among the
        Essenes, earthly and cosmic visions converged: here, the Messiah becomes in
        the Gnostic fashion a cosmic-primordial reality. The Essenes look forward
        prophetically to the crossing-point of converging lines; for Simon, he is a
        reality now, but transcends any individual embodiment: he exists as a Logos,
        or creative Word and does not descend to the perishable flesh, as the rest of
        this passage makes clear.

10.   Isaiah 40:6-8.

employs the terms secret[5] and manifest; it may, I say, in general, be affirmed that the fire, I mean the super-celestial fire, is a treasure, as it was a large tree, just such a one as in a dream was seen by Nabuchodonosor, out of which all flesh is nourished.[6] And the manifest portion of the fire he regards as the stem, the branches, the leaves, and the external rind which overlaps them. All these appendages, he says, of the Great Tree being kindled, are made to disappear by reason of the blaze of the all-devouring fire. The fruit, however, of the tree, when it is fully grown, and has received its own form,[7] is deposited in a granary, not flung into the fire. For, he says, the fruit has been produced for the purpose of being laid in the storehouse, whereas the chaff that it may be delivered over to the fire. Now the chaff is stem, and is generated not for its own sake, but for that of the fruit.

10. And this, he says, is what has been written in Scripture: "For the vineyard of the Lord of Sabaoth is the house of Israel, and the man of Judah is His beloved plant."[8] If, however, the man of Judah is the beloved plant, it has been proved, he says, that there is not any other tree but that man.[9] But concerning the secretion and dissolution of this tree, Scripture, he says, has spoken sufficiently. And as regards instruction for those who have been fashioned after the image of him, that statement is enough which is made in Scripture, that "all flesh is grass, and all the glory of flesh, as it were, a flower of grass. The grass withereth, and its flower falleth; but the word of the Lord abideth for ever."[10] The word of the Lord, he says, is that word which is produced in the mouth, and is a Logos, but nowhere else exists there a place of generation.

11. Now, to express myself briefly, inasmuch as the fire is of this description, according to Simon, and since all things are visible and invisible, and in like manner resonant and not resonant, numberable and not subjects of numeration; he denominates in the *Great Announcement* a perfect intelligible entity, after such a mode, that each of those things which, existing indefinitely, may be infinitely comprehended, both

11.   A confused summary. From what we can understand, it seems that Simon argued that everything visible, sounding and particular in our perceptible world has its reality in the invisible, infinite world. And from the fact that we are able to cognize things through an act of *gnosis*, he argued that they have a spiritual reality analogous to ours, that is, the universe consists ultimately of beings who express themselves in understanding and will, rather than of things. The Mandeans likewise believe in a world of 'counterparts.' 'For, as one priest told me,' relates Lady Drower, '"of all things there are two, an actual and its mabda (ideal or archetype)." Another explained that each individual on earth has his double (dmuta) or likeness ... and at the time of death the earthly individual leaves his earthly body and assumes the ethereal body of his double".' (Drower, Oxford 1960, p.40).

12.   Empedocles, fragment 109 (Diels). The citation is another attempt by Hippolytus to explain all heresy from Greek philosophy.

13.   The 'begotten' world did not, for Simon, come into being by a creative act, 'out of nothing.' It existed at first in a spiritual form — as Mind, Intelligence, etc. Later these spiritual powers find their external 'counterparts' in the externally existing heaven and earth, sun and moon and so forth. According to Iranian-Zoroastrian ideas, the world was fashioned by Ohrmazd in a state of pure light (cf. 'fire'), and only afterwards descended into the state of 'mixture' with material substance where it was corrupted by the influence of Ahriman. Further analogies with Zoroastrian thought will be noted below.

14.   Notice that the 'one who comes into being' out of the primal fire-stage is a being once more: the Logos, possessed of Mind etc. He is potentially the embodiment of the Hidden Power, the primal God. The term 'root' to describe an entity in the spiritual world is found in Hermetism and Christian Gnosticism.

15.   Simon now describes the world-process in dynamic terms. The original infinite power (God) goes forth into creation, becomes particular beings and things, and so loses himself, is scattered in the universe. But in those who come to *gnosis* he finds himself again and returns to the state of infinity as he was at the beginning. In past and future he is infinite: he stood and will stand forever. In the intermediate phase he is in individuals, who when they know this may claim like Simon to be 'the one who stands.' God is not exactly 'incarnated' in such an individual. Rather the moment of contact is a turning-point and a return to the spiritual state. But in the pattern of descent, individualization and return we have a model which — if translated into terms of history — could develop into an understanding in Christian, incarnational terms. In the older Mysteries, we should note the Zoroastrian teaching of the 'three Moments': Creation, Mixture and Separation (of spiritual and material).

16.   In the phase of descent, the six powers become the created universe, or made work, losing their infinite potential and atrophying into 'things.' Ideas about the six-days' 'work of creation' *(ma'aseh bereshit)* in the Jewish esoteric

speaks, and understands, and acts[11] in such a manner as Empedocles speaks of:

> For earth, indeed, by earth we see, and water by water,
> And air divine by air, and fire fierce by fire,
> And love by love, and also strife by gloomy strife.[12]

12. For, he says, he is in the habit of considering that all these portions of the fire, both visible and invisible, are possessed of perception and a share of intelligence. the world, therefore, that which is generated, was produced from the unbegotten fire. It began, however, to exist, he says, according to the following manner.[13] He who was begotten from the principle of that fire took six roots,[14] and those primary ones, of the originating principle of generation. And, he says, that the roots were made from the fire in pairs, which roots he terms "Mind" and "Intelligence," "Voice" and "Name," "Ratiocination" and "Reflection." and that in these six roots resides simultaneously the entire unlimited power potentially, however not actually. And this infinite power, he says, is he who stood, stands, and will stand.[15] Wherefore, whensoever he may be made into an image, inasmuch as he exists in the six powers, he will exist there substantially, potentially, quantitively, and completely. And he will be a power one and the same with the unbegotten and unlimited power, and not labouring under any greater deficiency than that unbegotten and unalterable and unlimited power. If, however, he may continue only potentially in the six powers, and has not been formed into an image, he vanishes, he says, and is destroyed in such a way as the grammatical or geometrical capacity in man's soul. For when the capacity takes unto itself an art, a light of existent things is produced; but when the capacity does not take unto itself an art, unskilfulness and ignorance are the results; and just as when the power was non-existent, it perishes along with the expiring man.

The Days of Creation[16]

13. And of those six powers, and of the seventh which co-exists with them, the first pair, Mind and Intelligence, he calls Heaven

tradition form the starting-point for Simon's reinterpretation from a Gnostic point of view. The unprepared introduction of a 'seventh power' points, in the first place, to the pattern of the six days of creation (Genesis 1) followed by the sabbath on which 'God rested from all his works.' Through the esoteric teachings, Jewish creation ideas had remained in touch with Mystery-experience. Simon, however, as we shall see, reinterprets them in the light of particular traditions which result in a radical swing in emphasis away from the glorious manifestation of God's work (as in Genesis) to a Gnostic evaluation of the material world.

17.   Cf. 'In the beginning God made the Heaven and the Earth' (Genesis 1:1). (But here they have a preceding spiritual reality in Mind and Intelligence).

18.   Isaiah 1:2.

19.   Here it emerges for the first time that the 'seventh power' is the reintegrated Godhead, which has recognized itself in the individual act of *gnosis* and realized its identity with the one who stood and will stand, that is, with God in his eternal being. Of the nature of this 'seventh power' we still have to learn below.

20.   Paired entities of this type are found in many Gnostic systems. Often they are called 'aeons,' and such a pairing is called a 'syzygy' (lit. yoking together!) In the system of Valentinus no less than thirty aeons exist prior to the material creation, and they are arranged in syzygies: the pattern is broken, however in the material world until restored by Christ. In Simon's system too we shall see that the division into sexual opposites is overcome in the future state and a deeper unity restored.

21.   Clearly not true in the sense of the system of the *Great Annunciation*. Rather, as Schmithals explains, Simon does assert his identity with the 'hidden power' — but that 'originally hardly denoted an individual person but rather the "Dynamis" (Power) also called "Christ" which is found on earth in all Pneumatics and can be active as redeemer in each of its parts. There is *one* Christ only above as He Who Stood or Will Stand. On earth Christ is found as the One Who Stands at all times in many ordinary men,' that is, Gnostics who are not thereby divine incarnations (W. Schmithals 1971, p.50). The Gnostic is redeemed *from* matter by the awakening of the seventh power. Schmithals argues that this conception of the Christ is not derived from the Church's conception of the earthly redeemer. The cosmic idea may rather form a prototype taken up by Christianity in historical terms, where the moment of embodiment becomes a unique Incarnation and effective in earthly reality rather than a rescue from it.

22.   Genesis 1:16 — the Fourth Day. The pattern of creation is evidently mirrored on a larger scale, and the 'three days prior to sun and moon' are regarded as three cosmic ages (aeons) before the origins of the material universe. The seventh power was already active at that time: hence one in whom it awakens could apply to himself the words of Proverbs 8:23, 25 ('Before all aeons I begot you,') originally applied to Sophia (Wisdom) and now identified in turn by Simon with the Spirit of God, his feminine aspect brooding on the waters. She is an 'image' of the potential seventh power.

23.   Genesis 1:2.

and Earth.[17] And that one of these, being of male sex, beholds from above and takes care of his partner, but that the earth receives below the rational fruits, akin to the earth, which are borne down from the heaven. On this account, he says, the Logos, frequently looking towards the things that are being generated from Mind and Intelligence, that is, from Heaven and Earth, exclaims, "Hear, O heaven, and give ear, O earth, because the Lord has spoken. I have brought forth children, and exalted them; and these have rejected me."[18] Now, he who utters these words, he says, is the seventh power — he who stood, stands, and will stand;[19] for he himself is cause of those beauteous objects of creation which Moses commended, and said that they were very good. But Voice and Name, the second of the three pairs, are Sun and Moon; and Ratiocination and Reflection, the third of the three pairs, are Air and Water;[20] and in all these is intermingled and blended, as I have declared, the great, the unlimited, the self-existing power.

14. When, therefore, Moses has spoken of "the six days in which God made heaven and earth, and rested on the seventh from all His works," Simon, in a manner already specified, giving these and other passages of Scripture a different application from the one intended by the holy writers, deifies himself.[21] When, therefore, the followers of Simon affirm that there are three days begotten before sun and moon,[22] they speak enigmatically of Mind and Intelligence, that is, Heaven and Earth, and of the seventh power, I mean the unlimited one. For these three powers are produced antecedent to all the rest. But when they say, "He begot me prior to all the Ages," such statements, he says, are alleged to hold good concerning the seventh power. Now this seventh power, which was a power existing in the unlimited power, which was produced prior to all the Ages, this is, he says, the seventh power, respecting which Moses utters the following words: "And the Spirit of God was wafted over the water;"[23] that is, says the Simonian, the Spirit which contains all things in itself, and is an image of the indefinite power about which Simon speaks, "an image from an incorruptible form, that alone reduces all things into

24.   The second short quotation from the actual words of the *Great Annunciation*.

25.   Or 'image.'

26.   In connection with the teaching about 'images' in the *Gospel of Thomas*, we
       should note here also saying 70 in that *Gospel*:
           Jesus said: When you bring forth that which you have in
           yourselves, that which you have will save you. If you do not have
           that in yourselves, that which you do not have in you will kill
           you.
       On becoming an image, and rebirth through the image, see also *Gospel of
       Philip* 67.

27.   1 Corinthians 11:32.

28.   Isaiah 44:2.

29.   In the mythological background to Genesis, the 'birth of the world' was
       indeed conceived as a kind of cosmic embryology. The Babylonian myth
       which provided a model for initiatory rebirth, for instance, described the
       chaos-monster Tiāmat sometimes as a giant foetus. Moreover, the paradise-
       garden of the Near Eastern temple-enclosures is sometimes also called 'Apsu'
       as it is formed from the body of the male monster, her consort, who is slain
       in the opening stages of cosmogony, provoking Tiāmat's vengeance. The
       king-god Marduk's struggle is thus the struggle to become human and be
       born in Paradise, fighting his way through the stages of animal forms
       represented by Tiāmat and her brood, corresponding to the pre-human
       phases echoed in embryology. In the myths, that is at once the creating of the
       ordered world, and a birth-process relived imaginatively so as to become a
       spiritual rebirth.
           Simon's interpretation ignores or argues away into allegory the entire
       Jewish tradition with its attempt to turn the myths into an historical account.
       Once again, the picture of the Spirit hovering over the waters is both cosmic
       creation and embryology and the 'image' through which we can be reborn.
       The old mythological imagery is not fully restored, but has been updated by
       a more detailed knowledge of the physiological aspects of birth. Nevertheless
       the direct linkage between creation-birth-salvation is powerfully reasserted.
           Similar ideas can be found in other Gnostics: e.g. the Naassenes, reported
       by Hippolytus V,9,14ff. See also the Nag Hammadi Tripartite Tractate Codex
       I 60:32–61:24: 'Thus it has been discovered that the (aeons) existed like a
       foetus ... While in the form of a foetus the infant is self-sufficient before ever
       seeing the one who sowed him.' In *Zostrianos* we find the spiritual ideal of
       'the purification of the unbornness,' that is, the return to the inner self-
       sufficient state of the aeons (Codex VIII 75:23).

order."[24] For this power that is wafted over the water, being begotten, he says, from an incorruptible form alone, reduces all things into order. When, therefore, according to these heretics, there ensued some such arrangement, and one similar to it of the world, the Deity, he says, proceeded to form man, taking clay from the earth. And He formed him not uncompounded, but twofold, according to His own image and likeness. Now the image is the Spirit that is wafted over the water; and whosoever is not fashioned into a figure[25] of this, will perish with the world, inasmuch as he continues only potentially, and does not exist actually.[26] This, he says, is what has been spoken, "that we should not be condemned with the world."[27] If one, however, be made into the figure of the Spirit, and be generated from an indivisible point, as it has been written in the *Announcement*, such a one, albeit small, will become great. But what is great will continue unto infinite and unalterable duration, as being that which no longer is subject to the conditions of a generated entity.

How then, he says, and in what manner, does God form man? In Paradise; for so it seems to him. Grant Paradise, he says, to be the womb; and that this is a true assumption the Scripture will teach, when it utters the words, "I am He who forms thee in thy mother's womb."[28] For this also he wishes to have been written so. Moses, he says, resorting to allegory, has declared Paradise to be the womb, if we ought to rely on his statement.[29] If, however, God forms man in his mother's womb — that is, in Paradise — as I have affirmed, let Paradise be the womb, and Edem the afterbirth, "a river flowing forth from Edem, for the purpose of irrigating Paradise," meaning by this the navel. This navel, he says, is separated into four principles; for on either side of the navel are situated two arteries, channels of spirit, and two veins, channels of blood. But when, he says, the umbilical vessels proceed forth from Edem, that is, the caul in which the foetus is enveloped grows into the foetus that is being formed in the vicinity of the epigastrium, now all in common denominate this a navel, these two veins through which the blood flows, and is conveyed from Edem, the after-

30.   Genesis 2:10-14.

31.   Cf. the Naassene teaching: 'Now this river that comes out of Eden, that is,
       from the brain' — for the child in the womb is considered to be essentially
       all head — '"is divided into four sources, and the name of the first is called
       Pheison; it is this which surrounds the whole land of Evilat; and there is gold
       there; and the gold of that land is good; and there is the fire-ruby and the
       green stone." This is the eye, which through its value and its colours confirms
       what is said. "And the name of the second river is Gihon; it is this which
       surrounds the whole land of Ethiopia." This is the ear, with its labyrinth of
       passages. "And the name of the third is Tigris; it is this which flows opposite
       Assyria." This is the (sense of) smell, because of the powerful flow of its
       current ... for this is the nature of the breath. "And the fourth river is
       Euphrates"; this is the mouth, through which prayer goes forth and
       nourishment comes in, which gladdens (Gk. *euphrainei)* and nourishes and
       characterizes the spiritual, perfect man' — given in Hippolytus, *Refutation of
       All Heresies*, V,9:15-18. The interpretation of the fourth river as the mouth is
       different from Simon's 'touch': however, on the mouth and its relation to the
       'spiritual, perfect man,' cf. VI,9:5 (end) above. The mouth is the 'place of the
       Lord,' forming the Logos or word. 'Characterizes' in connection with the
       'perfect man' born in initiation should be taken in the rather literal sense of
       'form an imprint' (Gk. *character)* cf. 'formed into a figure' or 'image' in Simon.

birth, to what are styled the gates of the liver; these veins, I say, nourish the foetus. But the arteries which we have spoken of as being channels of spirit, embrace the bladder on both sides, around the pelvis, and connect it with the great artery, called the aorta, in the vicinity of the dorsal ridge. And in this way the spirit, making its way through the ventricles to the heart, produces a movement of the foetus. For the infant that was formed in Paradise neither receives nourishment through the mouth, nor breathes through the nostrils: for as it lay in the midst of moisture, at its feet was death, if it attempted to breathe; for it would thus have been drawn away from moisture, and perished accordingly. But one may go further than this; for the entire foetus is bound tightly round by a covering styled the caul, and is nourished by a navel, and it receives through the aorta, in the vicinity of the dorsal ridge, as I have stated, the substance of the spirit.

15. The river, therefore, he says, which proceeds out of Edem is divided into four principles, four channels[30] — that is, into four senses, belonging to the creature that is being born, namely, seeing, smelling, taste, and touch; for the child formed in Paradise has these senses only.[31] This, he says, is the law which Moses appointed; and in reference to this very law, each of his books has been written, as the inscriptions evince. The first book is Genesis. The inscription of the book is, he says, sufficient for a knowledge of the universe. For this is equivalent in meaning with generation, that is, vision, into which one section of the river is divided. For the world was seen by the power of vision. Again, the inscription of the second book is Exodus. For what has been produced, passing through the Red Sea, must come into the wilderness (now they say he calls the Red Sea blood), and taste bitter water. For bitter, he says, is the water which is drunk after crossing the Red Sea; which water is a path to be trodden, that leads us to a knowledge in this life of our toilsome and bitter lot. Altered, however, by Moses — that is, by the Logos — that bitter water becomes sweet. And that this is so we may hear in common from all who express themselves according to the sentiments of the poets:

32.   Homer was 'the Bible of the Greeks,' and many Christian and pagan writers attempt to interpret it in mysterious senses in later times.

33.   The five books attributed to Moses (the Pentateuch) were held to be sacred and authoritative by the Samaritans as well as the Jews. Simon bases his metaphorical interpretation on the idea that these books form a complete whole, like the child in the paradise-womb — the view of the Samaritans, opposed to that of the Jews for whom they led on into the history of the chosen people. Nevertheless, we can see many signs of influence upon Simon from Jewish traditions close to those of the Essenes.

34.   On this analogy, see above VI,12:4.

35.   Isaiah 2:4. The persistent citation of Isaiah links the teaching again to the Essenes, for whom he was the prophet, and to Jesus, for whom his account of the 'Suffering Servant' of God was paramount.

> Dark at the root, like milk, the flower,
> Gods call it 'Moly,' and hard for mortal men
> To dig, but power divine is boundless. (*Odyssey*, X)

16. What is spoken by the Gentiles is sufficient for a knowledge of the universe to those who have ears capable of hearing.[32] For whosoever, he says, has tasted this fruit, is not the only one that is changed by Circe into a beast; but also, employing the power of such a fruit, he forms anew and moulds afresh, and re-entices into that primary peculiar character of theirs, those that already have been altered into beasts. But a faithful man, and beloved by that sorceress, is, he says, discovered through that milk-like and divine fruit. In like manner, the third book is Leviticus, which is smelling, or respiration. For the entire of that book is an account of sacrifices and offerings. Where, however, there is a sacrifice, a certain savour of the fragrance arises from the sacrifice through the incense-offerings; and in regard of this fragrance the sense of smelling is a test. Numbers, the fourth of the books, signifies taste, where the discourse is operative. For, from the fact of its speaking all things, it is denominated by numerical arrangement. But Deuteronomy, he says, is written in reference to the sense of touch possessed by the child that is being formed. For as touch, by seizing the things that are seen by the other senses, sums them up and ratifies them, testing what is rough, or warm, or clammy, or cold; so the fifth book of the law constitutes a summary of the four books preceding this.[33]

All things, therefore, he says, when unbegotten, are in us potentially, not actually, as the grammatical or geometrical art.[34] If, then, one receives proper instruction and teaching, and where consequently what is bitter will be altered into what is sweet — that is, the spears into pruning-hooks, and the swords into ploughshares[35] — there will not be chaff and wood begotten for fire, but mature fruit, fully formed, as I said, equal and similar to the unbegotten and unlimited power. If, however, a tree continues alone, not producing fruit fully formed, it is utterly destroyed. For somewhere near, he says, is

36.   Schmithals points out that in the older Mysteries, identity with the god was ascribed only to the few, the initiates, called in Gnostic terms the pneumatics (spiritual men, as opposed to the hylic or merely material men of earth). While the Great Annunciation clearly presupposes 'the Gnostic mythology' in this respect, Schmithals is right in seeing it as modified by the special influence of Judaism. It is the Jewish feeling for individuality which has universalized the teaching — paradoxical as it may sound — by bringing spiritual existence within the scope of everyone, at least as a possibility. 'The elimination of the cosmological dualism and the softening of the anthropological as well as the transformation of the pneumatic being into a possibility,' he says, 'is in my judgment characteristic of Jewish influence' (1971 p.42).

37.   Being 'begotten in the stream of waters' refers to baptismal rites of initiation which the sources on Simon and his teacher Dositheus mention repeatedly. Some of them connect them with the circles of John the Baptist — though as in the case of the Mandeans this link with a celebrity from the Christian tradition is likely to be artificial. Cf. however the Mandean polarity of fire and water.

38.   Cf. the account of Simon's pupil Menander, another Samaritan Gnostic: 'His disciples received resurrection through baptism into him, and they can no longer die, but remain without growing old and immortal' — Irenaeus, *Against Heresies* I,23:5. Resurrection here does not mean a future event, but more literally 'becoming a Standing One,' that is, attaining the state of the seventh power. Michael Goulder points out that the Samaritans did not believe in a 'resurrection of the dead,' an idea not found in the Pentateuch. 'The disciples of both Simon and Dositheus interpreted their master's teaching not in terms of resurrection but of immortality: Simon would stand, he would not be dissolved' — in J. Hick 1977, p.73. This passage in the Great annunciation shows that 'immortality' or 'being remade in similitude of an eternal nature' is connected rather with the beginning than the end. The unbegotten being 'wafted over the water' in baptismal regeneration reproduces the situation of the Spirit at the creation in VI,14:4f above. The experience of the cosmogony is at once a cosmic event, individual rebirth and salvation.

       Since the seventh power is latent in everyman, it is true in one sense that the Gnostic achieves a sort of self-redemption.

       Yet we miss the whole point if we take this in a modern way. For the self-redeeming is that of the hidden God, 'seeking itself, finding itself' in us. Self-redeeming is possible only for those who give up all their individual being, and allow the divine drama to be played out in their inner life. That could be done by the ancient initiates, the Gnostic pneumatics. The teaching of Simon opened it as a possibility to all. With Christianity, that possibility is actualized in an historical Event.

the axe which is laid at the roots of the tree. Every tree, he says, which does not produce good fruit, is hewn down and cast into fire.

The Standing One

17. According to Simon, therefore, there exists that which is blessed and incorruptible in a latent condition in every one — that is, potentially, not actually; and that this is He who stood, stands, and is to stand.[36] He has stood above in unbegotten power. He stands below, when in the stream of waters He was begotten in a likeness.[37] He is to stand above, beside the blessed unlimited power, if He be fashioned into an image. For, he says, there are three who have stood; and except there were three Aeons who have stood, the unbegotten one is not adorned. Now the unbegotten one is, according to them, wafted over the water, and is re-made, according to the similitude of an eternal nature,[38] a perfect celestial being, in no quality of intelligence formed inferior to the unbegotten power: that is what they say — I and you, one; you, before me; I, that which is after you. This, he says, is one power divided above and below, generating itself, making itself grow, seeking itself, finding itself, being mother of itself, father of itself, sister of itself, spouse of itself, daughter of itself, son of itself, mother, father, a unit, being a root of the entire circle of existence.

And that, he says, the originating principle of the generation of things begotten is from fire, he discerns after some such method as the following. Of all things, i.e. of whatsoever there is a generation, the beginning of the desire of the generation is from fire. Wherefore the desire after mutable generation is denominated "to be inflamed." For when the fire is one, it admits of two conversions. For, he says, blood in the man being both warm and yellow, is converted as a figured flame into seed; but in the woman this same blood is converted into milk. And the conversion of the male becomes generation, but the conversion of the female nourishment for the foetus. This, he says, is "the flaming sword, which turned to guard the way of

39.   Genesis 3:24. In a different idiom, we have here the same elements as the
        Essene prophecy concerning the Messiah who will re-enter Paradise and give
        humanity the fruit of the Tree of Life (p.138, note 24 above): the Gnostic
        version tells how this may be done inwardly, finding the creative forces at
        work in our birth/rebirth — and says nothing about an historical event to
        come. Moreover, the 'flaming sword' which the Essene Messiah is to
        'remove,' remains: only the Gnostic, the knower, can pass it. The 'fruit of the
        Tree of Life' is evidently the knowledge of the cosmic forces which form us
        as living beings.

40.   The concept of the 'seventh power' as including and indwelling the six
        cosmic powers cannot be derived from the Jewish 'teaching of creation'
        (ma'aseh bereshit), for that speaks only of God manifesting himself creatively
        in a series of aspects. It is strongly reminiscent, however, of the Zoroastrian
        doctrine that Ohrmazd is revealed in the Bounteous Immortals, the Creator
        Angels, yet is himself a seventh including but transcending them all.
        Moreover, three of the Zoroastrian powers are male and three female, while
        Ohrmazd himself is the fusion or wholeness. Simon presents a similar
        teaching as the conclusion of his system below. Once again, therefore, we see
        a direct influence of Zoroastrian ideas.

41.   A typical Gnostic expression. In context, it recalls the beautiful and compli-
        cated myth of the birth of Zarathustra (taken as the prototype of spiritual
        birth for the initiate). A 'fiery spark from above' represents the spiritual
        'seed,' or the 'Glory' which pre-exists his earthly appearance. In order for him
        to be born, substances have to be gathered together by means of a 'tall tree'
        (or haoma plant — cf. Tree of Life here) and through the milk of cows who
        have eaten grass watered by the magic rain which contains the living
        substance of the prophet in his cosmic reality. Cf. the Apocalypse of Adam
        which utilizes the legends; and note 43 below.

42.   Apsethus is described in Hippolytus, Refutation, immediately prior to his
        account of Simon.

43.   Gayomart, the Zoroastrian 'First Man' is the child of Ohrmazd and Spandar-
        mat (Bounteous Immortal of the Earth, a female) — and represents 'Man' in
        his archetypal existence. The apocalypse of Adam reproduces this myth too.
        In initiation, every Zoroastrian is taught that he is a creature of Ohrmazd, the
        heavenly Light, and also that 'My mother is Spandarmat': see H. Corbin 1977
        (p.15) for its spiritual significance.

44.   The third quotation from the actual text of the Great Annunciation. It is
        uncertain, in reality, how far the quotation extends, or whether Hippolytus
        resumes his summarizing procedure.

45.   Gk. 'silence.' Often the name in Gnosticism for a primordial being or Aeon:
        that is, nothing is yet outwardly manifest. Valentinus and his pupils also
        termed the feminine Aeon the Thought (Ennoia), the name found in the more
        legendary versions of Simon's teaching.

the tree of life."[39] For the blood is converted into seed and milk, and this power becomes mother and father — father of those things that are in process of generation, and the augmentation of those things that are being nourished; and this power is without further want, and self-sufficient. And, he says, the tree of life is guarded, as we have stated, by the brandished flaming sword. And it is the seventh power, that which is produced from itself, and which contains all powers, and which reposes in the six powers.[40] For if the flaming sword be not brandished, that good tree will be destroyed, and perish. If, however, these be converted into seed and milk, the principle that resides in these potentially, and is in possession of a proper position, in which is evolved a principle of souls, such a principle, beginning, as it were, from a very small spark,[41] will be altogether magnified, and will increase and become a power indefinite and unalterable, equal and similar to an unalterable age, which no longer passes into the unlimited age.

18. Therefore, according to this reasoning, Simon became confessedly a god to his silly followers, as that Libyan, namely, Apsethus[42] — begotten, no doubt, and subject to passion, when he may exist potentially, but devoid of propensions. And this too, though born from one having propensions, and uncreated though born from one that is begotten, when He may be fashioned into a figure, and, becoming perfect, may come forth from two of the primary powers, that is, Heaven and Earth.[43] For Simon expressly speaks of this in the "Revelation" after this manner:[44] "To you, then, I address the things which I speak, and to you I write what I write. The writing is this: there are two offshoots from all the Aeons, having neither beginning nor end, from one root. And this is a power, namely, Sigé,[45] who is invisible and incomprehensible. And one of these offshoots appears from above, which constitutes a great power, the creative Mind of the universe, which manages all things, and is a male. The other offshoot, however, is from below, and constitutes a great Intelligence, and is a female which produces all things. From whence, ranged in pairs opposite each other, they undergo conjugal union, and manifest an intermediate

46.   That is, God in his eternal reality, who undergoes division in cosmic evolution, but finds himself again when he 'becomes an image' in an awakened individual. 'Imagination' is thus the manifestation in us of the original creative power of God — not just its reflection through the 'products' of God's creative work, but an immediate spark of divinity in us.

47.   Self-consciousness — in God, and likewise in the Gnostic who re-enacts the divine drama or is its setting — is the catastrophic division which has to be overcome in the reintegration of the 'seventh power.' Gnosticism holds to the old, pre-conscious spirituality of the Mysteries. The moment of self-awareness is not held as self-discovery, but is a cosmic crisis leading to a reversion, or liberation from one's particular existence on earth.

48.   Simon describes at once a process going on in the mind of the Gnostic and the inner dynamics of the Godhead before it manifested itself outwardly in creation and so became the object of Jewish religious interest. the creation results from a process of division: yet the two are really 'in no wise different,' and the Gnostic transcends the creation by reintegrating the opposites (symbolized as above-below, male-female etc). in himself.

    In the process, the Christ — the Standing One — is actualized in a specific person. Yet there is no question of a real 'incarnation,' but of a 'knower' being united with the Standing One through release from his earthly, divided state. Only when this cosmic Christ-Mystery was joined to history in a positive vision did the Christian breakthrough become possible.

interval, namely, an incomprehensible air, which has neither beginning nor end. But in this is a father who sustains all things, and nourishes things that have beginning and end. This is He who stood, stands, and will stand, being an hermaphrodite power according to the pre-existent indefinite power, which has neither beginning nor end.[46] Now this power exists in isolation. For Intelligence, that subsists in unity, proceeded forth from this power, and became two. And that Father was one, for having in Himself this power He was isolated, and, however, He was not primal though pre-existent; but being rendered manifest to Himself from Himself, He passed into a state of duality.[47] But neither was He denominated Father before this power would style Him Father. As, therefore, He Himself, bringing forward Himself by means of Himself, manifested unto Himself His own peculiar intelligence, so also the intelligence, when it was manifested, did not exercise the function of creation.[48] But beholding him, she concealed the Father within herself, that is, the power; and it is an hermaphrodite power, and an intelligence. And hence it is that they are ranged in pairs, one opposite the other; for power is in no wise different from intelligence, inasmuch as they are one. For from those things that are above is discovered power; and from those below, intelligence. So it is, therefore, that likewise what is manifested from these, being unity, is discovered to be duality, an hermaphrodite having the female in itself. This, therefore, is Mind subsisting in Intelligence; and these are separable one from the other, though both taken together are one, and are discovered in a state of duality."

5. The *Poimandres* of Hermes the Egyptian

The transition to Christianity from the ancient world brought about, over the centuries, a gradual change in human consciousness. The result was above all a deepening of individual responsibility, of man's personal sense of relationship to the divine. For a long time there seemed to be no place within that development for Simon and his Faustian wisdom, his belief in the transfiguring power of imagination. Faust stood on the sidelines, a rejected and denounced figure.

But in due course he came once more to fascinate men's minds and stir their aspirations, and the question arose as to whether it was possible to take Faust into the Christian evolution. Man had developed his own ego: was it now strong enough not to be swept away and destroyed, or morally thrown off balance by the kind of cosmic longings which had motivated Simon and all later Fausts? These were questions which could not yet arise in first-century Samaria. Yet they arise inevitably for us in the modern world, and they exercised the imaginations of some of our greatest modern writers and poets — notably Goethe — as well as spiritual thinkers. In the light of the new picture of Christian origins, there arises at the same time the fascinating question of Faust's original setting. It appears that by taking Faust back into Christianity, we may actually be rediscovering the full potential of Christianity itself. Despite Goulder's tone of iconoclasm, his conclusion that 'the incarnational speculations introduced into the church by Simon Magus and his fellow Samaritans seem to me entirely dispensable,' on the other hand, continues the perspective of the orthodox view.

The rediscovery of Faust in modern times since the Renaissance was intertwined with the rehabilitation of another type, the Hermetic magus. The Hermetic writings were brought to the West from Byzantium, translated into Latin in great excitement by Marsilio Ficino, and were one of the major factors in transforming medieval thought into the approach to nature which we now call 'scientific.' The figure of the magus, familiar in the philosophy and mysticism of the sixteenth century, combines in one the Hermetic adept, the kabbalist and the Christian. Later, the elements of this synthesis disintegrated. The ideal of a 'Pansophia' or universal wisdom that would interpret the world at once scientifically and religiously lasted, however, until Newton. And in Newton's special form — for he was also an alchemist and an interpreter of the Apocalypse (Book of Revelation) — it lasted even until Darwin. What is interesting now is to see how science itself, in its origins, presupposes the Hermetic world-view as its spiritual foundation. It can be argued that the spiritual implications of modern science, to which official doctrine has never really faced up, remain those of its Hermetic origins — or at the very least, that science belongs like everything itself to its time, and can only be free from illusion if it understands its own history. Otherwise there is the danger of mistaking the current form of science for the only possible way of thinking! Rudolf Steiner stressed the need for science to be understood historically, not in order to bind it to an outdated form — but precisely in order to free us, to make us see that the scientific spirit must not be narrowly identified with the material domain in which it was successfully applied.

A further twist in the argument came at the beginning of our own century, when the comparative religionist Richard Reitzenstein published a study of the *Poimandres*, or first tractate in the 'Hermetic corpus': so it came to be called. He argued that this document presents a Gnostic teaching, like those of the Christian Gnostics known from the Fathers but here attached to the pagan Mystery-cult of the Egyptian god Thoth (identified by the Greeks with their Hermes). It had long been realized that the Hermetic writings were not as ancient as had first been thought. Reitzenstein provided them for the first time with a setting in the history of religions: and that setting turned out to be intimately related to early Christianity, and to the Gnostic movement which has increasingly come to seem an integral part of Christian beginnings.

The *Poimandres* takes its name from the divine being who gives to Hermes a revelation concerning the creation of the world, human beings and the spiritual destiny of the soul. It is around this knowledge that the Hermetic Mystery is centred, so that we have here in effect a statement of the origins of the cult, making the document crucial to our understanding of Hermetism as it is presented in the Greek texts. But there we come to the major problem: are these texts Greek or Egyptian? Is this a tradition deriving from authentic ancient Egyptian religion, or a deliberately exotic Greek concoction disguising Plato and the thinkers of the Stoic school and claiming for their ideas the bogus authority of the 'thrice-greatest Hermes'? Greek ideas there certainly are in abundance. W. Scott produced an edition of all the 'philosophical' Hermetica which has now once more become widely available, stressing in his commentary the absence of any real Egyptian background. But Scott also re-arranges the traditional texts in a most extraordinary, jigsaw puzzle-like way to suit his theories, and it might also be said that by choosing the 'philosophical' texts alone he makes his theory self-fulfilling. Other studies have examined the relation of the 'corpus' to the magical, alchemical and cosmogonical texts that go under Hermes' name, and found ample evidence of Egyptian links. The philosophical texts are, obviously, the very ones which go out of their way to adopt the language of Greek conceptual ideas and so where the Egyptian traditions are most effectively disguised.

The question is in practice often ambiguous. In another work from the *Corpus Hermeticum* Hermes comments on the issue himself. He says that his future readers, in an age 'when the Greeks think fit to translate these writings from our tongue into theirs':

will think that they are very simply and clearly written,
when in fact, on the contrary, they are unclear and hide
the meanings of the words ... Translation will bring about
a complete distortion and obfuscation of the text.
Expressed in the original language, the discourse conveys
its meaning clearly, for the very quality of the sounds and
the intonation of the Egyptian words contains in itself the
force of the things said.

This passage seems to come from a milieu in which the need to have the texts in Greek is recognized, and even foreseen by Hermes himself, but where the dangers of superficiality and the loss of the deeper dimension of the spiritual content was also evident. It tends to confirm the conclusion reached in his recent investigation of the Hermetica by Garth Fowden, namely that in them, 'even allowing for the presence of some characteristically Greek elements ... the overall atmosphere is Egyptian.'* They come from a milieu, he says

---

* Garth Fowden, *The Egyptian Hermes*, Cambridge 1986, p.32.

elsewhere in his book, 'that had been long and, so it seemed, irreversibly Hellenized in its language and thought-patterns; but that had not made it a Greek milieu.' The Hermetic writings are best understood as a manifestation of the 'durability of Egypt' and its spiritual traditions, though in a world where it had become necessary to speak an alien tongue and to think in alien terms.

Such were the very terms in which we characterized the Gnostic attitude, where the power of the ancient myths was still asserted, and led the initiates in the Mysteries still to a direct experience of the divine, but where the reality behind the myths could no longer be taken for granted, leading to a contradiction between outer and inner reality. Historical change brings about such crises: in the Hermetic case, the collapse of imperial Egypt and the conquest of the whole Mediterranean area by the Greeks and their colonization programme, which included the establishment of the huge Greek city of Alexandria with its cosmopolitan population. The timeless and universal validity of Egyptian ideas that was taken for granted by the myths and the cults of the gods and Pharaohs was challenged. Their values and spiritual truth had to be preserved — and, we can see from the Hermetic writings, were preserved — but there is henceforth a sense of living in two conflicting worlds.

The dual vision, we suggested earlier, crystallized in its most radical (i.e. Gnostic) form where there was contact with Judaism. It was the Jews who had themselves experienced the crises of historical change over and over again, and had adopted a thoroughly historical world-view as a result, where God no longer revealed himself in myths of eternal truth but in an ongoing special relation with his chosen people — the ones, in short, who were able to make the transition in consciousness to the historical vision, which is so much more demanding for the individual than the shared assurance of the myths. The Jews had accepted history; but where traditional ancient cultures felt the shock of collision, the Gnostic response was one way of conserving the mythological consciousness — alongside the new alien order that would not go away. It is not surprising that the Hermetic initiates in conquered Egypt should have been drawn to just such a Gnostic solution.

Thus it is not a contradiction with their native Egyptian background to see the Hermetica as belonging to the wider pattern of the 'spreading of ideas' which was giving new forms to the

Mysteries in Samaria, among the Essenes, and in Christianity. There is considerable evidence that the Egyptian priests and initiates saw the necessity of coping with the changing circumstances and the changes in consciousness that went with them at the time of Christian origins. That is when the textual evidence places our Greek texts; the *Poimandres* is generally dated in the first century AD. It embodies the Gnostic, rather than the Essene-type of new resolution, with the emphasis on the cosmic and mythological truth they knew from older cultic forms. But it is a response to the very issues which were tackled in all the developments we have studied, and the Hermetists were certainly aware of the ideas being formulated in Palestine and other parts of the Near East.

They must have known about the Essenes, if not about John the Baptist, because in the tractate from the Hermetic corpus which is called *The Bowl* (in Greek *Krater)* we hear about a kind of baptism, and in connection with it the call to the 'hearts of men' to be 'baptized in mind' — this is equivalent to the 'transformation of mind' *(metanoia,* often rendered 'repentance') mentioned in the Gospels and with parallels in the Dead Sea Scrolls. As among the Essenes, this is the prerequisite for attaining 'knowledge,' which here too means 'knowledge of God' and of 'the purpose for which you have been made,' just as in the *Hodayot.* The Hermetist says that God sent down with the baptismal *krater* a 'herald' *(keryx),* and in the Gospels' account of John the technical term *kerussein* is used for his proclamation. The baptismal rite and its special language point directly to the Jewish Mystery-circles and their initiatory procedures. Moreover, in the cosmological teachings of the Hermetica, Egyptian pictures are mingled with ideas which derive unmistakably from the Book of Genesis: most obvious is the 'holy word' ascribed to God in the *Poimandres,* 'Increase and multiply, all creatures and creations' which undoubtedly echoes Genesis 1:28; or the phrase taken from Genesis 1:12 — 'all things were multiplied after their kind' — which occurs a few lines later.

The Hermetists were in touch, then, with the esoteric interpretations of Genesis which constitute the *ma'aseh bereshit,* the lore of creation which is one branch of Jewish mystical teaching. But they know it in a form which is already Gnostic: the material world is described in the *Poimandres* from a dualistic viewpoint, as a trap and a prison for the soul which has 'forgotten' its divine nature, and become 'stupefied' or 'drunk' in oblivion. The one who would be

'baptized in mind' must come to hate the body. For the fall into
matter has divided man against himself, imprisoning the light in the
darkness, the free spirit within 'the framework' of Necessity or
Destiny:

> For this reason man, unlike all other creatures on earth, is
> dual in nature, mortal because of the body and immortal
> because of the essential Man. For being immortal and
> having authority over all things, he suffers the condition
> of mortals since he is subject to Destiny. Though he is
> superior to the framework, he has become a slave in it ...

This famous Hermetic summation contains all the elements familiar
from the Essene dualism of 'the Two Ways' — but here resolved in
the Gnostic way, with man's cosmic being and authority emphas-
ized rather than translated into history, into hope for the future. The
aim of the Hermetic Gnostic is to transcend nature and so 'ascend
to God.'

The new ideas thus reached the Egyptian adepts through Jewish,
Essene or similar esoteric channels. The elements of the Iranian
symbolism which still shine out in the Hermetic writings are best
understood as arriving in that way. Once we grasp the obscure
connections between the Mysteries at that time, the background of
the *Poimandres* starts to fall into place. Especially revealing is the
analogy between the opening vision and a similar one attributed to
a celebrated adept known to us under the sobriquet 'King
Nechepso.' He was not literally a king but a 'royal soul.' He may be
the one indicated in the *Apocalypse of Adam* as a 'son of the two
luminaries,' i.e. Sun and Moon: like the Pharaohs of an earlier time,
he was reborn in spirit as Horus, the royal child of lunar Isis and
the other-worldly sun-god Osiris. Historically, he appears around
the time of the Maccabees (second century BC) in Alexandria in the
guise of an authority on astrology, synthesizing traditional Egyptian
ideas with the advances made in Persia and Chaldea. On the
Egyptian side, we hear from one source of 'Nechepso, to whom the
all-powerful divinity of Hermes has revealed the secrets of this
science,' so that we may associate him with the Hermetic Mysteries,
in which connection he is often mentioned together with the priest
Petosiris.

A fragment tells us of his vision when, following the ways of the
early kings, he 'left earthly things behind in order to traverse the
heavens,' there 'to converse with immortal souls' and to receive 'the

divine holy thoughts.' In his trance, he saw a vast figure, clothed in darkness as in a gigantic cloak. Then 'a heavenly voice rang out,' revealing to him the secrets he so desired to know. The elements of the vision are so close to those of the opening vision in the *Poimandres*, that Martin Hengel is probably right to see a deliberate allusion. The initiation described by the writer of the *Poimandres*, in other words, is that founded by Nechepso when he gave the Hermetic Mysteries a renewed form that was in touch with developments elsewhere in the Near East. If the curious absence of a specific name in the text of *Poimandres* is indeed, as some have thought, a deliberately enigmatic gesture, the blank to be filled in should certainly read: Nechepso.

It is no objection to this view that the manuscripts of the *Corpus Hermeticum* have under the title of the first tractate the attribution 'of thrice-greatest Hermes.' The intention is there to indicate the source of the revelation in the Egyptian Mysteries, of whose teachings Hermes-Thoth is the spokesman and guardian. Any hierophant in the handing down of the Mysteries speaks in the name of the Mystery-god, and Nechepso would be no exception. His 'reform' of the Mysteries, introducing ideas of Greek and Babylonian mathematical astrology and the language of philosophy, would certainly have been presented as the fuller revelation of the primordial Mystery, not as a new direction. The *Poimandres* actually tells the story of the founding of the Mysteries. The knowledge of its revelation was offered to the masses, but they scorned and mocked it; only the few who were worthy received it. It is, then, the retelling of the foundation-myth of Hermetism in the version stemming from Nechepso's reform. A myth when retold ousts all previous versions of the myth, and history disappears. That is why in the traditions about Nechepso he is often spoken of as though he belonged to primordial times. What he offers is not his personal experience, but his affirmation of the archaic myth in living terms for his own time. Moreover, in the present text of *Poimandres* we must reckon with still further stages of retelling. In the period since Nechepso (*c.* 150 BC) to the first century AD the direction taken by the Hermetic Mysteries has gradually become a Gnostic one, arising as a resolution of tensions already there in Nechepso but coming to a head around the time of Christ.

For parallels to Nechepso's vision are not only to be found in pagan writings. Scholars have repeatedly noted similarities to the

Jewish apocalyptic writings, *Enoch*, Daniel, and so on. The 'divine voice' *(bat kol)* in particular is well-known from the esoteric tradition and even in the Rabbis. These resemblances again show that Nechepso and the Hermetic Mystery-circles were also in touch with esoteric developments in Palestine. Later, as we know, the spiritual encounter between Judaism and the Mysteries led to the Gnostic double vision. And that we can certainly detect in *Poimandres* and other parts of the Hermetic corpus.

When the Hermetic books came into Christian hands, some of the Fathers such as Lactantius (third to fourth century AD) were amazed to discover in them such startling statements of their own doctrines concerning God, the Logos, the creation, and the prophecy that the ancient order would end, but that though the ancient gods were no longer worshipped there would be a new revelation, that they hailed Hermes as a 'prophet of Christ.' We now know that the Hermetic Mysteries were in fact involved in the encounter which brought the Christian consciousness into being. The *Gospel of Thomas* finds its true place here in the picture. For it shows that long before the Hermetic literature became publicly know and caused, not for the last time, such a furore, there had been on the esoteric level a continuity between the ancient and the Christian Mysteries. The Gnostic affinities of *Thomas*, preserved as it was in the Gnostic library at Nag Hammadi, are a part of its Hermetic background. For its view of salvation as an inner awakening, a 'baptism in mind,' is precisely the fulfilment of the Hermetic hope. Here is Hermes' exhortation to self-deluded mortals:

> You men, where are you rushing in your drunkenness,
> you who have drained the undiluted doctrine of
> ignorance ...? Be sober and stop, look up with the eyes of
> your heart.

And here is the language of the Saviour in the *Gospel of Thomas:*

> Jesus said: I stood in the midst of the world, and I
> appeared to them in flesh. I found them all drunk, I found
> none of them thirsting; and my soul was afflicted for the
> sons of men, for they are blind in their heart and they do
> not see.

Gilles Quispel — a noted authority on the *Gospel* — has shown that the Hermetic Mysteries were active in Edessa, the town in Syria which was an important cultural centre for pagans and Christians alike, and which was connected in all the early legends with

Thomas the Apostle and his original teaching. It was almost certainly there that the *Gospel of Thomas* was written down, putting into fixed form the apostle's version of the teaching of Jesus. It was addressed in the first instance to those who could understand — who could grasp the 'mystery of interpretation' — which meant to begin with those whose background lay in the Mysteries of Egyptian Hermes. To them it could proclaim their hopes and Hermes' prophecies fulfilled.

Source: Corpus Hermeticum *I. Translated from the Greek by R.M. Grant from the only reliable text of the Hermetica: that of A.D. Nock and A.J. Festugière, published in four volumes (Paris 1945-1954).*

1.   Parallels with the vision of Nechepso and with Jewish apocalyptic visions in A.J. Festugière 1986, Vol.I, pp.314f. Most probably the initiated reader is expected to recognize the allusion to Nechepso — cf. M. Hengel 1974, pp.214f.

2.   As W. Scott points out (1985, p.12), the name of the visionary seems to be deliberately withheld, here and, still more unnaturally, in paragraphs 20 and 21. For a parallel 'calling,' cf. *Testament of Levi* above p.127 and the *Book of the Blessed* p.253 below.

3.   The name is unknown except here and in passages dependent on CH I. It might be derived from the Greek word *poimen* ('shepherd') together with that for 'man': but one would assume a resulting form 'Poimenandres,' which is what we find in the alchemist Zosimus, where however it is clearly secondary and made to obey Greek rules after the event, so to speak. A being called Poimael appears in the Nag Hammadi *Sacred Book of the Invisible Spirit*, described as an 'imperishable man' whose followers will 'by no means taste death.' The best interpretation of the name is therefore that of F.L. Griffith (in Scott 1985, p.16) that it comes from Egyptian, meaning 'knowledge of Re' (that is, of the Sun-god). In the *Sacred Book* the divinity's name is replaced by the termination *-el* (= God) in a manner common in forming divine names in esoteric Jewish and related literature (Codex III 66:1). (The *Sacred Book* has the alternative title *Gospel of the Egyptians*).

4.   The dualism of Light ('limitless ... serene and happy') and 'terrifying and abhorrent' Darkness comes once again ultimately from Zoroastrian thought — here it is interpreted in a Gnostic way, providing the backdrop to an account of the creation of the earthly world which is mainly in accordance with Egyptian traditions blended with the Book of Genesis. It serves, in other words to place the traditional 'creation' in an altered context. We are made aware that before and beyond the created world are the powers of Light and Darkness, where all things have their spiritual reality: creation is thus in one sense a fall into a lower mode of being.

5.   Genesis 1:2: the verb used is the same which refers to the creative Spirit in the Greek Bible. Genesis has no being called a Logos, however, but is being assimilated to another version of the myth. At his main centre of worship Hermoupolis Magna (al-Ashmunayn), the priests of Thoth developed a 'distinctive cosmogony,' explains Fowden, 'Hermoupolis being widely regarded as the oldest place on earth. So it was that Thoth acquired a leading role in the drama of creation itself, as a demiurge who called things into being

❊ The Poimandres ❊

The Vision and its Interpretation
One day, when I had begun to reflect upon the things that truly exist and my thoughts had soared aloft, while my bodily senses were bridled like those borne down by sleep through surfeit of food or fatigue of the body, it seemed to me that a being of vast, immeasurable size drew near[1] and called me by name[2] and said, "What do you wish to hear and see and by thinking come to learn and know?"

I replied, "Who are you?" And he said, "I am Poimandres,[3] the Mind of the Absolute Sovereignty. I know what you want, and I am with you everywhere."

I said, "I desire to learn the things that really exist and to understand their nature and to know God. How I desire to hear!" And he replied to me, "Keep in your mind the things you desire to learn, and I will teach you."

At these words he changed his form, and instantly everything opened up to me, and I saw a limitless vision, everything having become a light, serene and happy, and I was enraptured by the sight. After a little darkness, produced bit by bit, came bearing down, and it was terrifying and abhorrent, coiling itself in spirals like a serpent, as it seemed.[4] Then this darkness was changed into a kind of moist nature, indescribably shaken, and exuding smoke as from a fire, and emitting a kind of voice, an unutterable groaning. Then from it came an inarticulate cry, which it sent forth, like a voice of fire, and from the light ... A holy Logos came upon Nature, and an unmixed fire leaped forth from the moist nature upwards towards the height. It was light and swift and active, and the air, being light, followed the fiery spirit, rising up from earth and water to the fire, so that it seemed to be suspended from the fire. The earth and the water remained where they were, mingled together so that the earth could not be seen apart from the water. But it was moved in obedience to the spiritual Logos which was "borne over it."[5]

merely by the sound of his voice' (1986 p.23). The creative Word or Logos is therefore to be seen as a god, and a 'Son of God,' namely Hermes-Thoth himself.

Just as 'knowledge of Re' is actually a divine being, the supreme Mind, so the expressive agent or Word which gives it outer form is a divine being. Thoth was regarded as 'Lord of the emanations of Re,' that is, as the one who gave the Sun's spiritual potencies outward or lunar embodiment in writing or words. Thoth plays the part analogous therefore to the lunar God of Judaism as creator-demiurge.

6.   The vision rises to a higher intensity. The Light no longer appears undifferentiated, but is itself a spiritually creative, organizing power. Scott (1985 pp.27f) cites a parallel from Christian Gnostics who taught that Light was a spiritual entity, 'not something formless and unproductive, nor in need of anyone to put it to work. But having in itself boundless forms of living and differentiated beings, it shines down from above into the chaos below, at the same time giving light and producing form ...' — in Hippolytus, *Refutation of Heresies* VIII,9.

7.   Another version of the primal undifferentiated which gives way in the creation to a divided state, male-versus-female, above-versus-below, etc. Hermetic *gnosis* is the reintegration of the opposites, and so a knowledge of the original creative power, cf. Simon the Magus' 'seventh power.' The Nag Hammadi library contains a part of the Hermetic 'Initiatory Discourse' *(Logos Teleios)*, previously known in a somewhat bowdlerized version in Latin called the *Asclepius.* It teaches that the Hermetic Mystery has its 'representation' in 'the intercourse that takes place between the male and the female. For when the semen reaches the climax, it leaps forth. In that moment the female receives the strength of the male; the male for his part receives the strength of the female, while the semen does this. Therefore the mystery of intercourse is performed in secret ... And moreover these are holy mysteries, of both words and deeds, because not only are they not heard, but also they are not seen' — Codex VI 65:17-38. This is the 'sacred marriage' or *hieros gamos* of the Mysteries, and whether or not it is enacted literally its point lies in the spiritual 'unification' attained 'in secret.' It took special forms in Egypt, for instance, in the image of the sexual act in solitude of the creator: again, this is a condition which is reproduced in the initiate: see *Apocalypse of Adam* p.229 below.

Then Poimandres said to me, "Do you understand what this vision means?"

"I should like to know," I replied.

"That light," he said, "is I, Mind, your God, who existed before the moist nature which appeared out of the darkness. And the luminous Logos which came out of Mind is the Son of God."

"How so?" I asked.

"Understand it this way," he replied. "That which in you sees and hears is the Logos of the Lord, and your Mind is God the Father. The two are not separated from each other; life consists in their union."

"I thank you," I said.

"But think about the light," he said, "and understand this."

The Generation of the World

When he had said this he gazed at me a long time, so that I trembled at his appearance. Then, when he had raised his head, I beheld in my Mind the light consisting of innumerable powers which had now become a boundless ordered cosmos,[6] though the fire was surrounded by a mighty force, and being firmly held was kept stable. This is what I was thinking of as I looked at it, encouraged by what Poimandres told me. While I was thus struck with amazement, he spoke to me again: "You see by Mind the archetypal form, the primal principle, prior to the limitless beginning." That is what Poimandres said to me.

I said, "What about the elements of nature — whence did they arise?"

And again he replied to this, "From the Will of God, which having received the Logos, and beholding the beautiful cosmos, imitated it, since it was fashioned as an ordered world by its own proper elements and products, that is, souls.

"But Mind, which is God, being both male and female,[7] and existing as life and light, begot by a word another Mind, the Demiurge; and he, being God of fire and of spirit, created

8.   Gk. *heimarmene*. The term was used in Greek philosophy of later times to
        describe the system of natural law-governed nature, the domain of 'necessity.'
        Greek thought regarded it as a part of the 'harmony' of the cosmos, but the
        Poimandres later puns on harmony/heimarmene, regarding both as aspects of
        man's imprisonment here below

9.   The 'leaping up' of the spiritual Logos corresponds cosmically to the
        separation of the Sun, which now takes its place at the centre of a cosmic
        system; organizing Mind makes the inanimate material bodies revolve around
        it according to natural law *(heimarmene)*.

10.   The union of Logos and Mind corresponds to the Genesis account's shift to
        the plural ('Let us make man' — Genesis 1:26) and the subsequent combining
        of the divine names Elohim ('Gods') and Yahweh ('Lord') into one compound
        form, Yahweh Elohim (Genesis 2:4): cf. Steiner 1959, pp.45f, 83ff. The seven
        planetary 'Governors' are the Elohim in their separate aspects, in accordance
        with the widespread interpretation of Genesis in the esoteric tradition or
        ma'aseh bereshit. Man is at once the fusion of all the separate creative aspects
        or 'days' of divine activity, and the revelation of the primal unity from which
        they came forth.

        Man possesses himself, therefore, the creative power *(exousia,* here
        translated 'he received all power.') Cf. Simon's 'seventh power,' but also the
        giving of all *exousia* to Jesus in the Gospel of Matthew 28:18 and the Prologue
        to the Gospel of John where his followers are granted *'exousia* for their
        existence as sons of God' (John 1:12). The parallels with the Gospel of John
        have especially struck many scholars: God as Father, Life and Light; the Light
        shining; in the darkness; the interpretation of Genesis 1 ('In the beginning')
        as a pattern for the spiritual creation of the Logos in human beings; and, in
        the background, a baptismal mystery, etc. The similarity is explained by the
        contact of the Hermetic Mysteries with the esoteric baptizing sects of
        Palestine and the Gnostic tendencies arising there; the Gospel of John draws
        on an identical background as the starting-point for its understanding of
        Christ.

11.   The *Poimandres* now begins to explain why it is that Man, the synthesis of the
        creative powers and himself possessed of divine *exousia,* has become subject
        to perishable flesh, the laws of nature or the *heimarmene,* and to restless
        desire: its version of the Fall.

certain governors, seven in number to surround the sensible world with their circles. Their governing is called Destiny.[8] At once the Logos of God leaped out of the downward-moving elements into the pure region of Nature, just created, and united itself with the Demiurge Mind, for it was of the same nature as it, and thus the lower elements of nature were left to themselves, deprived of reason, and so became nothing more than mere matter. But the Demiurge Mind, joined with the Logos, surrounding the circles and compelling them to turn as they rush along, thus set his creatures revolving, and let them turn about from an invisible point of departure to an unfixed goal; for their revolution begins where it ends.[9] And the rotation of these, as Mind willed it, produces things that fly and the water, things that swim. Earth and water are now separated from each other, in accordance with the Will of Mind, and the earth brought forth from itself the animals that were in it, quadrupeds and reptiles, wild beasts and tame.

"But Mind, the Father of all, being life and light, gave birth to a Man like himself; with him he was pleased, as his own offspring, for the Man was very beautiful, bearing the image of his Father. For truly God was pleased with his own form, and he delivered all his creatures to him. Having observed the creation made by the Demiurge in the fire, Man himself desired to create, and permission was granted by the Father. So entering the creative sphere, where he received all power, he observed the things created by his brother; and the Governors were pleased with him, and each gave him a share in his own region.[10]

"Then having learned their substance and having received a share in their nature, he desired to break out of the bounds of their orbits, and to know the power of him who reigns over the fire. So Man, who possessed all authority over the world of mortal things and of irrational animals, bent down through the composite framework of the spheres, having torn off the covering, and showed to downward-tending Nature the beautiful form of God.[11] When Nature beheld the never-satiating beauty of the one who possesses in himself all the energy of the

12.   The 'Man' who figures in *Poimandres* is obviously identified in the reworking
       of Genesis with the biblical Adam; unlike the usual Adam or Man who sins
       and dies, however, this one remains as an essentially unaltered inner Man
       within all of us. These ideas came to the Hermetists not direct from the Bible,
       but in the Mystery-forms such as we see among the Mandeans, who have a
       whole teaching about 'the secret Adam,' whom we can rediscover and so
       regain Paradise through initiation. See E.S. Drower, Oxford 1960. The *Gospel
       of Philip* speaks of regaining the state 'when Eve was in Adam' and 'there
       was no death'; and Drower cites the views of some Jewish Christians who
       'say that Christ is Adam, the first-created (being) ... others say that he was
       created before all things, superior to the angels, ruling over all and called
       Christ' (p.96). Compare the Hermetic Man who is granted divine-angelic
       exousia, the Simonian Christ as a cosmic being, etc. For regaining Paradise in
       the historical-Essene version, see above Chapter 3.

13.   The word may mean that they were literally 'floating above the earth.'
       Although he has received a form from Nature, man was still embodied, it
       seems, only in fire and air, not yet in solid substance. Similarly, some
       Christian Gnostics such as Ptolemaeus, a follower of Valentinus, taught that
       when the Demiurge 'fashioned the universe, he made the earthly man, not
       out of this dry land but out of the invisible substance, taking him from the
       moving and flowing part of matter; and into him was breathed the soul-
       nature ... Finally he was clothed with a "coat of skin"; this is his flesh which
       is subject to sense-perception' (cf. Genesis 3:21) — in Irenaeus, *Against
       Heresies* 1,5,5. The seven Governors are connected with the planets, so that we
       have here the emergence of seven races of men each typical of one planetary
       influence.

Governors, and likewise the form of God, she smiled with love, for she had seen the image of Man's wonderfully beautiful form reflected in the water, and his shadow on the earth. And he, having seen in her this form like himself, reflected in the water, loved it and desired to live in it. With the will came the action, and thus he came to occupy a form devoid of reason. Nature, having received the form she loved, folded him to herself, and so they were united; for they passionately loved each other.

"For this reason man, unlike all other creatures on earth, is dual in nature, mortal because of the body and immortal because of the essential Man.[12] For being immortal and having authority over all things, he suffers the condition of mortals since he is subject to Destiny. Though he is superior to the framework, he has become a slave in it. And although created male and female because of his derivation from the bisexual Father, and sleepless from the unsleeping one, he is nevertheless overcome by love and sleep."

The Hidden Mystery
And after this ... "O my Mind, for I too love the teaching." And Poimandres said, "This is the Mystery which has been hidden until this very day. Nature, mingling in intercourse with man brought forth a marvel most marvellous. Since Man had in himself the nature of the framework of the Seven, which as I told you are composed of fire and spirit, Nature did not delay, but at once gave birth to seven men corresponding to the natures of the seven Governors, bisexual and sublime."[13]

After this I said, "O Poimandres, now I have the utmost point of desire and longing to hear. Do not leave the subject!"

And Poimandres replied, "Then keep still — I have not yet finished the first point."

"See, I am still," I said.

"So it came to pass, as I was saying, that the birth of these seven took place in the following way. Earth was female, and water the generative element; by the fire they were developed.

14.   The body too is an 'image' of the divine archetype, Man. Yet it is the merely
        outward reflection, to be distinguished from the 'essential Man.' The 'Fall,'
        according to the Hermetist, came when Man narcissistically loved his outer
        likeness and identified himself with it: he saw himself in terms of 'the
        framework,' explained himself in terms of nature. The solution to his, the
        human predicament, is therefore *gnosis* — the knowledge of Man's true place
        in the centre of the cosmic process, and the knowledge that the 'image' of the
        Man who has *exousia* is within. Cf. the Hermetically influenced *Gospel of
        Thomas* 84: 'When you see your likeness, you rejoice. But when you see your
        images which existed before you, and which neither die nor become manifest
        — how much will you have to bear!' The vision of the true 'image' imposes
        on us the hard path of regeneration — the forming of soul and of mind
        through the 'baptism' of CH IV *(The Krater)*.

15.   The term here is *erōs:* the desire for one who is other than oneself, from
        whom one is painfully divided. The Hermetic Mystery in the *Logos Teleios*
        speaks of the overcoming of such division through the overcoming of
        oppositions, the 'sacred marriage.' It must be achieved inwardly, otherwise
        all *erōs* remains endless and unsatisfying search, and we remain in the state
        of 'death,' division.
            In this 'holy word' the quotation from Genesis 1:22 is combined with a
        fundamental Gnostic saying, quoted in the *Chaldaean Oracles* as 'He who
        knows himself knows all things in himself.' Versions of it are known also
        from the Hermetic *Definitions* IX,4; the *Gospel of Thomas* III; the Nag Hammadi
        Book of Thomas the Contender Codex II 138:17f. See J.P. Mahé 1982, II, p.278.
        The oldest form is probably that in the *Definitions* (first century BC?).

16.   The Hermetist rejects the usual interpretation of Genesis in the Jewish
        tradition. His illumination by Poimandres enables him to see events rather
        against the backdrop of Light and Darkness: it is not that man has 'brought
        death into this world and all our woe' by sinning, but the human predica-
        ment is a part of the great cosmic struggle. His situation is not punishment,
        but a failure to grasp the reality of his role through knowledge, *gnosis*. Note
        that the visionary is not given the answer by Poimandres, but unfolds it
        himself out his 'reflection.' This is a further illustration of the principle
        expressed in the 'holy word' just cited, that in the content of self-knowledge
        is already given the whole knowledge of the cosmic 'system' which *gnosis*
        expresses.

17.   The text here is difficult to interpret and can best be reconstructed as the
        translator has taken it.

From the ether Nature took the spirit, and produced their bodies after the likeness of the Man. But the Man, being formed of life and light, changed himself into soul and mind, forming soul out of life and mind out of light.[14] And so all things in the sensible world continued until the end of a period and the beginnings of species.

"Now hear the teaching you have been longing to hear. When this period was fulfilled, the body uniting all things was broken by the will of God. For all living creatures, previously bisexual, were parted, as was man; they became on the one hand male, on the other, female. At once God spoke by a holy word, 'Increase and multiply, all creatures and creations, and let him who has a mind recognize himself as immortal, and know that the cause of death is love,[15] and know all the things that exist.'

"When God had spoken thus, Providence, by means of Destiny and the framework of the spheres, brought about unions and set births in process, and all things were multiplied after their kind. He who has recognized himself has come into that good which is best of all; but he who has loved the body, which comes from the deceit of love, remains wandering in the darkness, suffering in his senses the things of death."

"But what great sin," I asked, "have they committed, who are thus ignorant, so that they were deprived of immortality?"

"You seem to me, indeed," he said, "not to have reflected on what you have heard. Did I not tell you to think?"

"I am thinking," I replied, "and I remember, and I am grateful to you for it."

"If you understand," he said to me, "tell me why those who are in death deserve to die."

I replied, "It is because the source of the individual body is that abhorrent darkness,[16] from which the moist nature comes, and from which the body is produced in the sensible world, and by which death is nourished."

"You have understood correctly, O man," he replied; "but how is it that 'he who understands himself departs from himself,' as the word of God says?"[17]

18.   'The Man' here means the 'inner Adam,' comparable to the 'hidden' or 'secret Adam' within us of the Mandeans. Cf. the goal of 'finding the life of my Self' in the Mandean Mystery, where God is also referred to as the Life, and is symbolized in their thought by Light. All of which helps confirm that the Hermetic writer has been in contact with Mysteries in Palestine and the Jordan valley which stood in close relation to the Mandeans and Essenes, if not those exact groups. Compare also the Prologue to the Gospel of John, and the concept of 'eternal Life' which is related to the cosmic history of the Prologue. It is not a promise of future existence, but an inner reality: John 5:24f says 'He who hears my word and believes in him who sent me possesses eternal Life; he does not come to judgment, but has passed from death into Life ...' Cf. the Hermetic phrase below, 'depart again into Life.'

19.   This act of recognition is equivalent to the recognizing of Jesus as sent by God in the Gospel of John. Jesus is thus the 'true Man' — his expression 'Son of Man' is used in apocalyptic and Mystery texts to refer to the 'imprint' here below of the archetypal man above and points to ideas like those of the Hermetic and some Gnostic writings. See further Welburn 1991, pp.146ff, also 270ff (including a Hermetic parallel). The role of Mind in CH I is analogous to the *exousia* or divine creative power which works through Jesus. According to the Prologue of the Gospel of John that power is given to those who 'believe in his name,' that is, exactly the same terms as 'passing from death into life' to which it is thus equivalent, exactly as in *Poimandres*.

20.   The Hermetist maintains the old Mystery-attitude, that only the few, the initiates, share in the human condition fully. Contrast Simon the Magus' 'universalist' approach, attributing spiritual potential, at least, to all men.

21.   A typical figure in the Mysteries is the Guardian of the Threshold. He protects the spiritual aspirant from the chaotic energies he has not yet learned to master.

22.   A figure again suggesting Jewish influence: cf. the Essene idea of the Angel of Darkness which walks with man, etc. The Hermetic teaching is not the popular one of a tormenting devil from popular Judaism, but a similarly esoteric one: the 'punishment' of the ignorant man is simply the being delivered up to his own 'limitless appetites,' the only 'fire' which burns in him. The Essene doctrine was that these are entirely bad if orientated towards the 'Evil Tendency,' but all good if under the direction of the Good Inclination or Angel of Light (above, p.68, note 9). In the Nag Hammadi *Dialogue of the Saviour* Jesus teaches: 'If one does not know how the fire came to be, he will burn in it, because he does not know his root' (Codex III 134:1-4). Compare the Fire in the Mandean Mystery, at first frightening but mastered by the one who finds the Life of himself; and the *Gospel of Philip* 38 (see below).

I said, "It is because the Father of the All consists of light and life, and from him is begotten the Man."[18]

"You have spoken well," he replied. "Light and life, this is God the Father, from whom the Man is begotten. If then you learn that he is light and life, and that you too are formed from these, you will depart again into life." This is what Poimandres said.

"But tell me something more," I said. "How shall I depart into life, O my Mind? For God said, 'Let the man who has Mind recognize himself.'[19] Do not all men possess Mind?"[20]

"Watch your words, my friend!" he replied. "I myself, Mind, dwell with the holy and good, the pure and merciful, the pious; and my presence is a help to them, and at once they know all things and they worship the Father in love. And they give thanks, blessing and singing hymns in orderly fashion, with filial devotion. And before abandoning the body to its proper death, they despise the sense, since they know what the activities of the senses are. Nay, even more, I myself, Mind, will not permit the assailing activities of the body to take effect. I am the guardian of the gates and I lock the door against the entry of evil and shameful actions, cutting off their imaginations.[21] But I am far removed from foolish, evil, wicked, envious, covetous, murderous, and godless men. I yield place to the avenging demon,[22] and he applies to such a man the sharpness of fire, piercing his senses and arming him for still worse deeds of lawlessness so that he shall receive even harsher punishment. So the man does not cease having a desire for his limitless appetites, insatiably fighting in the dark, and this torments him and increases the fire upon him."

"You have taught me well, O Mind, all that I desired. Tell me just one thing more, about the ascent which takes place."

To this Poimandres replied, "First, in the dissolution of the material body, you deliver the body itself to be changed, and the form you possessed vanishes, and you deliver to the demon your character which is henceforth to be inactive, while the senses of the body return to their sources, of which they become part, and are once more identified with the Powers; but

23.   The soul after death ascends through the planetary spheres toward its cosmic origin. It constitutes a return to our 'essential Man' or primal being. In the *Gospel of Thomas* 49 Jesus says: 'Blessed are the solitary and the elect, for you shall find the kingdom. For you came forth thence, and shall go there again.' Many Gnostics claim to achieve the cosmic ascension already in this life, and so find themselves. In ancient Mysteries, as in the Mandean Mystery-recital, it is symbolized by the climbing of the world-mountain. The Gnostic group called the Ophites used a mandala or Diagram, which is related both to the layout of the Mithraic temples with their 'ladder'-like image of the cosmic stages, and to the kabbalistic figure of the Tree of Life. An important Gnostic account of the powers to be overcome or transformed in the spheres is the *Gospel of Mary* (published with the Nag Hammadi texts, also in R.M. Grant 1961, pp.65-68).

24.   The Mithraic temple layout, their *imago mundi,* included an 'eighth gate.' Most of the Christian Gnostics also use the term Eighth or 'Ogdoad' to refer to the spiritual realm, beyond the 'framework' or world of the seven spheres and the earth within them. Sometimes it is said to be the place of the divine Sophia.

25.   The description closely resemblances that of the Greek Mysteries given by Plutarch — see above, p.60 — especially the mention of 'gentle voices, and choric dances, and the majesty of holy sounds and sacred visions.'

26.   The technical term and the spiritual goal of the Mysteries. There is no reason to suppose, with Scott, that the word has been added by a later hand: it corresponds to the whole direction of thought of the *Poimandres.* The parallel with the Greek Mystery-language suggests that there may have been a ritual pattern behind the sequence of ideas. The continuing use of ritual is strongly suggested by the Hermetic document found at Nag Hammadi *On the Eighth and Ninth:* see the discussion in G. Fowden 1986, pp.104ff and 142ff. The Hermetic Mysteries were not merely 'literary' inventions, as used to be argued. The assimilation of Gnostic influence, stressing the validity of 'knowledge,' however, certainly leads in a direction away from the old 'enactment' Mysteries. The *Gospel of Thomas* shows a 'Hermetic Christianity' where the elements of ritual have receded into the background, and the 'preaching of knowledge' has taken central position.

27.   Compare Jesus' language in the Gospel of John, where he repeatedly asserts that he has been 'sent' by the Father to reveal him, and, just like the Hermetic initiate, so that through him 'the race of mankind may be saved by God.' Jesus is the focus of all that was formerly divided among all the initiates, and enacts their role as a unique individual.

28.   See *Gospel of Thomas* 28, already cited above, p.190, with a further Hermetic parallel.

29.   Scott (1985 p.9) thinks that the *Poimandres* differs from the other Hermetica in that it does not treat its 'knowledge' as secret. This is a complete misunderstanding. The legend of the founding of the Mystery-teaching given here explains precisely why the teaching, rejected and scorned by the many, is kept as a Mystery for the few.

anger and lust depart to the irrational nature. And so man henceforth presses upwards through the composite frame-work.[23] In the first zone he yields up the power to increase and decrease; in the second, the power to contrive evil, a deceit henceforth ineffective; in the third, deceitful lust, henceforth ineffective; in the fourth, arrogant ostentation, now deprived of its intended effects; in the fifth, unholy audacity and rash boldness; in the sixth, the lawless appetite given by wealth, henceforth ineffective; and in the seventh, the lie that sets a snare. Then, stripped bare of all that the powers in the frame-work had wrought in it, man enters the eighth nature,[24] possessing only his own proper power, and, together with the beings which are found there, he hymns the Father. Those who are present rejoice over his arrival; and being made like those with whom he dwells, he also hears a kind of sweet sound of certain Powers,[25] who dwell above the eighth nature, as they praise God. Then, moving in proper order, they mount up to the Father, and yield themselves to the Powers, and having themselves become Powers they enter into God. Such is the blissful goal of those who possess knowledge — to become God.[26] Why then do you delay? Now that you have received all things from me, should you not become a guide to those who are worthy, so that through you the race of mankind may be saved by God?"

The Preaching of Knowledge

Having said this to me, Poimandres mingled with the Powers. And after I had rendered thanks and had blessed the Father of the All, I was sent forth by him,[27] having been empowered and fully taught about the nature of the All and the supreme vision. And I began to preach to men the beauty of piety and of knowledge: "O ye peoples, men born of earth, you who have given yourselves up to drunkenness and slumber and ignorance of God, be sober, cease your debauchery, enchanted with the sorcery of irrational sleep!"[28] And as they heard this, they gathered about me with one accord.[29] And I said, "Men born

30.   The verb used is the same used by John the Baptist and Jesus, and whose root appears in the word *metanoia*.

31.   Cf. the language of 'the two Ways,' of Light and Darkness, in the Essene and early Christian writings. It is the reaction of mockery and rejection which leads to the founding of the Mystery for those few who receive Hermetic knowledge.

32.   The same word used in the Gospels for resurrection; compare too the Mandean Mystery, which took place on 'that great day when thou wast raised up,' Simon as 'the One Who Stands,' etc. The term may hide a reference to a Mystery-rite.

33.   In the *Gospel of Thomas* it says, 'These are the secret words which Jesus the Living spoke ... He who shall find the interpretation of these words shall not taste of death' (Prologue and 1). 'Ambrosial' water is, literally, water 'of immortality.' For 'sowing,' see *Gospel of Thomas* 9. The same parable appears in Mark 4:2-8, and in Mark 4:14-20 Jesus interprets it in terms of 'sowing the word.' And see the *Gospel of Philip* 16b.

34.   A technical term among many Gnostics for spiritual vision, which brings a union with the thing perceived. The state of ordinary consciousness is one of 'emptiness,' not containing the reality of the things perceived. 'The Fullness' or Pleroma is a name for the spiritual world, with many additional nuances of meaning.

35.   The initiate is not merely 'saved' by his *gnosis*, but becomes a participant in the creative work. The Egyptian Hermes or Thoth appears as a Creator or Demiurge through the power of the word, and the initiate, in whom is the Man or synthesis of creative powers, actualizes that power in his own utterance. With a somewhat different emphasis, we still have something close to Simon's 'seventh power,' and his doctrine of the Logos or spiritual Christ (p.164, note 9 above).

36.   This and the next verse strongly suggest once more the Prologue to the Gospel of John, which teaches that by the Logos 'all things were made' (1:3) and 'that he came to his own' (1:11) — even though in the Christian history it turns out that his own failed to know him as expected. Although the Hermetic hymn has been used by Christians, it is likely that the similarity comes from a common background influence from the esoteric baptizing sects who carried the Mysteries into the Jewish culture of the time of Jesus. The hymn has been studied recently and found to contain 'fragments of Jewish liturgy, prayers and worship formulae actually utilized in the worship life of Hellenistic Jewish synagogues in the diaspora' — B.A. Pearson in M.E. Stone 1984. Direct contact with Jews in Egypt, perhaps the Therapeutae or Alexandrian Essenes described by Philo, remains more plausible than the theory of Ludin-Jansen that the author of the *Poimandres* was himself Jewish.

of earth, why have you given yourselves over to death, when you have the power to partake of immortality? Repent,[30] you who have journeyed with error and kept company with ignorance! Free yourselves from the shadowy light, lay hold on immortality, forsaking corruption!"

And some of them mocked me and stood apart, for they had given themselves over to the way of death;[31] others threw themselves at my feet and begged for instruction. I raised them up[32] and became the guide of mankind, teaching the doctrine of how and in what manner they should be saved. And I sowed in them the words of wisdom, and they were nourished with the ambrosial water.[33] And when evening came and the sun's rays were beginning to decline completely, I bade them give thanks to God. When they had completed the thanksgiving, each of them betook himself to his own bed.

But I wrote down for myself the benefaction of Poimandres, and being filled[34] with what I had wanted I greatly rejoiced. For the sleep of the body became wakefulness of the soul, and the closing of the eyes true vision, and my silence gestation with the good, and the utterance of the word a birth of good things.[35] And all this came to pass for me when I received it from my Mind, that is, from Poimandres, the Logos of the Absolute Sovereignty. And so, being divinely inspired by the truth, I have come. Therefore with all my soul and strength I give praise to God the Father:

"Holy is God, the Father of the All.

"Holy is God, whose Will is accomplished by his own Powers.

"Holy is God, who wills to be known and is known by his own.[36]

"Holy art thou, who by Logos has constituted all existing things.

"Holy art thou, of whom all Nature was born as the image.

"Holy art thou, whom Nature has not formed.

"Holy art thou, who art more mighty than all Power.

"Holy art thou, who art greater than all eminence.

"Holy art thou, who art superior to all praises.

37.   The last words seem to express the actual fulfilment of the Mystery, as the
       speaker 'enters into life and light.' Cf. the exclamations added at the end of
       the Mandean Mystery-recital. The speaker identifies himself fully at the end
       with the divine Man possessed of *exousia*. He does not disappear, however,
       but becomes a part of the creative Light itself, shining out into the darkness
       of ignorance in human souls. Cf. *Gospel of Thomas* 24b: 'There is a light within
       a man of light, and it gives light to the whole world. If it does not give light,
       there is darkness.' Also Gospel of John, 1:5.

"Accept the pure spiritual sacrifices from a soul and heart uplifted to thee, O inexpressible, ineffable one, named only by silence! Grant me this prayer, and fill me with power, who implore thee that I may never fall away from the knowledge which is fit for our nature; that with this grace I may illuminate those of our race who are in ignorance, my brethren, thy sons. Yea, I believe, and bear witness. I enter into life and light. Blessed art thou, O Father; thy Man longs to share with thee in the work of sanctification, even as thou hast given all authority unto him."[37]

6. *The Apocalypse of Adam*

The *Apocalypse of Adam* was unknown until the discovery of the Nag Hammadi Library, where it is to be found (in Coptic translation) among the documents of Codex V. It is not the most outwardly spectacular of the writings that were rediscovered in the Gnostic Library, but it yields up its secrets gradually and has turned out to be in some ways the most amazing of all.

Its presence in the Library makes it virtually certain that the *Apocalypse* was being used by Egyptian Gnostics in the early centuries of Christianity. The owners of the Library were most likely followers of Valentinus. However, the investigations by scholars of the special contents of the *Apocalypse* has convinced many that it is not a Gnostic work — at least in the sense of being written by a special group expressing Gnostic doctrines. Although the Gnostics of Christian times took up its ideas, there is much to support the idea that they were taking over an earlier source. There is no explicitly Christian material in the *Apocalypse*, but much that in the words of Martin Krause 'goes back to Old Testament and late Jewish traditions, to apocryphal Adam literature' and similar writings.*
Further research has confirmed its manifold connections with the Jewish esoteric writings of the Essene and closely related traditions. In its form, for instance, the *Apocalypse of Adam* reminds us immediately of the *Testaments of the Patriarchs*; for its scene is laid in the seven hundredth year of Adam's life since the birth of his son Seth, and we know from the ancient Greek version of the Old Testament that the old texts of the Bible gave that figure for the end of Adam's life. Thus Adam is on his death-bed when he gives this 'revelation' to his son of the future course of history up to the last days. Compare the opening formulae of the *Testaments* — for instance, *Gad:*

> A copy of the testament of Gad, concerning what he said
> to his sons in the one hundred and twenty-seventh year of
> his life, saying 'I was Jacob's ninth son ...'

or of *Levi:*

---

* Krause, in W. Foerster (ed), *Gnosis. 2. Coptic and Mandaic Sources*, Oxford 1974, p.15.
See further my *Beginnings of Christianity*, Edinburgh 1991, pp.44ff.

> The copy of the words of Levi, what things he
> appointed to his sons, according to all they should do,
> and what things should befall them until the day of
> judgment ...

The claim of the document to come from Adam is not to be taken literally, any more than the *Testaments* were really traditions preserved from patriarchal times. It is a visionary work in the Essene or some related school, where the seer projects himself back into the past — here, to the very start of human history — in order to survey the rhythms of time and then follow their pattern as it reaches a 'fulfilment' in the actual future. 'Adam' is a sort of spiritual mirror into which the initiate looks, gazing into the past so as to see over his own shoulder the resolution of events in the time to come.

The structure of a 'Testament' makes instant sense of many features of the *Apocalypse of Adam*, and like the *Testaments* of *Levi* and *Judah* it is especially concerned with the coming of a messenger, called 'the Illuminator.' In fact, by analogy with the prophecies contained in the *Testaments* of *Levi* and *Judah*, in the apocalypse called the *Second Book of Enoch* and other esoteric Jewish works, we recognize him as the Messiah — not interpreted in the conventional way as a great leader sent by God, but in accordance with the profoundly spiritualized Essene or Enochian tradition. He is himself a revelation of the Light, and the stories of his birth in thirteen different incarnations are themselves parables, 'Imaginations' of his spiritual significance rather than literal histories. To be 'born' in the ancient Mysteries was an experience for the initiated: ordinary people were not able to rise as individuals to an appreciation of the wonder, the miracle of origination. Each 'birth' of the Illuminator is a new beginning, the bringing of some new quality into earthly history, and so a divine miracle or revelation. The different stories use the symbolism of different Mysteries, and collectively reveal a sequence of incarnations in the several civilizations of the ancient world. The special qualities of the Mystery-streams then flow together in his final appearance as the Royal Messiah, the climactic incarnation which still lies in the future for the actual visionary who wrote the *Apocalypse of Adam*.

The absence of Christian allusions, and the close parallels to the *Testaments of the Patriarchs*, etc. supports the contention of Alexander Böhlig that the author of the *Apocalypse* belonged to a pre-Christian baptizing sect similar to the Mandeans or the Essenes. Towards the end of the document we hear about 'the guardians of baptism,' who are called by the mysterious names Michev, Michar and Mnesinous, and who are subjected to sharp criticism. In view of the Messianic expectations centred on the reappearing prophet, and the apocalyptic structure of the writing, we may infer that it comes from some wing of the Essenes which had begun to develop in a more Gnostic direction and become critical of the baptismal lustrations and water-rites of the Essenes such as we know from Qumran. The ideas of the cycles of time which the author employs are again reminiscent of Iranian-Zoroastrian thought, blended with materials from the Book of Genesis — the same synthesis which we find in the Scrolls from Qumran, though with the Iranian features coming more strongly to the fore. Writing probably in the first century BC, the visionary looks back on the twelve incarnations of the prophet which were already known in the different Mysteries, and sees a pattern which will be completed in the impending future, 'so that the desire of those powers may be fulfilled.' The Illuminator who had been 'born' in all the ancient Mystery-centres will appear one more time: he will be the fulfilment, the Messiah.

Can we decipher the identity of the reappearing one? Here we touch upon the most striking revelation of the *Apocalypse of Adam*. In its riddling way, it gives us just enough information to recognize the figure it points to if we have 'ears to hear.' In the first of the birth-legends is also one of the clearest allusions. It says:

> Now the First Kingdom says of him that he came from ...
>
> a Spirit ... heaven.
>
> He was nurtured in the heavens.
>
> He received the Glory of that one and the Power.
>
> And he came to the bosom of his mother.
>
> And thus he came on the water.

Anyone in the Zoroastrian tradition would recognize the legend of the prophet's birth here identified as his first in the cycle of revelations. It is unmistakably that of Zarathustra himself:

> As the Religion says: When Ohrmazd created the creation
> of Zarathustra, then (first) was his Glory. Then the
> creation of Zarathustra sped down from before Ohrmazd
> to (the heaven of) the Endless Light; from the Endless
> Light it sped down to the sun; from the sun it sped down
> to the moon; from the moon it sped down to the stars;

and from the stars it sped down to the fire in the house of
Frahim-ruvanan-Zoish. From that fire it sped upon Zoish's
wife, at the time when she bore the daughter who became
Zarathustra's mother.

Even this summary version in the *Denkard* contains all the elements
of the 'First Kingdom' story. The heavenly origins of the prophet,
long prior to his birth here below; his nurturing in the several
realms of the heavenly spheres; his receiving of the Glory as his
primary attribute, even as the kernel of his existence. All the
identifications serve to show that in the visionary universe of the
Apocalypse of Adam the figure behind the revelation was precisely
indicated. The one who has appeared many times in the cycles of
time in the centres of the Mysteries is the original prophet of Light,
Zarathustra. And it is he who will come again as the Messiah.

Rudolf Steiner had already uncovered the connection which the
Apocalypse of Adam unfolds in fascinating detail, and which the Dead
Sea Scrolls showed in their blending of Iranian and Jewish ideas in
the doctrines among the Essenes. Steiner saw in their teachings the
real background of the Gospel of Matthew, with its infancy legends
and the account of the 'virgin birth.' The Essene ideas, he said,

> were based upon cosmic Mysteries, whose aim was to
> prepare from the purified blood of the Hebrew people —
> blood which showed the influence of the cosmic order —
> a body for the reincarnation of the great initiate
> Zarathustra. For it is of the figure of Zarathustra, of him
> and no other, that the Gospel of Matthew primarily
> speaks.*

From his spiritual sources of investigation, Steiner reached the
Mystery behind the so-misunderstood 'virgin birth.' Once we realize
that it is a part of the Mystery-language of Zoroastrianism, concerning the 'miracle' of the reappearance of the prophet in his different
incarnations, we have for the first and only time in modern Bible-
study an objective starting-point for the elucidation of its real
meaning. It is in fact part of the symbolic language — the language
of spiritual Imaginations from the Mysteries.

For the scriptures relate of Zarathustra that upon his death his life
or 'spiritual seed' was not lost, but hidden in the depths of a dark
lake. It consisted of 'light and power,' and some say that at night it

---

* Rudolf Steiner, *The Gospel of St Matthew*, London 1965, p.83.

could be seen shining up to the surface like three lamps. Moreover, the story is connected with the Zoroastrian idea of the 'cycles of time,' and points to several further incarnations of the prophet at cosmically determined stages of the world's unfolding. The last of the incarnations is the 'World Saviour' or Saoshyant. But the manner of the birth of all them is the same:

> And for each, when his own time comes, it will be thus: a
> virgin will go to Lake Kayansih to bathe; and the Glory
> (of Zarathustra) will enter her body, and she will become
> with child. And so, one by one, they will be born thus,
> each at his own time.

In the mythological, pictorial language of the ancient world, the Zarathustra-legend embodies the teaching of the passing on of the divine 'Glory,' the spiritual essence of Zarathustra, from his first appearance to his subsequent reincarnations. And exactly so in the *Apocalypse of Adam* does each incarnation of 'the Illuminator' or prophet of Light receive the Glory. The picture of birth from the waters of the lake through a pure virgin, as Alexander Böhlig has noted, is itself reproduced in the enigmatic formula given by all the 'Kingdoms': *And thus he came on the water.* Virgin-birth is explicitly mentioned in the legends of several of the 'Kingdoms.' Even if the *Apocalypse* did not contain in the 'Thirteenth Prophecy' a reference to the Enochian or Essene Messiah, some of the parallels to the Gospel of Matthew would be striking. In the past, Steiner's idea and similar ones which recognized a Zoroastrian background have been rejected, on the grounds that no source near enough in space or time to the events in Palestine could be found to support it. Any such objection is now rendered obsolete by the discovery of that astounding document, the *Apocalypse of Adam*.

Source: The Nag Hammadi Library, *Codex V 64:1–85:32. Translated from Coptic by George MacRae; edited by Douglas M. Parrott.*

1.   For the 'testamentary' significance of opening formula, cf. the introductory remarks, above p.211f.

2.   The version of the Fall told here is close to that of the *Poimandres* and anticipates Christian Gnosticism. The 'essential Man' of the Hermetic retelling of Genesis, though 'higher than the framework,' became trapped within it; the Man originated, as here, from a higher world than the 'demiurge Mind' which fashioned the material world. The treatment of Adam and Eve in the *Apocalypse of Adam* also resembles the Hermetic version in that primal Man is evidently both male and female in one — the immortal state to be regained through the Hermetic Mystery — and through his feminine aspect possesses intrinsic spiritual knowledge. On the other hand, there is nothing to suggest dependence on Hermetic sources. Rather, the *Apocalypse* represents the kind of Jewish esoteric teaching which we have seen influenced the Hermetica. The interest in Egypt shown later in the work shows that points of contact with Egyptian ideas were recognized and in later 'Sethian' traditions were developed further.

3.   The 'Glory,' evidently an attribute of the 'essential Man,' is mentioned again in relation to the prophet or Illuminator, who thus restores man's primal state before he was 'enslaved' to nature and the lower God. The Glory is part of the Zoroastrian background which can be seen clearly once we have identified the prophet indicated. The Genesis-story has thus been interpreted in the light of Iranian ideas. According to the Iranian myth, the First Man was Gayomart. R.C. Zaehner says: 'Gayomart himself is said to have sprung from Spandarmat, the Earth, and the seed from which he grows was planted by Ohrmazd himself, Spandarmat's own father' (1975): the Illuminator (Zarathustra) fulfils this pattern again in the legend of the Eleventh Kingdom below. The original Man or Gayomart, however, fell victim to the attack of Ahriman, the Dark power. Like the Adam-Eve portrayed in the *Apocalypse* 'he does not fall in any theological sense, he is simply overpowered by overwhelming force and dies' (Zaehner 1975 p.74). On his death, his seed enters the Earth and from it springs the first couple, Mashye and Mashyane, sprouting like a rhubarb-plant: 'It was as if their hands were clapped to their ears, and they were joined the one to the other, joined in limb and form, and over the two hovered the Glory. So closely were they linked together that it was not clear which was the male and which was the female. The Glory which had been created by Ohrmazd and which accompanied them and is the Glory of mankind, was given to them' (*Bundahishn* or 'Iranian Genesis,' in Zaehner 1975 pp.75f). Unlike the heavenly-earthly Gayomart, though, Mashye and Mashyane become separate, sin and forfeit the Glory, which flees away from them. Henceforth it manifests only in connection with certain special leaders and spiritual teachers, and pre-eminently Zarathustra.

✳ The Apocalypse of Adam ✳

Paradise and the Fall

The revelation which Adam taught his son Seth in the seven hundredth year, saying, "Listen to my words, my son Seth.[1] When God had created me out of the earth along with Eve your mother, I went about with her in a glory which she had seen in the aeon from which we had come forth. She taught me a word of knowledge of the eternal God. And we resembled the great eternal angels, for we were higher than the God who had created us[2] and the powers with him, whom we did not know.

"Then God, the ruler of the aeons and the powers, divided us in wrath. Then we became two aeons. And the glory in our hearts left us, me and your mother Eve, along with the first knowledge that breathed within us. And it (glory) fled from us;[3] it entered into ... great ... had come forth, not from this aeon from which we had come forth, I and Eve your mother. But it (knowledge) entered into the seed of great aeons. For this reason I myself have called you by the name of that man who is the seed of the great generation or from whom (it comes). After those days the eternal knowledge of the God of truth withdrew from me and your Mother Eve. Since that time we learned about dead things, like men. Then we recognized the God who had created us. For we were not strangers to his powers. And we served him in fear and slavery. And after these (events) we became darkened in our hearts. Now I slept in the thought of my heart.

"And I saw three men before me whose likeness I was unable to recognize, since they were not from the powers of the God who had created us. They surpassed ... glory, and ... men ... saying to me, 'Arise, Adam, from the sleep of death, and hear about the aeon and the seed of that man to whom life has come, who came from you and from Eve, your wife.'

"When I had heard these words from the great men who were standing before me, then we sighed, I and Eve, in our

4.   Adam fulfils the function for the seer-author of the *Apocalypse* of the patriarchs such as Levi or Judah for the writer of the *Testaments*. He represents the wholeness of vision to be regained, standing at the beginning of an unfolding pattern which will be completed in the actual future, that is, soon after the first century BC when the *Apocalypse of Adam* was probably composed. The content of Adam's revelation is the rhythms or cycles of time. The broad threefold division of history again recalls Iranian teachings concerning 'the Three Times.' The substance of the account is based, however, on Genesis once more.

5.   See Genesis 6:17. The Flood is sent by God to punish sinful and rebellious humankind. The motive appears in other accounts of the Flood, such as Plato's in the *Timaeus*, where the continent that was destroyed is called Atlantis. In the *Apocalypse*, the special motive of the creator-God is to wipe out all traces of the 'first knowledge' of a higher state. Humankind are to know only the material world and the God who made it, nothing of a 'higher world.' The usual Jewish tradition accepts that viewpoint; but the *Apocalypse* tells the story from the perspective of the Mysteries.

6.   The *Apocalypse* indicates the migration of peoples, led by 'great angels,' escaping the Flood but not descended from the family of Noah.

7.   That is, Noah's sons and family. MacRae (in Charlesworth 1983, p.713) emends the text to include Noah by name, but probably the story is being retold from previous sources and assumes familiarity among readers with the outline of the story already. Cf. the similar attitude to biblical events in the *Testaments of the Patriarchs* e.g. pp.119ff above.

8.   Son of Prometheus and hero of the Greek version of the Flood story. There are many links between the story of Prometheus, the rebel god or Titan, and the myths in *Enoch* etc, concerning the rebel angels, illicit 'knowledge' of heavenly secrets, the Flood and the state of humankind. 'The generations' — that is, the Gentiles.

hearts. And the Lord, the God who had created us, stood before us. He said to us, 'Adam, why were you sighing in your heart? Do you not know that I am the God who created you? And I breathed into you a spirit of life as a living soul.' Then darkness came upon our eyes.

"Then the God, who created us, created a son from himself and Eve, your mother, for ... in the thought of my ... I knew a sweet desire for your mother. Then the vigour of our eternal knowledge was destroyed in us, and weakness pursued us. Therefore the days of our life became few. For I knew that I had come under the authority of death."

Prophecy of the Flood
"Now then, my son Seth, I will reveal to you the things which those men whom I saw before me at first revealed to me:[4] after I have completed the times of this generation and the years of the generation have been accomplished, then ... slave ...

"For rain-showers of God the almighty will be poured forth so that he might destroy all flesh of God the almighty, so that he might destroy all flesh from the earth by means of that which is around them, along with those from the seed of the men to whom passed the life of the knowledge, that came from me and Eve, your mother. For they were strangers to him.[5] Afterwards great angels will come on high clouds, who will bring those men into the place where the spirit of life dwells ... [6] glory ... there ... come from heaven to earth. Then the whole multitude of flesh will be left behind in the waters.

"Then God will rest from his wrath. And he will cast his power upon the waters, and he will give power to his sons and their wives[7] by means of the ark along with the animals, whichever he pleased, and the birds of heaven, which he called and released upon the earth. And God will say to Noah, whom the generations will call Deucalion,[8] 'Behold, I have protected you in the ark along with your wife and your sons and the wives and their animals and the birds of heaven, which you called and released upon the earth. Therefore I will give the earth to you — you and your sons. In kingly fashion you will rule over

9.   According to Genesis 9:18f and Jewish tradition building upon it, Noah's
       three sons Shem, Ham and Japhet escaped the Flood in the ark, and
       afterwards their children formed the ancestors of all humanity. The old Greek
       translation of the Bible shows that some texts at least reckoned their sons as
       twelve in all. In this version, however, they encounter the remnants of older
       cultures preserving the 'first knowledge' in their Mysteries.

10.   Probably Egypt; for it is there that, despite the negative evaluation of Egypt
       in most Jewish traditions, that the *Apocalypse* acknowledges a survival of the
       'first knowledge.'

11.   The knowledge of the Mysteries does not survive in its original form. The
       'other race' is absorbed into the development of the 'twelve kingdoms' which
       spring from the sons of Ham and Japhet. There it continues to protect
       humankind from evils and sinful desires, and the cultures which are later
       represented by their birth-legends of the Illuminator each have a part of the
       spiritual knowledge which needs to be fused back into oneness, restoring the
       state of the beginning. The twelve kingdoms can be identified concretely by
       the legends which are later cited for each of them in turn, and should be
       understood as spread out from this original point both in space and in time,
       reaching up to the juncture at which the author-seer actually writes. The
       enigmatic 'other people' mentioned at the end may be the children of Shem,
       the Jews.

12.   Sakla appears in many Gnostic writings as a derogatory name for the
       Demiurge or lower God of material creation. It may derive from the Semitic
       word meaning 'fool.'

13.   The Flood has not produced the effect — the wiping out of the 'first
       knowledge' — which the creator-God wished. The Mysteries have survived
       and their knowledge has been taken up in Egypt and elsewhere, even
       affecting the creator-God's special people. What follows is a retelling of the
       Exodus. (A surprising number of scholars were misled by the mere mention
       of 'fire' in the catastrophes to assume it had something to do with Sodom
       and Gomorrha). The creator-God leads his people out of the influence of the
       Mystery-knowledge and brings punishment through volcanic upheaval upon
       the rest of humankind.

it — you and your sons. And no seed will come from you of the men who will not stand in my presence in another glory.'

"Then they will become as the cloud of the great light. Those men will come who have been cast forth from the knowledge of the great aeons and the angels. They will stand before Noah and the aeons. And God will say to Noah, 'Why have you departed from what I told you? You have created another generation so that you might scorn my power.' Then Noah will say, 'I shall testify before your might that the generation of these men did not come from me nor from my sons[9] ... knowledge.'

"And he will ... those men and bring them into their proper land and build them a holy dwelling place.[10] And they will be called by that name and dwell there six hundred years in a knowledge of imperishability. And angels of the great light will dwell with them. No foul deed will dwell in their hearts, but only the knowledge of God.

Egypt and the Exodus
"Then others from the seed of Ham and Japheth will come, four hundred thousand men, and enter into another land and sojourn with those men who came forth from the great eternal knowledge. For the shadow of their power will protect those who have sojourned with them from every evil thing and every unclean desire. Then the seed of Ham and Japheth will form twelve kingdoms, and their seed also will enter into the kingdom of another people.[11]

"Then ... will take counsel ... aeons ... who are dead, of the great aeons of imperishability. And they will go to Sakla their God.[12] They will go in to the powers, accusing the great men who are in their glory.

"They will say to Sakla, 'What is the power of these men who stood in your presence, who were taken from the seed of Ham and Japheth, who will number four hundred thousand men? They have been received into another aeon from which they had come forth, and they have overturned all the glory of your power and the dominion of your hand.[13] For the seed of Noah

14.   The expunging of Mystery-knowledge is thwarted once more. The eternal
       God sends his messengers, and it is actually they who lead the people out of
       Egypt. The *Apocalypse* seems to indicate that the Jewish tradition too kept the
       primordial knowledge in its esoteric teaching. Those sent are the angelic
       beings subsequently named as Abrasax, Sablo and Gamaliel, angels of the
       Four Luminaries who are sometimes identified with the Four Living
       Creatures before God in Ezekiel 1:5ff. A fuller account of these angels is to
       be found in the *Sacred Book of the Invisible Spirit* or *Gospel of the Egyptians* from
       Nag Hammadi, Codex III 52:19–53:9. The *Sacred Book* is later and explicitly
       Christian, but is related at many points to the *Apocalypse of Adam*.

15.   The biblical account of the Exodus includes mention of signs and many
       plagues — devastation caused by natural catastrophes and disturbances.
       These include 'darkness' (Exodus 10:21-23), a 'pillar of cloud' and a 'pillar of
       fire' (Exodus 13:21); the volcanic events continue up to the revelation on
       Sinai: 'Mount Sinai was covered with smoke, because the LORD descended
       on it in fire. The smoke billowed up from it like smoke from a furnace, the
       whole mountain trembled violently' (Exodus 19:18); God remains hidden in
       'thick darkness' (20:21).

16.   The 'clouds of light' leading the people of knowledge are perhaps spiritual
       — cf. Exodus 10:23 with its supernatural light for the Israelites. But they may
       also be the pillar of cloud/fire which 'brought those men out of the fire and
       the wrath,' out of the reach of the hostile powers.

17.   Those who receive the Mystery-knowledge anew within the Jewish stream
       are best identified with the Essenes, from some branch of whom the
       Apocalypse comes. It was they who felt that they were living in the company
       of angels (see especially p.94, note 7 above). It is they who took up the
       teachings of the Illuminator (Zarathustra) mentioned immediately below; and
       they used the 'plant' imagery both for their own Community and for the
       Messiah — cf. the 'trees' planted by the Illuminator below, and again cf. p.96,
       note 8 above.

18.   In context the phrase is obscure: the presence of the Illuminator at the Flood
       and the Exodus has not been mentioned. It might mean rather that we are
       now passing to consider a third way in which the 'first knowledge' of the
       Mysteries has been revealed among men.

19.   The title is used in the Zoroastrian tradition for the Prophet of Light,
       Zarathustra.

20.   Attempts have repeatedly been made to find in the prophetic passages con-
       cerning the Illuminator materials which show a Christian influence, for
       instance, the idea of a 'suffering Messiah,' and so on. However, no such inter-
       pretation is necessary or demonstrable. Everything can be explained from an-
       cient traditions without recourse to the Christian transvaluation of suffering
       and victory. The Illuminator is a power of the Light, and attracts the enmity
       of the Dark 'powers' in the legends of Zarathustra, for example. The other
       detailed identifications given for the Kingdoms below are all based on the
       concept of a 'struggle,' but not of redemptive suffering and death. It remains
       unclear whether the description given at the beginning of the sequence here

through his son has done all your will, and (so have) all the powers in the aeons over which your might rules, while both those men and the ones who are sojourners in their glory have not done your will. But they have turned (aside) your whole throng.'

"Then the God of the aeons will give them (some) of those who serve him ...[14] they will come upon that land where the great men will be who have not been defiled, nor will be defiled by any desire. For their soul did not come from a defiled hand, but it came from a great commandment of an eternal angel. Then fire and sulphur and asphalt will be cast upon those men, and fire and (blinding) mist will come over those aeons,[15] and the eyes of the powers of the illuminators will be darkened, and the aeons will not see by them in those days. And great clouds of light will descend, and other clouds of light will come down upon them from the great aeons.[16]

"Abrasax and Sablo and Gamaliel will descend and bring those men out of the fire and the wrath, and take them above the aeons and the rulers of the powers, and take them away ... of life ... and take them away ... aeons ... dwelling place of the great ... there with the holy angels and the aeons. The men will be like those angels, for they are not strangers to them.[17] But they work in the imperishable seed.

The Illuminator

"Once again, for the third time,[18] the Illuminator[19] of knowledge will pass by in great glory, in order to leave (something) of the seed of Noah and the sons of Ham and Japheth — to leave for himself fruit-bearing trees. And he will redeem their souls from the day of death. For the whole creation that came from the dead earth will be under the authority of death. But those who reflect upon the knowledge of the eternal God in their hearts will not perish. For they received (it) from one of the eternal angels ... illuminator ... will come upon ... that is dead ... of Seth. And he will perform signs and wonders in order to scorn the powers and their ruler.[20]

is a general one intended to characterize all the appearances, or whether it is already looking forward to the fulfilment. The collection of the birth-legends may have existed separately from the document as we now possess it, and perhaps formed its original kernel.

21.   The notion that a spiritual person attracts more enmity and suffers from persecution in this world is not specifically a Christian one. It is, however, already strongly developed among the Essenes, who are perhaps seeing in the Illuminator their own type of prophet, like the persecuted Teacher of Righteousness. MacRae (in Charlesworth 1983, p.715) may be quite correct, therefore, in seeing the influence of the 'Suffering Servant' idea from Isaiah 42:1 but not in the sense of the Christian usage he supposes. In short, we may likely be witnessing the formation of Christian language, rather than seeing it reflected in the *Apocalypse of Adam*. The phrase 'upon whom the holy spirit has come' recalls the imparting of the holy spirit through initiation in the *Community Rule*, and MacRae himself points out that the phrase 'suffer vengeance in the body of his flesh' used at Qumran presents a close parallel.

22.   An allusion to the Zarathustra-legend, identifying the Illuminator in his first incarnation of the series as the founder of the Zoroastrian religion, the prophet of Light and Darkness. See above, pp.213ff: Zarathustra was created and nurtured in the highest heaven before descending to be born on earth. Historically, the Prophet lived in prehistoric times in ancient Iran.

23.   The Glory was the divine core of Zarathustra's being, from which his heavenly form originated. As a spiritual radiance it was possessed by the first man also. The Zoroastrian story of the Fall relates that it was lost when the first couple, Mashye and Mashyane, sinned and fled away to the depths of the waters. The *Apocalypse of Adam* echoes the Zoroastrian myth in its version of the Fall, and the receiving of the Glory by the Illuminator in each of his births among the twelve Kingdoms points to a Zoroastrian Mystery too. The Glory, lost to humanity in general at the Fall, will be restored through the work of the Saoshyants or World-Saviours. They 'possess the Glory,' which is as much as to say that they are reincarnations of the eternal essence of Zarathustra, the only man able to retain that spiritual connection. The last, or *the* Saoshyant will restore it in its fullness, leading to the Transfiguration or spiritualization of the Earth.

24.   The formula alludes to the legend of the birth of the Saoshyants, each being born from a pure virgin who comes to bathe in the waters which conceal the Glory at the appropriate time.

25.   The birth-story is that of the archaic hero Zal (also called Dastan). The legend gives an imagination of the heavenly origin of the human spirit, nurtured by the miraculous bird Simurgh. The great prophet (or hero) from whom he was descended is Sama Kereshasp, important in Zoroastrian lore.

26.   This birth story is that of another archaic Iranian hero, Faridun, a dragon-slayer behind whom one can discern a Mystery of the natural cycle and the yearly renewal of life. The stories about him connect with the myths of the god Mithra.

"Then the God of the powers will be disturbed, saying, 'What is the power of this man who is higher than we?' Then he will arouse a great wrath against that man. And the glory will withdraw and dwell in holy houses which it has chosen for itself. And the powers will not see it with their eyes, nor will they see the Illuminator either. Then they will punish the flesh of the man upon whom the holy spirit has come.[21]

"Then the angels and all the generations of the powers will use the name in error, asking, 'Where did it (the error) come from?' or 'Where did the words of deception, which all the powers have failed to discover, come from?'

> "Now the First Kingdom says of him that he came from
> ... a Spirit ... heaven.
> He was nurtured in the heavens.[22]
> He received the Glory[23] of that one and the Power.
> And he came to the bosom of his mother.
> And thus he came on the water.[24]

> "And the Second Kingdom says of him that
>   he came from a great prophet. And a bird came,
>   took the child who was born and carried him
>   to a high mountain.
> And he was nurtured by the bird of heaven.
> An angel came there and said to him,
>   'Arise! God has given you glory.'
> He received glory and strength.[25]
> And thus he came on the water.

> "The Third Kingdom says of him that
>   he came from a virgin womb. He was cast out
>   of the city, he and his mother; he was taken
>   to a desert place.
> He nurtured himself there.[26]
> He came and received glory and power.
> And thus he came on the water.

27.   The story is easily recognizable as a variant on the celebrated tale of Solomon and the Queen of the South (Sheba). See 1 Kings 10:1-13 and the legends which grew up in Ethiopia, preserved in the *Kebra Nagast* or 'Epic of the Kings.' The Ethiopian version claims that Solomon seduced the Queen and took her virginity: she bore him a son Menelek who founded the Ethiopian dynasty. Solomon's use of magical and demonic aid also features in the legend. The *Apocalypse* seems to complicate the story: the virgin escapes from Solomon's pursuit, and it is another virgin whom he takes instead. However, the original virgin gives birth to the wonder-child, the Illuminator. Oral versions of the Menelek story sometimes include two women and introduce the themes of dual appearance and look-alikes. The *Apocalypse of Adam* is much older than the known Ethiopic sources, and probably reproduces a primary form of the myth which has been adapted to nationalistic purposes in the *Kebra Nagast*.

28.   That is, Ethiopia. The Fourth Kingdom is thus identified, and the Illuminator appears as a spiritual leader and king, the spiritual though not the physical 'son of Solomon.' Historically, Solomon reigned c.1000 BC.

29.   The story is that of a sun-hero, who seems almost identical with the sun itself — the 'drop from heaven' which descends into the sea every evening and is 'brought forth again to heaven' every morning. Specifically, it is the story told of the Armenian sun-hero (later deified) Vahagn.

30.   Indian mythology relates that the seed (creative power) of Shiva, god of ascetics and yogis, was hidden in a lake full of lotus-flowers, watched over by the star-goddesses of the Pleiades. The Goddess, Parvati, drank from the lake and gave birth to Skanda. He was reared by the Pleiades and became a great yogi, who by his spiritual powers saved the world from the demon Taraka.

31.   According to Babylonian myth, the king-god Marduk was born from a drop of water in the *apsu* or abyss. He fought against the dragon Tiãmat and her brood, but was initially defeated and imprisoned in the dark interior of the world-mountain (that is, the underworld). He was rescued by the god Nabu, and subsequently defeated the dragon and ascended into heaven. It may appear inappropriate that a myth about a god should be applied to the Illuminator. However, in a yearly festival the king of Babylon enacted the part of Marduk in secret rites, while the great poem of Marduk's struggle and victory was recited. The Seventh Kingdom thus indicates an incarnation as a king in Babylon.

"The Fourth Kingdom says of him that
he came from a virgin ...

Solomon sought her, he and Phersalo and Sauel and his
armies which he had sent out. Solomon also sent out his army
of demons to seek the virgin. And they did not find the one
they sought; but the virgin who was given to them was the one
they brought. And Solomon took her.[27]

But the virgin conceived and gave birth to the child. She
nurtured him on the borders of the desert.[28] When he had been
nourished, he received glory and power from the seed from
which he had been begotten.

And thus he came on the water.

"And the Fifth Kingdom says of him that he came
from a drop from heaven.
He was thrown into the sea. The deep received him
and brought him forth to heaven.[29]
He received glory and power.
And thus he came on the water.

"And the Sixth Kingdom says of him ... she came down
to the world below in order to gather flowers.
She became pregnant with the desire of the flowers.
She gave birth to him in that place.
The angels of the flower-garden nurtured him.
He received glory there and power.[30]
And thus he came on the water.

"And the Seventh Kingdom says of him:
he is a drop. It came from heaven to earth.
Dragons brought him down to caves.
He became a child.
A spirit came to him and took him on high,
to the place from which the drop had come.[31]
He received glory there and power.
And thus he came on the water.

32.   The celebrated myth of the birth of Mithra from the rock, depicted in many
       of the Mithraic temples. Again, the import of the myth is not to make of the
       Illuminator a god, but to describe his initiatory 'birth.' In the Mithraic
       Mysteries the adept was reborn by analogy with the god, with whom at the
       highest grade he was virtually identified. Several ancient sources describe the
       reappearance of Zarathustra as Zaratas in the sixth century BC in Babylon,
       when he is said to have founded the Mithraic Mysteries.

33.   The story indicates the Orphic Mysteries of Greece, deriving from Orpheus,
       who was the son of a Muse. Themes of androgyny are important in the
       Orphic myths, although this particular myth is not known from elsewhere.
       Ancient sources know of a 'Greek Zoroaster' or 'Zoroaster of Proconnesus';
       and the island of Proconnesus in Ionian Greece was in fact a centre of Orphic
       Mysteries. There, then, the Illuminator was 'born.'

34.   The myth is that of the Egyptian creator-god Atum. Every Pharaoh was said
       to 'sit upon the throne of Atum,' and reigned in the power and authority of
       the creator. The Tenth Kingdom thus indicates a Pharaonic incarnation. Since
       the Eighth Kingdom points to the sixth century BC, this one must be late in
       Egyptian history.

35.   The myth of Gayomart, the Iranian first man — see above note 3.

36.   Another Egyptian myth. 'The two luminaries' or 'stars' is an Egyptian
       expression for the sun and moon (cf. Fowden 1986, p.57). This incarnation
       must be in post-Pharaonic times (cf. Tenth Kingdom). The great adept 'king
       Nechepso' is probably indicated — see above pp.188f.

"And the Eighth Kingdom says of him that a cloud
    came upon the earth and enveloped a rock.
He came from it.[32]
The angels who were above the cloud nurtured him.
He received glory and power there.
And thus he came on the water.

"And the Ninth Kingdom says of him that one
    of the nine Muses separated herself.
She withdrew to a high mountain and dwelt there
    for a time so as to desire herself alone,
    that she might become male-female.
She fulfilled her desire and conceived from her desire.
He was brought forth.[33]
The angels who were over the desire nurtured him.
And he received glory there and power.
And thus he came on the water.

"The Tenth Kingdom says of him that his god loved
    a cloud of desire.
He begot him in his hand, and cast upon the cloud
    above him some of the drop.
And he was born.[34]
He received glory and power there.
And thus he came on the water.

"And the Eleventh Kingdom says of him that
    the father desired his own daughter.
She herself became pregnant from her father.
She cast ... a tomb out in the wilderness.
The angel nourished him there.[35]
And thus he came on the water.

"The Twelfth Kingdom says of him that he came
    from the two luminaries. He was nurtured there.[36]
He received glory and power.
And thus he came on the water.

37.   After 'the twelve kingdoms' who derive from Ham and Japhet after the
       Flood, the mention of a Thirteenth Kingdom is unexpected (cf. above note 11
       however). The text avoids mentioning explicitly the sons of Shem, or Jewish
       people deriving from Noah's third son. This is a 'mystery' which we have to
       deduce in order to find the 'fulfilment.'

38.   An allusion to the Jewish circumlocution for God, the ruler of the universe:
       'He who spoke and it came into being' (see Genesis 1:3ff). In the *Book of Enoch*
       Chapters 48-49 we learn that God uttered one name even before he made the
       world: the name of the Messiah, which stays hidden however until the time
       of his earthly appearance. It is this name which 'receives a mandate' now.
       Zarathustra is born as the Messiah. Whereas the twelve Kingdoms and the
       incarnations they indicate all lie in the past for the actual author of the
       Apocalypse, this one belongs to the 'fulfilment' — the completion of the
       pattern in the future: see introductory remarks, above pp.211ff.

39.   The inclusion of a Fourteenth Statement is still more surprising than the
       mention of a Thirteenth Kingdom. It does not come from another Kingdom,
       and does not tell a birth-story. Thus it cannot be the indication of a further
       incarnation. Rather it gives the eternal dimension to the final or Messianic
       appearance, which is revealed to be much more than the traditional Jewish
       expectation. In the Messiah a consciousness of the 'Undefiled One of Truth,'
       that is, the Light itself, which is Ohrmazd's body as Truth is his spirit, is
       embodied. There are parallels with the last section of the *Testament of Levi*
       (above p.137f) and with *Enoch* 104:2 as well as Daniel 12:3. But the full
       uniting of the significance of the Thirteenth with the Fourteenth prophecies
       could only come about in Christianity, when 'the desire of those powers was
       fulfilled.'

40.   In Zoroastrian tradition, the last age of the world is preceded by a 'struggle
       against the powers,' that is, the powers of Ahriman, Spirit of Darkness. In the
       struggle human beings play a role. Afterwards comes the 'Transfiguration of
       the Earth,' or spiritualization of the material world and of humanity. The
       Apocalypse of Adam presents a vision recalling Zoroastrian ideas as well as
       Jewish apocalyptic.

41.   Resurrection is part of the spiritualization-process, as in the more 'evolution-
       ary' versions in Zoroastrianism: immortality is achieved, not bestowed.
       Contrast the usual apocalyptic idea that the dead will be raised, then judged
       and some rewarded with eternal life. Closest to the *Apocalypse* is the Iranian-
       influenced thought of the Essenes, where inner reality becomes outer reality,
       and the body becomes immortal 'as the soul is already immortal' (see above
       p.100 note 12).

42.   It seems likely that the harangue against the 'guardians of baptism,' who
       have defiled the living water, represents a development away from the kind
       of Essene ritualism we know from Qumran. The *Sacred Book of the Invisible
       Spirit* (closely related to the *Apocalypse of Adam*) records disputes about the
       place 'where Seth planted his seed,' or which community possesses his true

"And the Thirteenth Kingdom[37] says of him that
    every birth of their ruler is a word.
And this word received a mandate there.[38]
He received glory and power.
And thus he came on the water, in order that
    the desire of those powers might be fulfilled.
But the generation without a king over it says that
    God chose him from all the aeons.
He caused a knowledge of the Undefiled One of Truth
    to exist in him, which said:
'Out of an alien air, out of a great Aeon,
    the great Luminary has come forth.

And he has made the generation of those men whom he has chosen for himself shine, so that they should shine upon the whole aeon.'[39]

The Struggle against the Powers

"Then the seed, those who will receive his name upon the water and that of them all, will fight against the power.

    And a cloud of darkness will come upon them.[40]

"Then the peoples will cry out with a great voice, saying, 'Blessed is the soul of those men because they have known God with a knowledge of the truth! They shall live forever, because they have not been corrupted by their desire, along with the angels, nor have they accomplished the works of the powers,[41] but they have stood in his presence in a knowledge of God like light that has come forth from fire and blood.

"'But we have done every deed of the powers senselessly. We have boasted in the transgression of all our works. We have cried against the God of truth because all his works ... is eternal. These are against our spirits. For now we have known that our souls will die the death.'

"Then a voice came to them, saying,

"'Micheu and Michar and Mnesinous, who (are) over the holy baptism and the living water,[42] why were you crying out against the living God with lawless voices and tongues without law over them, and souls full of blood and foul deeds? You are

revelation: see Welburn 1991, pp.59-62. It too mentions the guardians by name (Codex III 64:15 and 64:20), apparently without criticism. The *Sacred Book* comes from a Christian stage of the tradition, but the names also occur in the Nag Hammadi work *Zostrianos* in Codex VIII, a non-Christian work with detailed discussion of initiatory baptism; and they occur once more in *Trimorphic Protennoia* from Codex XIII — a work which is intimately related to the Gospel of John (Welburn 1991, pp.261ff). Their baptism seems to stand at the point where pre-Christian Mysteries, Essenism, Gnosticism, and Christian origins meet!

43.   The 'high mountain' as a place of revelation is important in the Zoroastrian version of the last days, or Transfiguration. The Saoshyant or World-Saviour prophesied by Zarathustra was expected to be born on a mountain top when a star came to earth. Other versions say the prophecy telling of his birth was hidden on a mountain peak. The *Sacred Book* which, like our *Apocalypse*, is a revelation of Seth, claims that 'he placed it in the mountain that is called Charaxio, in order that, at the end of the times and eras, by the will of the divine Self-begotten ... it may come forth and reveal the incorruptible, holy race of the great Saviour' (Codex III 68:12-22). The form 'Charaxio' probably reproduces the Iranian name for the place where Ohrmazd and the Creator-Spirits appear to direct events at the Transfiguration of the Earth, that is, Mount Hukhairya. The *Apocalypse of Adam* is hostile to book-wisdom, and speaks not of finding a written revelation, but the actual presence of the divine or angelic beings upon the mountain, the 'rock of truth.'

44.   The knowledge, that is, is passed down by oral tradition or more accurately by living experience passed on from spiritual 'father' to 'son.' Those with the knowledge form a 'spiritual race' — the one which has no king over it and no physical bond of race or family. An element of this Gnostic community of scattered 'sparks' of light was certainly necessary to transform the Essene community of the 'true Israel' into the Christian community, united across cultural and racial divisions by inner connection as the 'Fourteenth Statement' foreshadows.

full of works that are not of the truth, but your ways are full of joy and rejoicing. Having defiled the water of life, you have drawn it within the will of the powers to whom you have been given to serve them.

"'And your thought is not like that of those men whom you persecute ... desire ... Their fruit does not wither. But they will be known up to the great aeons, because the words they have kept, of the God of the aeons, were not committed to the book, nor were they written. But angelic (beings) will bring them, whom all the generations of men will not know. For they will be on a high mountain, upon a rock of truth.[43] Therefore they will be named "The Words of Imperishability and Truth," for those who know the eternal God in wisdom of knowledge and teaching of angels forever, for he knows all things'."

These are the revelations which Adam made known to Seth his son. And his son taught his seed about them.[44] This is the hidden knowledge of Adam, which he gave to Seth, which is the holy baptism of those who know the eternal knowledge through those born of the word and the imperishable illuminators, who came from the holy seed: Yesseus, Mazareus, Yessedekeus, the Living Water.

The Apocalypse of Adam

7. *The Book of the Blessed* by Justin the Gnostic

In his wide-ranging *Refutation of Heresies*, Hippolytus of Rome, who gave us the summary and quotations from Simon's *Great Annunciation*, has preserved the substance of another extraordinary book: Justin's *Baruch*. It takes its name from a mysterious angelic being who appears repeatedly and speaks to men; but the designation is no more than the Hebrew word for 'the blessed one,' and does not yet reveal who he really is. We may more correctly render the title therefore *The Book of the Blessed*.

Nothing is known about Justin, its author, save what we can infer from Hippolytus and the contents of his book. From them we gather that he was a Christian Gnostic, who taught a system of cosmic mythology involving three primordial Beings. The highest God is called simply 'the Good,' and he is distinct from the Creator-God, called by the biblical title Elohim. And there is also from the beginning a feminine Earth-Spirit known as Edem, whose name is to be connected both with Eden or the state of Paradise, and with the kabbalistic *'adamah* (Earth) that forms part of the earthly Adam's soul. The celebrated kabbalistic scholar Gershom Scholem noticed that Justin's ideas belong to the stream of Jewish esotericism and that, like much else in the *Book of the Blessed* 'this tellurian soul of Adam stems from older Jewish speculation.'[*] However, Justin's teaching was not in any narrow sense Jewish, because it included an account of Christ and refers to the Gospel of Luke, and it mentions a more obscure mission of the Blessed One to the gentiles through the agency of 'the prophet Hercules.' His book was extant in the second century AD, but clearly has its roots further back. Its form of Christianity is one which drew its categories from the Mysteries and from the esoteric Judaism that was in touch with them — from that world we have been exploring throughout this book.

We can glean some of the details about its esoteric background from the later parts of the book, in which we hear how Elohim, the

---

[*] G. Scholem, *On the Kabbalah and its Symbolism*, New York 1969, p.164.

Creator, desires to ascend into the higher, purely spiritual regions and in doing so finds himself in the presence of the Good — the higher divinity previously unknown to him. A light now shines upon him that is far brighter than the light he made in the created world, and he hears a divine voice which promises that he will know 'things that eye hath not seen, and ear hath not heard, and which have not entered into the heart of man,' i.e. purely spiritual Mysteries. He swears an initiatory oath. In fact, as Geo Widengren the comparative religionist points out, he is acting as the prototype of the pneumatic, the initiate in the Mystery to which Justin belonged:

> We observe how the Pneumatic, who has been initiated
> into the mysteries and made perfect, in everything is
> acting with Elohim as his pattern. He swears the same
> oath, he enters like him into the presence of the Good One
> ... He drinks of the living water, in which the Pneumatic is
> said to have his ablution (Hippolytus, V,27:3). However, it
> is expressly stated that he drinks of this living water,
> which nevertheless is styled a *loutron* (bath) and which is
> mentioned as the water in which Elohim underwent his
> purification, as well as that wherein the Pneumatic gets
> his bath of purification. The baptism in this water
> accordingly means at the same time an ablution in the
> water of Life and a drinking thereof, hence a kind of
> communion.*

We recognize rites essentially similar to those of the Mandeans (which incidentally also involve drinking the water), constituting a pattern of cosmic initiation through baptism, with a symbolism of light, and so on. The description looks back to the Near Eastern complex of ideas about the water of life, which Justin terms 'a bath, a fountain of life-giving, bubbling water' suggesting that baptism took place in 'living' or flowing water as among the Essenes and other of the baptizing groups — but also looking forward to the 'bubbling spring' from which Thomas drinks (*Gospel of Thomas* 13) and to the water 'welling up to eternal life' (Gospel of John 4:14) and the 'communion' of Christianity.

Contact with several different Mysteries must be assumed in

---

* Geo Widengren, in *The Saviour God*. Essays presented to E.O. James, Manchester 1963, p.211.

order to explain the details of Justin's teaching. For instance, Edem is said to have a double form: a woman to the middle, but below a coiling snake. Herodotus mentions a Scythian snake-woman, but despite Hippolytus' satisfaction in deriving Edem from the Greek historian it is highly unlikely that she really comes from there. Much more convincing is a recent argument that her form is that of Isis-Thermouthis, the Egyptian Mystery-goddess in a special cultic representation. Whether or not Justin came from Egypt (a disputed point), therefore, he seems to have had inside knowledge of Egyptian Mysteries that were not known, so far as we are aware, outside Egypt itself.

More important to the mythological system as a whole are ideas that we have met before in our studies, reflecting the influence in Jewish Mystery-circles of the thought of Iran. The supra-cosmic light, brighter than any created radiance, which Elohim/the initiate sees, for example, recalls the Iranian divinity of Light. Coupled with the name of the highest God, i.e. 'the Good,' it is a sure sign of Zoroastrian interest in the shaping of Justin's work. 'There can be little doubt,' says M. Marcovich, 'that the Just God is the God of Law, Retribution and final Justice, while the Good God is best explained as an *alien, extra-cosmic, unknowable god*, say, the Iranian Ahura Mazda (or Ohrmazd).'* The combination of Iranian with Jewish concepts no longer surprises us since the discovery of the Dead Sea Scrolls showed us the extent of the influence which Iran exerted on the new Mysteries within Judaism. The deciphering of the *Apocalypse of Adam*, which indicates the future destiny of the reappearing Prophet of Light or Illuminator, goes far toward explaining the motive behind the meeting of the two different traditions. And in fact it is the *Apocalypse of Adam* which for the first time enables us to make fuller sense of Justin's altogether remarkable myth.

Thus the marriage of Heaven and Earth which produces Man (Adam) in the *Book of the Blessed* recalls the Iranian myth of Man (Gayomart) which is applied by the Eleventh Kingdom to the Illuminator. Gayomart was the child of Heaven (Ohrmazd) and Spendarmat (Earth). In his eleventh incarnation, therefore, the Illuminator was restoring the primal Glory of Man before he fell — or better, before he was divided, and lost his original nature under

---

* Marcovich, M. *Studies in Graeco-Roman Religion and Gnosticism*, Leiden 1988, p.95.

the impact of Ahriman. The narrative part of the *Apocalypse of Adam* uses this idea to reinterpret the biblical version of Adam and Eve, originally one but 'divided in great wrath' by the Demiurge. In Justin, it is Heaven and Earth (Elohim and Edem) who are separated and bring about the loss of Paradise: but since each of them is present as soul and spirit in Adam their child, the myth amounts to virtually the same thing. At any rate, we are witnessing the interpretation of the Genesis-story in essentially the same terms. The account seems different also in that Elohim ('Father of all created things' and identified with Heaven) is the father of Justin's Man — but once Elohim has united himself with the Good, the myth of his efforts to rescue the scattered sparks of his spirit here below in humanity and draw them to follow him above likewise becomes identical in their implication with the *Apocalypse*.

The question arises therefore as to the relationship between the angelic messenger Baruch ('the Blessed') and the messenger of Light, the Illuminator in the *Apocalypse*. Is it possible that they are the same? That they are both, in short, Zarathustra?

The Zarathustra-legend, echoed by the *Apocalypse of Adam*, attributes to Zarathustra a heavenly origin and pre-existence in the divine realm. In Jewish terms, that might well be described as an 'angelic' state. Moreover, Iranian thought makes great use of the notion of a 'messenger,' or 'apostle,' in relation to spiritual teachers — and 'angel,' of course, means 'messenger,' even though the implications of the term are somewhat different; it might have seemed the most appropriate term that could be found in the circumstances. The brilliant (if sometimes over-enthusiastic) scholar R. Reitzenstein already recognized this idea earlier this century, and concluded that 'what has happened is that Baruch actually has been identified, in a Jewish-Gnostic circle, with Zarathustra and has been viewed as "the emissary" and son of God.'* But he did not yet have the *Apocalypse of Adam* — only late reflections of its lost teaching, in which Baruch ('the Blessed' Being) had been confused with another Baruch, the scribe of Jeremiah! Outside the esoteric circles where the teachings were understood, all sorts of confusions were possible and perhaps inevitable. Eventually we even meet the idea that Jeremiah's scribe Baruch apostatized from Judaism and wrote the Zoroastrian scriptures. But from all such nonsense Justin's *Book of*

---

* R. Reitzenstein, *Die hellenistischen Mysterienreligionen*, Leipzig 1920, p.60.

the Blessed is wholly free, and now that we possess the *Apocalypse of Adam* we are able to recognize its version of the mission of Zarathustra in its original purity and power, shorn of the later misunderstandings which corrupted it.

The enemy of the Blessed One — Zarathustra — in his repeated missions to Earth to rescue the spirit trapped in humanity is Edem, and the 'angels' which she too possesses. Her antitype to Baruch, the third angel, is Naas whose name clearly reproduces the Semitic word for serpent, *nahash*. Divided from Elohim and resentful of his parting from her, Edem has become a vindictive power which leads her to be identified with many mythological figures and some biblical ones. She sends Naas to thwart the work of the Blessed One. In the legends of the Kingdoms in the *Apocalypse of Adam*, there are frequent references too to the fight against dragons, etc. and we may see in Naas not only the 'subtle serpent' of Genesis, but the mythic opponents of the sun-hero in many of the ancient mythologies and Mysteries.

One serpent-slayer in mythology was Hercules, who in other respects is also a typical sun-hero. By the time of early Christianity, certainly, his twelve labours had come to be interpreted in up-to-date astrological terms as referring to the signs of the zodiac. But Justin's mention of him as a 'prophet' to the Gentiles seems to do more than invoke the general notion of a sun-hero. A specific reference is clearly intended which eludes us — or at least did so until the find of the amazing *Apocalypse of Adam*.

In the light of the *Apocalypse* we soon spot the allusion: the twelve heroic acts of the sun-hero are being used to characterize in pagan Mystery-language the twelve incarnations of the hero of Light. As an agent of Baruch-Zarathustra, this Hercules however can rightly be called a Prophet, and the *Apocalypse of Adam* uses the term (see the Second Kingdom) in exactly that sense for one who bears heroic testimony to the Light. And the *Apocalypse* enables us to identify the connotations of 'Hercules' exactly too. For the reference is not to the ancient Greek hero, but to one of those other figures whom the Greeks in their way identified with their own gods. Classical writers mention, in fact, a 'Syrian Hercules,' an 'Egyptian Hercules,' and so forth. In the *Apocalypse of Adam*, the Fifth Kingdom told the birth-story of Vahagn — and he is one of those whom the Greeks called a Hercules. Indeed, the tale told of him is the one which features in the *Book of the Blessed*, the tale of the hero's temporary subjection by the queen who has taken him captive, Omphale (interpreted as a guise of the vindictive Edem). In the eastern version, Vahagn is subdued by Astlik whose name means 'the Little Star,' an epithet of the love-and war goddess Ishtar, whose planet is Venus. And the story appears again in the Zoroastrian scriptures. For Verethragna (= Vahagn) is mentioned in the *Vahman Yasht* as a 'Prince,' to whom are applied prophecies similar to the ones about the reappearing Prophet or the Saoshyant. But for a period of thirty years he is held in subjection by a Woman, interpreted astrologically as the influence of Venus. His time will come, however: 'when the star Jupiter comes to its culminating point and casts Venus down, the sovereignty comes to the Prince.' When that happens he will be made manifest as what he is — the bearer of the Glory, the power of Light, the prophet Zarathustra.

The *Apocalypse of Adam* also solves the mystery which shocked the pious Hippolytus and has offended some modern scholars too, making them argue that Justin's book must have been interpolated or misrepresented in Hippolytus' source. For nothing in it has caused so much scandal as the identification of the Good, the Light, with Priapus, the phallic god of fertility. 'What a demeaning role for a manifestation of the Iranian Ahura Mazda!' (M. Marcovich — who nevertheless believes, rightly, that the identification is Justin's).

The explanation lies once more in the ancient habit of recognizing in foreign gods the essential qualities of one's own, and calling them by familiar names. We need to ask who lies behind the classical name. And the *Apocalypse of Adam* furnishes the answer. The Sixth Kingdom describes an incarnation of the Illuminator in terms derived from India. He is born as Skanda, son of the mysterious and great god Shiva, Lord of ascetics and of lovers, master of insight, of paradoxes and contradictions, the Destroyer of illusion. That would make him a great yogi, able to redirect the energies which the techniques of meditation are intended not to abolish but to transform. Energies such as those of sex are tremendous powers which may either enslave or liberate. Yoga, in the cult of Lord Shiva, is a way to control our energies in order to achieve liberation. In representing him in the form of the *lingam*, the phallus, and showing his ecstatic union with the Goddess, the Indian cults are not forgetting his ascetic and world-denying nature. That is exactly the paradox of the myths about him. It is our minds which are inadequate, which are locked in their single categories and find only 'contradiction,' not reality which is at fault. From Shiva's divine perspective, that of ultimate reality, the creative force in the *lingam* is at the same time the manifestation of the creative spirit, and world-denial converges with passionate affirmation of the world in every aspect.

The unexpected apparition of the phallic Priapus is not a demeaning of the Light, therefore, but an expression of all-inclusive affirmation drawn from the East. He is the Lord Shiva, the highest and most mysterious aspect of the Hindu God. The *Book of the Blessed,* like the other documents assembled here, draws on a world-wide range of religious experience before pointing to 'Jesus, the Son of Man' as its fulfilment. That breadth was, tragically, not grasped by orthodox Christianity. But it can be grasped once more by us today; it should be a power which immeasurably deepens our vision, for only in that way can it bring us closer together.

Source: report on the teachings of Justin the Gnostic, in Hippolytus, Refutation of All Heresies *V, 26:1–27:5. Translated from the Greek by J.H. MacMahon.*

1.   It is characteristic of Gnostic systems that they trace back the world we know to certain pre-existing roots or principles. There is some similarity to early Greek philosophy in this, but the difference of emphasis is enormous. In fact, the Gnostics contrast their view with the Greek starting-point, which posits the unformed matter which makes up the world we know and explains its present condition by means of an organizing principle (that is, what is sometimes called chaos and form or idea): 'Though all the gods of the world and men say that nothing existed prior to Chaos, I shall demonstrate that they all erred, since they do not know the structure of Chaos, nor its root ...,' says the author of *On the Origin of the World* (Codex II 97:24-29). The Gnostic goes back to something radically prior to the world we know. The model for this is most likely Iranian dualism: some Iranian theologies add to Light and Darkness the Void (Vayu) which originally separated them. 'The Good' in particular suggests the pure goodness of the Zoroastrian Ohrmazd — cf. the introductory remarks above.

2.   On 'Edem,' see introductory comments. Hippolytus' suggestion that her form comes from the story in Herodotus, *Histories* IV, 8-10 is unconvincing. Most plausible is R. van den Broek's suggestion that she is a form of Isis (above p.237).

3.   The name of the Creator-god in Genesis 1. Hence we have to do here again with an esoteric interpretation of the *ma'aseh bereshit* or account of creation (cf. Simon, *Poimandres,* etc). Themes such as the 'paradisal' condition when the sexes were undivided are dramatized especially on the cosmic level as the union of Elohim and Edem, who are also present in earthly man. Thus Justin comes particularly close to the Iranian myth of Ohrmazd-Heaven and Spandarmat-Earth who beget Man (cf. *Apocalypse of Adam*). Human origins are preceded, however, by the generation of the cosmos and the twelve angels who constitute the zodiac, together with their earthly reflections.

4.   The list of angels corresponding to the signs is regrettably incomplete, but probably uses the same system as the Ophite Diagram of the Gnostics (preserved in Origen, *Against Celsus* VI, 24-38), commencing with Leo. The archangels Michael, Gabriel, etc. stand at the points of the 'fixed cross.' The other names also represent angels or aspects of divinity, e.g. Essaddaeus = El Shaddai; for Amen cf. Revelation 3:14; Baruch = the Blessed; the idea that the divine names actually refer to angels or to specific forms of manifestation of God is, of course, one of the foundation-stones of the kabbala or Jewish esoteric tradition.

5.   In many Gnostic systems the pre-existing angels or aeons are grouped in pairs, likened to male and female and called *syzygies* ('unions'); *syzygy* is also used to describe the union of the soul with the spirit or higher self in the adept through *gnosis*. The Gnostic version of the Fall is usually associated

❋ On the Teachings of Justin the Gnostic ❋

Elohim and Edem

Justin makes the following statement. There are three unbegotten principles of the universe, two male and one female.[1] Of the male principles, however, a certain one is denominated the Good, and it alone is called after this manner, and possesses a power of prescience concerning the universe. But the other is father of all begotten things, devoid of prescience, and invisible. And the female principle is devoid of prescience, passionate, two-minded, two-bodied, in every respect answering the description of the girl in the legend of Herodotus, as far as the groin a virgin, and in the parts below resembling a snake, as Justin says. But this girl is styled Edem and Israel.[2] And these principles of the universe are, he says, roots and fountains from which existing things have been produced, but that there was not anything else. The Father, then who is devoid of prescience, beholding that half-woman Edem, passed into a concupiscent desire for her. But this Father, he says, is called Elohim.[3] Not less did Edem also long for Elohim, and the mutual passion brought them together into the one nuptial couch of love. And from such an intercourse the Father generates out of Edem unto himself twelve angels. And the names of the angels begotten by the Father are these: Michael, Amen, Baruch, Gabriel, Esaddaeus ...[4] And of the maternal angels which Edem brought forth, the names in like manner have been subjoined, and they are as follows: Babel, Achamoth, Naas, Bel, Belias, Satan, Sael, Adonaeus, Leviathan, Pharao, Carcamenos, and Lathen.[5]

Of these twenty-four angels the paternal ones are associated with the Father, and do all things according to His will; and the maternal angels are associated with Edem the Mother. And the multitude of all these angels together is Paradise, he says, concerning which Moses speaks: "God planted a garden in with the breaking of this male-female balance, with catastrophic results. The names of Edem's angels are a mixture of divine and demonic and the un-recognizable. Achamoth = Wisdom, or Sophia, who plays an important role in many Gnostic systems and may have done so in parts of Justin's which Hippolytus does not quote.

6.   Genesis 2:8.

7.   In Jewish esoteric interpretation the plural name Elohim (cf. here 'angels of Elohim') is taken to refer to the separate aspects or angels of God (see *Zohar* 64b).

8.   Adam is thus the synthesis, like the Adam-Eve of the *Apocalypse of Adam*. G. Scholem relates the ideas in Justin to Jewish esoteric traditions connected with the golem and with the woman who existed before Eve was made from Adam's rib. 'It is maintained, surprisingly enough, in traditions from the second century, that Genesis 1:24: "Let the earth bring forth living soul," refers to the spirit *(ruah)* of the first Adam, which accordingly is not a pneuma blown into him, but an earth-spirit, a vital potency dwelling in the earth' (Scholem 1969, pp.163f). He admits however that: 'Here as so often the Aggadah goes back to ideas far removed from the Biblical text.' Behind the version in the *Apocalypse of Adam* we can in fact discern the Iranian myth of the marriage of Heaven and Earth and their child Man or Gayomart. ('Aggadah' = the traditional Jewish legends, often read or told at festivals).

9.   Genesis 1:28.

10.   Eve here is produced alongside Adam 'in like manner' and like him possesses a soul and spirit from earth and heaven respectively, just as he does. The biblical subordination of Eve to Adam as produced from his rib is not mentioned. Hence we should not read the 'dowry' myth as expressing Eve's inferiority. The point is primarily that, as in Hermetic thought, marriage reproduces the state of paradise or original wholeness — a spiritual mystery of which outer union is no more than an image. Elohim also gives his own power, his own spirit, to the human 'seal' of their union; and the aim was not to deprive Edem of her power but to 'replenish the earth,' that is, Edem herself, through mutual giving and receiving. Cf. p.251 below: 'For the soul is Edem, but the spirit Elohim, and each of these exists in all men, both females and males.'

Eden towards the east,"[6] that is, towards the face of Edem, that Edem might behold the garden — that is, the angels — continually. Allegorically the angels are styled trees of this garden, and the tree of life is the third of the paternal angels — Baruch. And the tree of the knowledge of good and evil is the third of the maternal angels — Naas. For so, says Justin, one ought to interpret the words of Moses, observing, "Moses said these things disguisedly, from the fact that all do not attain the truth." And, he says, Paradise being formed from the conjugal joy of Elohim and Edem, the angels of Elohim receiving from the most beauteous earth, that is, not from the portion of Edem resembling a monster, but from the parts above the groin of human shape, and gentle in aspect, make man out of the earth.[7] But out of the parts resembling a monster are produced wild beasts, and the rest of the animal creation. They made man, therefore, as a symbol of the unity and love subsisting between them; and they depute their own powers unto him, Edem the soul, but Elohim the spirit.[8]

And the man Adam is produced as some actual seal and memento of love, and as an everlasting emblem of the marriage of Edem and Elohim. And in like manner also Eve was produced, he says, as Moses has described, an image and emblem as well as a seal, to be preserved for ever, of Edem. And in like manner also a soul was deposited in Eve, an image from Edem, but a spirit from Elohim. And there were given to them commandments, "Be fruitful, and multiply, and replenish the earth,"[9] that is, Edem; for so he wishes that it had been written. For the entire of the power belonging unto herself, Edem conferred upon Elohim as a sort of nuptial dowry. Whence, he says, from imitation of that primary marriage up to this day, women bring a dowry to their husbands, complying with a certain divine and paternal law that came into existence on the part of Edem towards Elohim.[10]

And when all things were created as has been described by Moses — both heaven and earth, and the things therein — the twelve angels of the Mother were divided into four principles, and each fourth part of them is called a river — Phison, and

11.   Again we meet the mystique of the great rivers — cf. p.173f above. As among
       the Mandeans, the rivers are treated as images of the heavenly water such as
       the Jordan — their name for any flowing water in which baptism is
       performed. Later (pp.255f below) we learn that the archetypal baptism of
       Elohim takes place in the waters 'above the firmament.' These waters are the
       ethereal formative forces, which are conceived as flowing down (as here) into
       the realm of 'the Mother,' and as ascending (baptism of Elohim). When
       flowing down into the Mother, they are described by Simonian and other
       Gnostics as forming the child in the womb; when flowing upward, they bring
       about 'rebirth,' or spiritual generation.

12.   Lit. 'satrapic' — based on the analogy of the Persian regional governors or
       satraps.

13.   The 'angels' are clearly connected with the zodiac. However, Babel is
       identified with Venus, and the description of them as 'moving around'
       suggests that they are primarily the planets which 'rule' over particular signs
       and at intervals enter them.

14.   Elohim, the Creator, is identified with the 'upward tending,' or spiritualizing
       power. He becomes, after completing the creation, the archetype of the
       initiate who aspires to a knowledge of what is higher than the created world.
       This identification is characteristic of the earliest forms of Gnosticism. The
       theme of 'mounting aloft' goes back to the Mysteries of Babylon (cf. the
       Mandean Mystery) and the ascent of the cosmic mountain, as did the creator-
       god Marduk after his conquest of chaos and the dragons. The ascent theme
       connects with the Genesis-account through Genesis 2:3: see Rudolf Steiner
       (1959, p.133) for a description of spiritual and cosmic processes underlying
       these events.

15.   Marcovich suggests that this extra-cosmic light, far surpassing the created
       light made by Elohim, may be the old Iranian or Vedic *rokah*, the supernatu-
       ral radiance of the gods (1988, p.103). Ohrmazd's nature is the Boundless
       Light, which existed from eternity, according to the *Bundahishn*. The initiate's
       experience of cosmic ascent was likewise one of 'illumination,' on the pattern
       of Elohim's vision. In the Mithraic Mysteries, water-rites were combined with
       symbolism of illumination for the grade of *nymphus* or 'Bride.'

16.   Psalm 117:19.

17.   Psalm 118:20.

18.   This Mystery-formula is also cited by Paul, 1 Corinthians 2:9. It is attributed
       to Jesus in the *Gospel of Thomas* 17, and there are allusions or parallels to it in
       apocalyptic writings, but its original source is unknown.

19.   Psalm 110:1.

20.   A typical Gnostic theme is that of the scattered sparks of light or spirit which
       have been cast into the world and are to be 'gathered' back into the
       archetypal, spiritual Man. The practical consequence of this Gnostic idea has
       sometimes been extreme asceticism: however, here it is emphasised that
       Edem has her rightful place in the picture, so that destroying the earthly
       nature in order to liberate the spirit would be a violation which cannot unite
       us to the Good.

Gehon, and Tigris, and Euphrates, as, he says, Moses states.[11] These twelve angels being mutually connected, go about into four parts, and manage the world. Holding from Edem a sort of viceregal[12] authority over the world. But they do not always continue in the same places, but move around as if in a circular dance, changing place after place, and at set times and intervals retiring to the localities subject to themselves.[13] And when Phison holds sway over places, famine, distress, and affliction prevail in that part of the earth, for the battalion of these angels is niggardly. In like manner also there belong to each part of the four, according to the power and nature of each, evil times and hosts of diseases. And continually, according to the dominion of each fourth part, this stream of evil, just like a current of rivers, careers, according to the will of Edem, uninterruptedly around the world. And from some cause of this description has arisen the necessity of evil.

When Elohim had prepared and created the world as a result from joint pleasure, He wished to ascend up to the elevated parts of heaven, and to see that not anything of what pertained to the created laboured under deficiency. And He took His Own angels with Him, for His nature was to mount aloft,[14] leaving Edem below: for inasmuch as she was earth, she was not disposed to follow upward her spouse. Elohim, then, coming to the highest part of heaven above, and beholding a light superior to that which He Himself had created,[15] exclaimed, "Open me the gates, that entering in I may acknowledge the Lord; for I considered Myself to be Lord."[16] A voice was returned to Him from the light, saying, "This is the gate of the Lord: through this the righteous enter in."[17] And immediately the gate was opened, and the Father, without the angels, entered, advancing towards the Good One, and beheld "what eye hath not seen, and ear hath not heard, and what hath not entered into the heart of man to conceive."[18] Then the Good One says to him, "Sit thou on my right hand."[19] And the Father says to the Good One, "Permit me, Lord, to overturn the world which I have made, for my spirit is bound to men. And I wish to receive it back from them."[20] Then the Good One

21.   Cf. the seductive Nature of the Hermetic *Poimandres* (above p.197f) and the
       Gnostic myth of the 'seduction of the archons' which appears in variant
       forms in many systems, including Manichaeism. It is connected with the
       creation of earthly (sometimes Fallen) Man, the separation of the sexes etc.
       It seems more ambiguous than the biblical version, reflecting the Gnostic
       viewpoint. For the Gnostic, everything hinges on recognizing the truth of the
       situation: not to understand the world into which we have been 'thrown' is
       to be imprisoned by it; to recognize our condition is already to transcend it.

22.   That is, the Hebrew *nahash*, 'serpent.' Cf. Introductory notes (p.239).

23.   That is, the pre-existing 'emissary,' Zarathustra, who was created in the
       condition of 'the Glory,' the radiance of pure spiritual being, according to
       Zoroastrianism and the *Apocalypse of Adam* (First Kingdom). In Justin he is
       apparently only one out of a circle of twelve. Whether he has any link with
       the 'Third Emissary' of Manichaeism remains unclear, though certainly
       Zarathustra was highly important in Mani's understanding of the different
       streams in the history of salvation. On the name, or rather title Baruch, 'the
       Blessed,' see p.238.

24.   The manifestation of the Blessed One in Paradise is surprising and seems to
       contradict his identity with Zarathustra — cf. introductory section. However,
       the key to understanding lies in the concept of the Glory.
           Gayomart or primal Man-Woman, according to Zoroastrian myth echoed
       in the *Apocalypse of Adam*, possessed the Glory or spiritual radiance which
       denotes his quality of kingship or prophetic and priestly power. The Glory
       was transmitted to the first human pair, but they forfeited it through sin.
       Only a few received the Glory in subsequent times: kings (who ruled by
       cosmic authority, on the analogy of the divine world-order which they
       represented to men) or spiritual teachers. The full revelation of the Glory in
       fact only came through Zarathustra, whose spiritual essence, created before
       the world began in heaven, was the Glory in the spiritual world. Those who
       possessed the Glory in the fullest sense were Zarathustra's 'spiritual sons' (=
       reincarnations), the Saoshyants. In the appearances of Zarathustra, the nature
       of Gayomart is restored, so that we find the remarkable statement in
       Zoroastrian writings: 'The religion of Zarathustra is the nature of Gayomart,
       and the nature of Gayomart is the religion of Zarathustra' — *Bundahishn*
       XXXV,1. See the further discussion in F.H. Borsch 1967, pp.76ff.
           In Justin's *Book of the Blessed*, Baruch is the angel of Elohim, that is, of the
       spirit which is actually in Adam and Eve. He is the Glory which is present
       in paradisal Man — and that Glory, lost by humanity in general, appears
       again in its essence in Zarathustra.

replies to him, "No evil canst thou do while thou art with me, for both thou and Edem made the world as a result of conjugal joy. Permit Edem, then, to hold possession of the world as long as she wishes; but do you remain with me." Then Edem, knowing that she had been deserted by Elohim, was seized with grief, and placed beside herself her own angels. And she adorned herself after a comely fashion, if by any means Elohim, passing into concupiscent desire, might descend from heaven to her.[21]

The Sending of Baruch
When, however, Elohim, overpowered by the Good One, no longer descended to Edem, Edem commanded Babel, which is Venus, to cause adulteries and dissolutions of marriages among men. And she adopted this expedient in order that, as she had been divorced from Elohim, so also the spirit of Elohim, which is in men, being wrung with sorrow, might be punished by such separations, and might undergo precisely the sufferings which were being endured by the deserted Edem. And Edem gives great power to her third angel, Naas,[22] that by every species of punishment she might chasten the spirit of Elohim which is in men, in order that Elohim, through the spirit, might be punished for having deserted his spouse, in violation of the agreements entered into between them. Elohim the father seeing these things, sends forth Baruch, the third angel[23] among his own, to succour the spirit that is in all men. Baruch then coming, stood in the midst of the angels of Edem, that is, in the midst of Paradise,[24] for Paradise is the angels, in the midst of whom he stood, and issued to the man the following injunction: "Of every tree that is in Paradise thou mayest freely eat, but thou mayest not eat of the tree of the knowledge of good and evil," which is Naas. Now the meaning is, that he should obey the rest of the eleven angels of Edem, for the eleven possess passions, but are not guilty of transgression. Naas, however, has committed sin, for he went in unto Eve, deceiving her, and debauched her; and such an act as this is a violation of law. He, however, likewise went in unto Adam, and had unnatural

25.   Another surprising connection: see Rudolf Steiner (1965, pp.63ff) on the
       nature of the 'Sun-mystery' transmitted from Zarathustra through Moses as
       a spiritual event. Justin presumably intends us to understand that this 'Sun-
       mystery' is the inner meaning of the Mosaic laws, grasped by the initiated,
       since 'Moses said these things disguisedly, from the fact that all do not attain
       the truth' (p.245 above). Steiner describes the source of the revelation as the
       'etheric body' of Zarathustra.

26.   Or better: 'Father Elohim had fled,' that is, to the Good.

27.   The prophets carry on the revelation to Moses; but in the orthodox interpreta-
       tion of the Bible, Justin suggests, the spiritual meaning has become overlaid
       by the external dead letter, and the worldly concerns which afflict any
       religion. In these he sees the corrupting spirit of Naas. The notion that the
       meaning of the biblical texts could only be known to illuminated interpreta-
       tion is central to the commentaries and prophetic collections of the Essenes
       in the texts from Qumran (the 'Dead Sea Scrolls.') The Gnostics developed
       the concept of unconscious meaning considerably further. Many of the
       techniques of interpretation originate in the methods of interpreting dreams,
       oracles and so on, in the Mysteries.

28.   The *Apocalypse of Adam* uses the term 'prophet' to refer to a hero who
       manifests the Glory, such as the father of Zal (Second Kingdom). Hercules is
       the name for a sun-hero of a certain type and stage of initiation. The hero
       Vahagn (Verethragna, etc). was a Hercules-figure who appears as one of the
       incarnations of the Illuminator in the *Apocalypse of Adam*.

29.   The twelve labours of the classical Hercules came to be connected with the
       signs of the zodiac, and that idea is here applied to the twelve angels of
       Edem.

30.   The Omphale myth is retold in the Armenian legends about their 'Hercules,'
       Vahagn. The Fifth Kingdom in the *Apocalypse of Adam* indicates that he is an
       incarnation of the Illuminator, and stories about him are told in the
       Zoroastrian *Vahman Yasht*. He is to be dominated by a Woman, until his star
       (Jupiter) is exalted above hers (Venus).

intercourse with him; and this is itself also a piece of turpitude, whence have arisen adultery and sodomy.

Henceforward vice and virtue were prevalent among men, arising from a single source — that of the Father. For the Father having ascended to the Good One, points out from time to time the way to those desirous of ascending to him likewise. After having, however, departed from Edem, he caused an originating principle of evil for the spirit of the Father that is in men. Baruch therefore was despatched to Moses,[25] and through him spoke to the children of Israel, that they might be converted unto the Good One. But the third angel Naas, by the soul which came from Edem upon Moses, as also upon all men, obscured the precepts of Baruch, and caused his own peculiar injunctions to be hearkened unto. For this reason the soul is arrayed against the spirit, and the spirit against the soul. For the soul is Edem, but the spirit Elohim, and each of these exists in all men, both females and males. Again, after these occurrences, Baruch was sent to the Prophets, that through the Prophets the spirit that dwelleth in men might hear words of warning, and might avoid Edem and the wicked fiction, just as the Father had fled from Elohim.[26] In like manner also by the prophets, Naas, by a similar device, through the soul that dwells in man, along with the spirit of the Father, enticed away the prophets, and all of them were allured after him, and did not follow the words of Baruch, which Elohim enjoined.[27]

Ultimately Elohim selected Hercules, an uncircumcised prophet,[28] and sent him to quell the twelve angels of Edem, and release the Father from the twelve angels, those wicked ones of the creation. These are the twelve conflicts of Hercules which Hercules underwent, in order, from first to last, namely, Lion, and Hydra, and Boar, and the others successively.[29] For the say that these are the names of them among the Gentiles, and they have been derived with altered denominations from the energy of the maternal angels. When he seemed to have vanquished his antagonists, Omphale (now she is Babel or Venus)[30] clings to him and entices away Hercules, and divests him of his power, namely, the commands of Baruch which

31.   The Armenian versions are also pessimistic: Vahagn was not able to overcome the goddess Astlik ('Little Star,' a euphemism for the decadent pagan goddess Ishtar whose cult persisted despite the influence of Zoroastrianism). The *Vahman Yasht* throws its hopes on the distant future and the final coming of the Saoshyant.

32.   Luke 1:5.

33.   The situation suggests the Lukan nativity scene with its shepherds on the hills; the background is provided by the closely analogous calling of Levi, the archetypal Priest, in the *Testaments of the Twelve Patriarchs* (see p.127 above). Further discussion of the implications in Welburn 1991, pp.132-34. The Jesus of Luke's Gospel suddenly shows marvellous wisdom at the age of twelve (Luke 2:41-51) evidently because he was united at that age with the spirit of the Illuminator, or Blessed One.

34.   In the prototype of the scene in the *Testament of Levi*, the message is also followed by a heavenly ascension during which Levi learns the secrets of God. Jesus fulfils the pattern, however, not by having a vision, but by the actual events of his death and resurrection.

35.   Jesus thus reveals the true message which has been hidden and overlaid in the scriptures of Moses and the prophets. The idea that the Messiah would solve all the apparent contradictions in the Law is well-known in Judaism. Many of the Essene 'illuminated' interpretations actually point to the Messiah as their meaning.

36.   A possible rendering of the Greek of John 19:26.

37.   Another surprising turn in the narrative. On the meaning of this identification, cf. introductory remarks pp.240f.

38.   The name Priapus is ingeniously made to mean the pre-existence of the Good by being derived from the Greek for 'fashion before' *(prin-poiein)*.

Elohim issued. And in place of this power, Babel envelopes him in her own peculiar robe, that is, in the power of Edem, who is the power below; and in this way the prophecy of Hercules remained unfulfilled, and his works.[31]

Jesus and the Mysteries

Finally, however, "in the days of Herod the king,"[32] Baruch is despatched, being sent down once more by Elohim; and coming to Nazareth, he found Jesus, son of Joseph and Mary, a child of twelve years, feeding sheep.[33] And he announces to him all things from the beginning, whatsoever had been done by Edem and Elohim, and whatsoever would be likely to take place hereafter, and spoke the following words: "All the prophets anterior to you have been enticed. Put forth an effort, therefore, Jesus, Son of man, not to be allured, but preach this word unto men, and carry back tidings to them of things pertaining to the Father, and things pertaining to the Good One, and ascend to the Good One, and sit there with Elohim, Father of us all."[34] And Jesus was obedient unto the angel, saying that, "I shall do all things, Lord," and proceeded to preach. Naas therefore wished to entice away this one also. Jesus, however, was not disposed to listen to his overtures, for he remained faithful to Baruch.[35] Therefore Naas, being inflamed with anger because he was not able to seduce him, caused him to be crucified. He, however, leaving the body of Edem on the accursed tree, ascended to the Good One; saying, however to Edem, "Woman, thou retainest thy son,"[36] that is, the natural and earthly man. But Jesus himself commending his spirit into the hands of the Father, ascended to the Good One. Now the Good One is Priapus, and he it is who antecedently caused the production of everything that exists.[37] On this account he is styled Priapus, because he previously fashioned[38] all things according to his own design. For this reason, he says, in every temple is placed his statue, which is revered by every creature; and there are images of him in the highways, carrying over his head ripened fruits, that is, the produce of the creation, of which he is the cause, having in the first instance formed,

39.   Hippolytus can perhaps not bear to report that Priapus as god of fertility is generally shown with huge erect phallus. It is this, however, which presumably first suggested his symbolic equivalence to the Shiva, the myth of whose extraordinary creativity also figures in the cycle of the *Apocalypse of Adam* (Sixth Kingdom). The Illuminator or Blessed One was born as his mystical son, Skanda. The summary of the *Book of the Blessed* here seems to break up into not-very-clearly reported fragments dealing with various myths as indicators of the Blessed One.

40.   Leda, according to Greek myth, was raped by Zeus in the form of a swan. From the union were born Helen (prominent in the legends attached to Simonian *gnosis)* and the *Dioscouri* (Castor and Pollux). Ganymede was a handsome youth abducted to heaven by Zeus in the guise of an eagle. Danaë, locked by her father in a tower, was visited by Zeus as a shower of golden rain and impregnated with his child, the hero Perseus.

41.   Isaiah 1:2. Hippolytus hastily summarizes further scriptural interpretation, which makes the traditional prophecies apply to inner realities: the heavenly spirit and the earthly soul within us all. Although we do not know how extensively the interpretations dealt with Isaiah, it is worth pointing out Isaiah is rich in Messianic allusions which were already developed by the Essenes, later by Christians.

42.   Expanded from Isaiah 1:3.

43.   Psalm 110:4. This psalm was used or closely connected with those involved in the royal initiations of ancient Israel. Royal and priestly rites were combined by the Essenes; cf. the *Testament of Levi* (above pp.133f). Elements from very ancient rites were revived: but a new synthesis was created which also reflected the influences of Iran and Babylon. The initiatory oath is typical of Mysteries everywhere. The Essenes were said to be bound by a formidable oath, and early Christians are said to have taken an initiatory oath after baptism.

44.   See note 18 above.

according to His own design, the creation, when as yet it had no existence.[39] When, therefore, he says, you hear men asserting that the swan went in unto Leda, and begat a child from her, learn that the swan is Elohim, and Leda, Edem. And when people allege that an eagle went in unto Ganymede, know that the eagle is Naas, and Ganymede Adam. And when they assert that gold in a shower went into Danaë and begat a child from her, recollect that the gold is Elohim, and Danaë is Edem.[40] And similarly, in the same manner adducing all accounts of this description, which correspond with the nature of legends, they pursue the work of instruction. When, therefore, the prophet says, "Hearken, O heaven, and give ear, O earth; the Lord hath spoken,"[41] he means by heaven, Justin says, the spirit which is in man from Elohim; and by earth, the soul which is in man along with the spirit; and by Lord, Baruch; and by Israel, Edem, for Israel as well as Edem is called the spouse of Elohim. "Israel," he says, "did not know me, Elohim; for had he known me, that I am with the Good One, he would not have punished through paternal ignorance the spirit which is in men."[42]

Hence also, in the first book inscribed "Baruch," has been written the oath which they compel those to swear who are about to hear these mysteries, and be initiated with the Good One. And this oath, Justin says, our Father Elohim sware when He was beside the Good One, and having sworn He did not repent of the oath, respecting which, he says, it has been written, "The Lord sware, and will not repent."[43] Now the oath is couched in these terms: "I swear by that Good One who is above all, to guard these mysteries, and to divulge them to no one, and not to relapse from the Good One to the creature." And when he has sworn this oath, he goes on to the Good One, and beholds "whatever things eye hath not seen, and ear hath not heard, and which have not entered into the heart of man;"[44] and he drinks from life-giving water, which is to them, as they suppose, a bath, a fountain of life-giving, bubbling water. For there has been a separation made between water and water; and there is water, that below the firmament of the

45.   Based on Genesis 1:6f, but ideas about the heavenly waters of the baptismal
       river Jordan are prominent in the Mandean Mystery. The Mandean baptismal
       rites, like those here, involved drinking from the water.

46.   That is, ensouled, belonging to the *'adamah.*

47.   Hoseah 1:2.

wicked creation,[45] in which earthly and animal[46] men are washed; and there is life-giving water, that above the firmament, of the Good One, in which spiritual and living men are washed; and in this Elohim washed himself, and having washed did not repent. And when, he says, the prophet affirms, "Take unto yourself a wife of whoredom, since the earth has abandoned itself to fornication, departing from following after the Lord;"[47] that is, Edem departs from Elohim. Now in these words, he says, the prophet clearly declares the entire Mystery, and is not hearkened unto by reason of the wicked machinations of Naas. According to that same manner, they deliver other prophetical passages in a similar spirit of interpretation throughout numerous books. The volume, however, inscribed "Baruch," is pre-eminently to them the one in which the reader will ascertain the entire explanation of their legendary system to be contained. Beloved, though I have encountered many heresies, yet with no wicked heresiarch worse than this Justin has it been my lot to meet.

8. *The Gospel of Philip*

Christian Mysteries

When the Church began to expand, spreading the Christian message through the 'inhabited world,' it was perhaps inevitable that the more esoteric ideas which transformed the old expectation of a Messiah, and an 'Age to Come' into inner realities attained by a development in consciousness should be blurred by popularization. In its drive to win over the people, the Church needed to be highly organized, have clear lines of authority. Such structures rapidly emerged, crystallizing around the figure of the bishop ('overseer.') On the inner side, a clearly defined 'orthodoxy,' a 'right belief' was required. Out of the rich weave of the early traditions, a few were selected to be the focus of the great campaign to win souls.

The loss of virtually all the others meant that the fascinating confluence of ideas and images which we can now begin to trace once more could no longer be grasped. Only the Old Testament background was accepted as valid, and the Christ-Event came to seem an external, historical happening somehow independent of man's inner participation. Conversely, those 'Gnostics' who insisted upon the reality of an inner event and a cosmic dimension were rejected as 'heretics,' starting in the second century. Inevitably, they were led to contrast their views with the outward, historical concept of Christ in the Church. The polarization which resulted reversed the whole direction of the Christian evolution, the impetus behind the beginnings of Christianity we have sketched. Spiritual currents that had flowed together and enriched one another were turned into opposite channels once again.

When the discoveries at Nag Hammadi restored to modern humanity the contents of the world that had been suppressed by the emerging Church, it seemed at first as though the new texts would show an 'alternative' Christianity — a type of Christianity that had been fostered in opposition to the mainstream. The *Gospel of Thomas* was initially described as a 'Gnostic Gospel'; the *Gospel of Philip* was thought to be a Valentinian work. Of course, some of the writings from Nag Hammadi were the products of groups which can be defined by their opposition to institutional Christianity, and all were probably used by one such group — the one which assembled the library itself. But scholarship has increasingly recognized that such groups inherited much that had originally belonged to the mainstream. Rather than being 'offshoots,' some of them at least were evidence of the Christian Mysteries which continued transformed in the earliest communities.

With the changing perspective, new light was shed in particular on one of the most enigmatic aspects of Christian beginnings: the origins of the sacraments. The Christian sacraments have a long history. They have also played an unusually large role in the controversies among Christians in relatively modern times. The Reformation was at least in part a reflex of the changed experience of the Mass among certain large groups of peoples in Western Europe, necessitating much rethinking of the theology it implied. And on a smaller scale today, changes in the Anglican liturgy, especially as regards language, continue to raise passions, cause spiritual distress, and are as passionately argued to be necessary. Such a vital history of change in the ritual is unusual in wider religious terms, perhaps uniquely Christian. It is inconceivable that Buddhists or Hindus could be seriously divided over ritual practice. Zoroastrianism suffered for several centuries a major ideological schism, yet both sides appear to have happily celebrated the same rites together. The Christian sacraments, on the other hand, have been a constant source of diversity and creativity. The need to understand the centrality of sacramental experience is therefore important, indeed especially so if we are to grasp the sacramental needs of humanity for the present and for the future.

All this makes it the more mysterious when we find that the sacraments appear in early Christianity in what seems an oddly sudden and inorganic way. In the Gospels as we have them handed down, Christ is presented as having performed no ritual act whatsoever. In Paul there is a great deal about baptism and receiving the Holy Spirit; but this too became largely remote from the life of the Church after Baptism had become a sacrament for infants and no longer affirmed 'conversion' on the part of an adult.

What do we know, then, about the communal religious activity of the first Christians? We can form some impression from a surviving letter of Clement, who was evidently a Greek-speaking Jew and a Christian leader in Rome in the first century. His kind of Christianity is very different from Paul's in that is assumes as natural and unquestioned the continuing validity of the Jewish Law and a Jewish way of life among Christians. He knows none of Paul's violent new paradoxes of righteousness and grace. And his extracts from Christian prayer and liturgy also point to the Jewish heritage: they are simply adaptations and slight developments of synagogue services.

Now the synagogue, of course, was not the Temple. The Temple in Jerusalem has been for the Jews the only place on earth where a legitimate priestly cult could be carried on; the synagogues grew up as centres of study, reading and prayer, but there were no priests and no sacramental acts. When the Romans destroyed the Temple in the year 70 after a long and bloodthirsty war, Jewish priesthood and cult alike came to an end, leaving the synagogues and their rabbis the undisputed spiritual leaders of a bruised and scattered Israel. In contrast, within Christianity Clement's kind of Christian synagogue worship rapidly died out. But where then did Christianity derive its rich sacramental life? Discoveries in the twentieth century have at last begun to shed new light on this perplexing problem and suggest that we look not to Rome but to Syria and its great metropolis of Antioch.

For it is to Antioch that we can trace one of the 'new Gospels,' which are really very old Gospels long lost and newly come into our possession from the desert sand. The *Gospel of Philip* is a collection of traditions handed down by the disciple of that name, the kind of oral traditions which we know circulated before any written Gospels existed. At a certain stage, the traditions were written down by his followers to preserve them as memories faded. That happened quite early in this case: it happened at any rate before the authoritative sifting of traditions into the New Testament, since the writer betrays no knowledge whatsoever of any such collection. He does know of one other type of Christianity — and again this points to an early date — namely that of Paul. Toward Pauline ideas he is certainly drawn. But they do not provide the groundwork of his Gospel.

Now if you go to the *Gospel of Philip* expecting to find a Gospel like that of Matthew, Mark, Luke or John, you will be surprised or disappointed. Its approach is very different. It does contain

traditions about Jesus (and about Mary his mother, Mary Magdalene, Joseph, and naturally Philip the apostle); it also includes
isolated 'sayings' of the Lord, as they were termed, which again
links it with the earliest kind of Gospels. All in all, it contains 127
short paragraphs. But most of these make no immediate reference
to the life or teaching of Christ. They are concerned with Adam and
Eve, Abraham, the Holy Spirit, Jews and Christians, flesh and spirit,
Paradise and the fall, knowledge and creativity. And they come one
after another in what at first seems a confusing sequence, or rather
inconsequence.

In fact, it seems hard to see how anyone could have made any
sense of this Gospel at all, until one notices that the themes are
grouped not around ideas, but around certain experiences. Those
experiences keep shifting the context of the ideas so that they have
to be rethought. And gradually, as they are rethought and re-
grouped they begin to form a rich whole, with a 'spiralling' effect
as their significance and full interrelationship becomes manifest.
And those central, cohesive experiences are sacramental experiences.

Five sacraments are referred to and they are so enwoven into the
texture of the Gospel as to form the whole grounding of its form
and content. Indeed, the best theory about the book is that it was
used among the community of Philip-Christians in those early days
to prepare a candidate for Baptism. For that he had to have a sound
grasp of Christian 'knowledge' in outline, and after Baptism and
Anointing he would be admitted to the Eucharist as a full Christian.
Probably before Baptism he would study the book with a teacher
and would be allowed to possess or consult it himself only afterwards. Its contents would only make full sense to him, in fact, when
the experiences alluded to in the text became realities and he
entered upon the sacramental life.

So, then, not long after the time of Clement and his Christian
synagogue, we find in the East a community with a highly developed sacramentalism at the heart of its life and thought. An
extraordinary contrast! It is worth looking in a little detail at the
rites they performed.

Baptism is extremely prominent in the *Gospel of Philip*, and the
references to it suggest a vivid picture of Christian practice when
we put them together in imagination. It is clear that Baptisms were
performed all together, at Easter. The candidates have been
prepared by fasts and vigils, by earnest instruction and solemn

instigations. They approach the significant day with trepidation, for they are to die to their former existence. The water is not the spoon-sprinkling we see in many churches today but a plunge into 'the waters of death,' a complete submersion in which the self is washed over and is abolished by the swirling water. The death-symbolism, and the fear of utterly losing the sense of identity in the amorphous-ness of the element, of being 'poured out,' is stressed. It is only because of what Jesus achieved in his death and resurrection that man can survive the ritual ordeal:

> Even as Jesus perfected the water of baptism, so he
> poured out death. Therefore we descend into the water,
> but not unto death — so that we should not be poured
> out. When the wind (or spirit) of this world blows, it
> makes the winter come. When the Holy Spirit (or wind)
> blows, the summer comes.

These words have a strong ritual feel: perhaps they were recited as the one being baptized descended into the water.

The seemingly unconnected passage about the winter and summer actually points to another essential element of the rite, its cosmic significance. Easter is clearly acknowledged as the festival of Christ's death, which enables the Christian to be reborn from this world into the eternal world. But the ousting of the 'spirit of this world' (one could say, the exorcism) and the inbreathing of the Holy Spirit is experienced in a kind of continuum with nature. Easter is also a spring celebration of the transition from death to new life in the world of plants and animals, as the wind changes and the hard winter drought of the Middle East breaks up, a cosmic event. And likewise the death and resurrection of Christ was enacted at one time in history, but it reveals an eternal and cosmic deed, in that 'he laid down his soul from the beginning of the world.' In its theology of these matters, this early Gospel is far from orthodox by the later standards of the Church.

The baptized candidate rises up from the waters, from his inner death and rebirth, and declares 'I am a Christian.' We should remember that the term Christian was coined in Antioch (Acts 11:26) and the taking of the name was evidently an act of commitment. However, the right to take it must be bestowed by inner experience during the baptismal rite. Those who do not experience anything but merely go through the outward procedure and speak the words do not really possess the name, but 'receive it on loan';

and, it is added ominously, from those who receive on loan payment is demanded. But if the name was rightly claimed, the candidate would ascend from the waters and be clothed in a white garment symbolizing his new life and pure inner state. The references to fire as well as water, together with what we know of early practice elsewhere, make it virtually certain that the baptized Christian was also given a lighted taper. This may have represented the spirit called into life by rebirth, just as the waters represented the death and dissolution of the old self. Thus: 'By water and fire the whole place is purified, the manifest by the manifest, the hidden by the hidden.'

The fire-symbolism led over into the next stage of the proceedings: for Baptism was not complete without the further sacrament of Anointing (equivalent, really, to a modern Confirmation). It is said that there is 'fire' in the Anointing, apparently referring to the oil. The inner disposition of oil is to spread, to expand, and in ancient alchemical terms the expanding tendency is referred to as the 'sulphur' or 'fire' principle. Its polar opposite is 'salt,' which alchemically refers to the crystallizing, precipitating or hardening tendency. The *Gospel of Philip* several times refers to Baptism as if it were an alchemical 'transmutation' of the soul, and in a role that cannot be quite reconstructed salt too played a part in the rites. It stood for the divine Sophia, who is mystically the mother of the regenerate Christian. Outwardly, the text says, salt results in sterility; but this is not an outward but an inner birth. Hence of the Sophia it is declared that 'she is barren, and her children are many.' The symbolism of the elements reminds us of other Jewish-Christian groups in the East, who performed Baptism before 'the seven witnesses.' These were oil, salt, and earth; the angels of prayers; heaven, water and the holy spirits, the last probably being actualized in the flames carried by the candidates or perhaps candles burning on the altar.

It will be clear by now that the sacraments are understood in this early *Gospel* as far more than gestures of incorporation into the community of Christians. There is an element of process, or initiation through definite stages. So now there are further stages, as we come to the third sacrament, the Eucharist. The cup is referred to as 'the cup of prayer' (perhaps watched over by angels of prayer). The drinking of the water and wine will lead to the receiving of the Christ within ('the perfect Man'):

> The cup of prayer contains wine and water, being
> appointed as the type of the blood over which thanks is
> given, and it is full of the Holy Spirit and belongs to the
> wholly perfect Man. When we drink this, we shall receive
> for ourselves the perfect Man.

In a certain sense the inner process here reaches its goal. And yet there is still more to come. With regard to the bread, however, the *Gospel* touches on a very interesting problem of the role of the celebrant, the 'holy man' who officiates at the rite. For it appears that the efficacy of the rite is partly dependent on his spiritual condition. The spirit works through him to sanctify the substances and acts of the ritual. And the spiritual forces of the 'perfect Man' can work on even into man's physical body through the bread. Yet this depends on the total spiritualization which the 'holy man' has attained:

> The holy man is altogether holy, including his body. For if
> he has received the bread, he will make it holy, or the
> cup, or all the rest which he receives he purifies. And how
> will he not purify the body also?

The presence of this 'holy man' at the eucharistic table, and the absence of the terminology of priesthood, once more points to the early origins of the *Gospel of Philip*.

Many further dimensions of the Eucharist experience are hinted at in the *Gospel*. For example, it is repeatedly described as a re-entering of Paradise and eating from the Tree of Life, forbidden to fallen man. We have met this symbolism among the Essenes, in the *Testaments of the Patriarchs*, and in related traditions; subsequently it features among the Syrian Fathers. We know that it goes back to the Mysteries of the ancient Middle East. Its form in the *Gospel of Philip* reminds us especially of Babylonian myths, such as Gilgamesh who went searching for the Plant of Life.

But I have still to say something of the remaining two sacraments referred to in the *Gospel*. For the entry into the Eucharistic life is sufficient for the Christian, and permits him to 'laugh at' the power of the world:

> Thus it is with the bread and the cup and the oil, even if
> there is something else more exalted than these.

The 'something else more exalted' refers to those Christians who desire a higher initiation, and can receive it in the sacrament of the Bride Chamber. It is clear that this was not a rite of marriage in the external sense, but the union of the soul with its divine arche-type:

> While the union in this world is man and woman, the
> place for the power and the weakness, in the Aeon the
> likeness of the union is something other.

The ritual Bride Chamber was an 'image of the All,' of the eternal world (the Aeon). The Christian initiate could there join his own being in a higher sense to that of the 'perfect Man':

> For this one is no longer a Christian but a Christ.

The language is that of the Mysteries, applied with hitherto un-precedented boldness to Christianity. The Mystery initiates 'became Osiris' or 'Attis' or 'Mithras.' This higher Mystery of union can be described only in riddling terms to 'those outside.' Yet it is not darkness which hides it from us; but 'it is revealed to him alone, not hidden in the darkness and the night, but hidden in a perfect day and a holy light.'

Equally fascinating is the other sacrament — the 'Redemption.' It was apparently a rite for the dead, helping to ensure the passage of the soul into the higher world, and could probably be performed only by a 'higher Christian' initiate, although the community may have played some part. It is also possible that it might have been performed for a living man as a still higher degree of initiation. It might be the original of the practice still found among medieval heretics, who performed the *Consolamentum* (or last rites) for those who were already able to live the life of a pure spirit while yet on earth. It has its closest parallels among the Mandeans, who perform a *masikta* for the soul of the dead — a rite in which the officiating priest accompanies the soul into the other world and effects its rebirth into eternity.

The Mandeans are a clue to the whole picture which the *Gospel of Philip* reveals. Many further parallels could be mentioned in regard to the dramatic baptismal process, the imagery of water and fire, cosmic ascent (cf. 'I climbed the mountain' in the Mandean Mystery). At one stage, indeed, the *Gospel* quotes from a Mandean secret scroll a passage about Light and Darkness, life and death and transcending dualities through initiation. This not only shows the antiquity of the Mandean teachings which have been handed down to the twentieth century. It brings us full circle in our exploration of the Mysteries and Christian beginnings. It shows that the emergence of Christian sacramentalism flowed directly from the stream of the Mysteries, present in Palestine in Mandean form and influencing the Jewish sects of the Essenes, John the Baptist, and so on. It provides unequivocal evidence, for the first time, of the involvement in the earliest Christianity of the representatives of the ancient Mysteries — indicated by Rudolf Steiner from his spiritual researches long before the Nag Hammadi texts were discovered. They were able to provide Christianity with a sacramentalism that the Jewish heritage failed to give, indeed could never have given: the whole history of Judaism consists in the narrowing down and final disappearance of cultic activity. Moreover, we can point to a specific Mystery-stream in the background of the Mandeans and the traditions of the *Gospel of Philip*. Their Mysteries are based on the same fusion of ancient Babylonian and Iranian teachings which we find in the rites of Mithra, the sun-genius, whose cult spread from the East and in its pagan form was widely diffused through the Roman Empire.

Many of the same features appear, as they have done in so many of the documents we have studied in this book: the water rites of baptismal purification, the multiple grades or stages of knowledge, the two winds (or spirits), the Plant of Life which is a symbol of the god, the rite of 'Bride' *(nymphus)*, and so on. The orthodox Christian Fathers were later to be deeply embarrassed to note the similarities between Christian and Mithraic rites: but we can see that it was through contact with these Mysteries that Christianity was able to evolve, and gradually transform, its own necessary sacramental structure. It kept alive the mythic experience of the eternal reality, the timeless truth in the depth of the soul, which gave its meaning to the historical event:

> He who came into being before the All was begotten
> again. He who was anointed at first was anointed again,
> he who was redeemed redeemed again.

Long after the pagan Mithraic Mysteries had died out, and the Mandeans fled preserving their doctrines in obscurity in the marshes of Iraq, the Mystery-stream lived on in a new form, brought ever more into the light of day, in Christian celebration.

But how did the timeless Mystery-Christ connect with the historical event? Does not the *Gospel of Philip* rather belong, some scholars have pointedly asked, to a marginal, mystical tendency in early Christianity that was duly rejected by the historically hard-headed Church? I said earlier that the *Gospel*'s theology was far from orthodox: is it not simply a Gnostic system, of the kind which ignored or devalued the historical Christ? Close parallels are to be found especially in the teachings of one Marcus, a disciple of Valentinus who cultivated a sacramental life and taught that the outward acts reflected the primordial events in the realm of the aeons. He even performed the rite of the Bride Chamber, so some direct connection with the *Gospel* is certain. After all, then, does it not turn out that the *Gospel of Philip*, with its Mystery connection, belonged to some divergent minority group, a Gnostic sect?

In reality, the evidence is not so simple. Marcus' teaching is full of the technical terms of his master, Valentinus; the *Gospel of Philip* contains none of them, and where its terminology does overlap uses concepts such as 'the Middle,' for instance, in non-Valentinian ways. Why should the *Gospel*, if it was fashioned for the use of a special Gnostic group, have avoided any reference to Valentinus' central ideas, his aeonology, and so on? It does not make sense. In fact, the *Gospel* has little close relation to the doctrines of the Gnostic master, but only to the special modifications brought into it by Marcus, so that it is better to suppose an influence the other way. Marcus is much easier to understand as a Valentinian who went back to a tradition of Christianity that was rooted in the Mysteries, i.e. the *Gospel of Philip*, as the parting of the ways between the Gnostics and the developing orthodoxy of the Church took sharper forms. He then interpreted it in the spirit of Valentinus and produced a Gnostic system out of it, with typical Gnostic language but an unusual stress on the sacraments.

His task was a relatively simple one. If one gathers together the Mystery-ideas in the *Gospel* — the eternally repeated or always happening cycle of redemption, the reattaining of Paradise, the seizure of freedom, fusion with the god in the Bride Chamber — and opposes them to the historical figure of Jesus, to earthly events which are time-bound, and so forth, one has a ready-made Gnostic theology. The point is, however, that in the *Gospel of Philip* these ideas have not been drawn together in that way and opposed to the earthly fact. A tendency in that direction is there in the background: already in the Mandean Mystery the clash with Judaism points toward the world of later Christian Gnosticism. But in the *Gospel* that tendency is countered by a different one — or several different ones, which emphasize the words of the historical Jesus, traditions from the Old Testament, ideas from the letters of Paul, ideas about the holiness even of the body when it is penetrated by the Christ-power. The traditions of the 'sayings of the Lord' are linked rather exactly to those which we find in the Gospel of Matthew. It is by no means clear, however, whether the sayings were already embedded there when they reached the author of the *Gospel of Philip*, or whether they were still oral tradition. Likewise, similarities to the Gospel of John are repeatedly encountered, but may indicate a shared background rather than a knowledge of the text.

The whole situation suggests something more fluid, much earlier, than the consolidation of 'historical Christianity' on the one hand and the specifically Gnostic Christian groups on the other. It suggests a more exciting vista into the formative stage of Christianity, and an indication of the milieu in which Christianity took root. It shows us a flourishing Mystery-community, inheriting many riches from ancient Babylon and Iran, in touch with or perhaps developing out of the Mandean esoteric baptizing movement. And it was they who were able to take up the message of Jesus, and to see in his deeds and words the earthly manifestation of the Mystery-god. It was they who could begin to balance their cosmic revelation against the redemptive appearance of the Christ on earth. It was in these circles of the Mysteries that the words of Jesus were preserved as authoritative utterances, and with them the over-whelming, all-transforming implications of his 'coming into the world.' The *Gospel of Philip* shows us a point in the process where earthly and cosmic are still coming together in the tentative and difficult understanding of the new direction to the Mysteries that he has given, not a stage at which they are falling apart. The rediscovered fragment of the 'Secret Mark,' as we shall see, enables us to go still further. For it suggests that Jesus himself moved in circles just such as these, and performed a Mystery-rite for Lazarus when he, like many an ancient initiate, was 'raised from the dead.' The *Gospel of Philip* may turn out not only to be the missing link in the lost history of the sacraments, but a point of contact also with the setting of Jesus in the Mysteries of his time.

Source: Nag Hammadi Codex II. Translated from the Coptic by K.H. Kuhn after the German version by Martin Krause. The numbering of the paragraphs is that suggested by H.M Schenke.

Note numbers here refer to the paragraph numbering.

1ff.   The opening statements have the character of a *rite de passage:* they offer categories (Hebrew, slave, dead) which define the existential state of mankind from which the pupil is implicitly asked to detach himself. By recognizing the condition of unredeemed humanity, the pupil immediately finds himself on a threshold. Many ideas are raised which will come round again and again, and will in due course be attached to the sacramental nodes around which the loose structure of the *Gospel of Philip* hangs.

   The categories used do not imply any sense of 'Gnostic' self-definition over against the body of 'ordinary' Christians. On the contrary, though there are parallels with Gnostic groups and with Valentinus' disciple Marcus in particular, it is evident that these are a part of the thought-world of the whole community, which sees itself simply as the community of 'Christians' (cf. 6). Over against it stand 'heathens' and 'Jews.' Nor is there any reason to assume that such a community must have been a marginal or unusual one. In style and content, notes W.W. Isenberg, 'the *Gospel of Philip* resembles the orthodox catechisms from the second through fourth centuries' (in Robinson 1988, p.141); there are passages, confessed R.McL. Wilson, which suggest the Gnostic doctrines refuted by Irenaeus, 'but curiously there are others where the closest parallels are to be found not in Irenaeus' discussion of Gnostic theories but in his own Demonstration of the Christian faith' (Wilson 1968, p.97). The use of Syriac words in some parts of the *Gospel* make it probable that it comes from Antioch, one of the major centres of earliest Christianity. It provides evidence for the Mystery influences upon Christianity in its formative stages: only later were such ideas rejected and became the property of special, 'Gnostic' groups.

6.   Evidently those who came to Christianity were generally from a Jewish background.

7.   The first mention of a Mystery-theme which will recur: initiation clearly took place at a specific time, namely Easter; but the festival is treated not only as commemorating the historical event but as a cosmic turning-point, like the old spring or autumn festivals of the Mysteries. The regeneration of the Christian initiate is part of the awakening of life from death in cosmic nature, the winter giving way to summer. Cf. especially 109. On the cosmic festivals underlying the Christian one, see the interesting perspective of Rudolf Steiner (1968).

9.   In terminology the *Gospel of Philip* is close here to the Gospel of John. In the latter we also read that Christ 'came' into the world, or from the Father, or in an absolute sense that he simply 'came,' as here: see R. Bultmann (1955,

✽ The Gospel of Philip ✽

1. A Hebrew man produces a Hebrew and he is called thus: "proselyte." But a proselyte does not produce a proselyte. On the one hand there are men just as they come into being and they produce others, but there are other men for whom it suffices to come into being.

2. The slave seeks only to be free. But he does not seek after the property of his master. But the son is not only son, but he ascribes to himself the inheritance of the father.

3. Those who inherit dead things are themselves dead and inherit dead things. Those who inherit that which is alive are alive, and they inherit that which is alive and things that are dead. The dead do not inherit anything; for how should the dead inherit? If the dead man inherits that which is alive he will not die, but the dead will live the more.

4. A heathen man does not die, for he has never lived that he should die. He who has believed in the truth has lived. And this one is in danger of dying. For he is alive only since the day Christ came.

5. The world is created, the cities are adorned, that which is dead is carried out.

6. In the days when we were Hebrews, we were orphans. We had only our mother. But when we became Christians, we acquired father and mother.

7. Those who sow in winter reap in summer. The winter is the world, the summer is the other aeon. Let us sow in the world that we may reap in summer. Therefore it is fitting for us not to pray in winter. What (or: He who) comes out of the winter is the summer. But if someone reaps in winter, he will not reap but pluck out (Saying 8) as the multitude. Thus he will not bring forth any fruit. Not only will it come forth ..., but also on the Sabbath ... is without fruit.

9. Christ came to ransom some, to save others, and to redeem others. He ransomed the strangers, he made them his own, and he separated his own whom he had deposited as pledges

p.34) for the many references. According to the Prologue he came 'to his own' — a concept also found here; and the phrase rendered 'deposited his soul' is found in John in the form 'laid down his life,' since 'soul' and 'life' are both modern renderings of the same word. It does not seem that the author of *Philip* is alluding to the Gospel of John, however: rather the *Gospel* seems to use similar ideas and stands in a related tradition.

The coming of Christ, and his laying down his soul, are treated as eternal, cosmic realities of which his earthly advent is a revelation.

10.   A quotation from the Mandéan 'secret scroll' *The Thousand and Twelve Questions:* 'Observe, that light and darkness are brothers, emanating from one mystery, and the trunk retains both (in itself)' — the 'trunk' or torso being an expression for the macrocosmic Adam, of whom the opposites are the right and left sides. The context of the Mandean teaching is baptism: 'Whoever is not marked with the sign of darkness will not be established or approach the baptism and be marked with the sign of life': E.S. Drower (Berlin 1960, No.95, pp.264f). On 'being established,' see 11 below.

11.   The spiritual world consists of things which are 'firmly established,' in contrast to earthly, perishable things: in Mandean thought we learn of a realm of eternal images ('World of Counterparts,') described in terms deriving from Zoroastrianism as light-images, etc. Similar ideas underlie the *Gospel of Philip* — cf. 51 and commentary.

Language stands in an ambiguous relationship to this realm. On the one hand, words (names) lead us astray, and trap us in a system of deceit because they do not contain reality. On the other hand names are necessary rungs on our ascent to the single truth which 'brought forth names in the world for our sakes.' We must recognize the creative source of language, not become stuck in its products.

12.   The 'name' of the Father used by Jesus in the Gospel of John is 'I AM,' which in Judaism appears as a name of God: cf. R.E. Brown (1971) for detailed references. For instance when challenged in John 18:5 Jesus says 'I AM' — 'but the fact that those who hear it fall to the ground when he answers suggests a form of theophany which leaves men prostrate with fear before God' (1971, Appendix IV, p.534). Here in the *Gospel of Philip* we probably have the same meaning: 'those who have this name' are the ones who know that the 'I AM' is the God in us, our divine self which was revealed in its fullness in Christ; 'in it' he 'became the Father.' Those who do not have it nevertheless 'speak of it,' that is, they are always saying 'I,' but do not understand its deeper implications.

according to his will. Not only when he appeared did he deposit the soul when he wished, but since the day when the world was in existence he deposited the soul. At the time when he wished, then he came first to take it, for it had been deposited as a pledge. It fell among the robbers and was taken prisoner. But he saved it and he redeemed the good in the world and the evil.

10. The light and the darkness, life and death, right and left are brothers one for another. It is impossible that they separate one from another. Therefore neither are the good good, nor are the evil evil, nor is life life, nor is death death. Therefore each one will dissolve into its original from the beginning. But those who are exalted over the world are indissoluble and eternal.

11. The names that are given to worldly things contain a great error. For they turn away their heart from things that are firmly established to those that are not firmly established. And he who hears "God" does not perceive what is firmly established, but he has perceived what is not firmly established. So also with the "Father" and the "Son" and the "Holy Spirit," and "life" and "light," and the "resurrection" and the "church," and all other names: they do not perceive things that are firmly established but they perceive those that are not firmly established unless they have learned the things that are firmly established. The names which are heard are in the world to deceive. If they were in the aeon, they would not be named in the world on any day, nor would they be put among worldly things. They have an end in the aeon.

12. One single name is not pronounced in the world, the name which the Father gave to the Son; it is exalted above every name, which is the name of the Father. For the Son would not become Father except he put on the name of the Father. Those who have this name know it, but do not speak of it. But those who have it not do not know it, but speak of it. The truth has brought forth names in the world for our sakes, because it is impossible to learn it without names. One and only is the truth. It is manifold, and that for our sakes, to teach this one alone in love through many.

13.   The deceiving system of words, if divorced from the 'truth' which 'brought them forth,' is the model for the cosmic system of deceit now described mythologically as that of the hostile archons or world-rulers. They imprison us — by trapping us in the limitations of our meaning, cutting us off from the creative source.

14.   Here begins an important theme: the true food of man. Cf. Steiner 1968, pp.40ff. The *Gospel of Philip* connects here with themes in the *Gospel of Thomas* (e.g. Saying 11: 'They that are dead are not alive, and they that live shall not die. In the days when you were eating that which is dead, you were making it alive. When you come into the light, what will you do?') and with the question of sacrifices which was important in Jewish-Christianity. 'Eaters of dead things' or of sacrifices ('when they offered them up they died') feed only the earthly man; but being sustained in this way is not in the full sense 'life.' Many people are in reality to be numbered among 'the dead.' Those who are truly alive offer themselves to God, but they are not destroyed in sacrificing themselves for they find eternal life. This is *Thomas'* 'they that live shall not die': cf. below, 21. Also *Gospel of Thomas* 7.

15.   Christ is here described as a Mystery-god, like Osiris 'who delivered mankind from their destitute and brutish manner of living ... by showing them the fruits of cultivation' (Plutarch, *Isis and Osiris* 13) or like Bacchus spreading the knowledge of cultivation through the world, as does Tripto-lemus in the Eleusinian Mysteries. Christ appears as the founder of a Mystery, and gives to its initiates truly human existence. Cf. Gospel of John: 'Do not work for the food which perishes, but for food that endures to eternal life, which the Son of Man will give you' (6:27) and: 'I AM the living bread that came down from heaven.' (6:51) Again the *Gospel of Philip* does not allude directly to John — rather, it shows us the Mystery background of the sayings in John's tradition.

17.   *Philip* combats the idea that Mary is the mother of Jesus in a crudely miraculous way, and that the Holy Spirit fathered him. In fact, says the *Gospel*, the Holy Spirit is the real Mother and Mary's 'virginity' has a mystical rather than a literal meaning. The idea of the Holy Spirit as the feminine aspect of God is general in Jewish-Christianity, for instance in the so-called *Odes of Solomon* (actually early Christian hymns of baptism and initiation from Syria): and see Steiner 1965, pp.79ff. The 'virgin whom no power defiled' is mythologically the divine Sophia, another feminine aspect of divinity, outwardly 'barren' but inwardly creative (see 35f below). Mary is apparently the earthly representative of the Eternal Feminine, and in 32 below seems to be a triple goddess or archetypal Mother-Sister-Wife. The 'virgin birth' of Jesus is the prototype of the spiritual birth of the true Man through the Mysteries, and points to his 'father in heaven' in a spiri-tual-mystical way. *Philip* supports this idea from Matthew 16:17: Jesus had an earthly father in the normal way, but the inner reality of his 'virgin birth' is understood by the initiated (see 82 below).

18.   A saying of Jesus not known from elsewhere. It appears to concern the observance of the boundaries between inner and outer truth, so as not to confuse spiritual with material reality (cf. the 'virgin birth.')

13. The archons wanted to deceive man, for they saw that he had an affinity with those that are truly good. They took the name of those that are good and gave it to those that are not good, but they might deceive him by the names and that they might bind them to those that are not good. And afterwards if they do them a favour, they make them depart from those that are not good and put them among those that are good, whom they knew. For they wanted to take the free and make him their slave for ever.

14. There are powers which give food to man for they do not want him to be saved, that they may exist for ever. For if man is saved, there will be no sacrifices for the powers. And they offered up animals to the powers ... These were offered up to them. They offered them up alive, but when they offered them up they died. Man was offered up to God dead and he lived.

15. Before Christ came there was no bread in the world. Like the Paradise, the place where Adam was, it had many trees as food for the beasts. It had no wheat as food for man. Man fed like the beasts. But when Christ, the perfect man, came, he brought bread from heaven that man should feed on the food of man.

16a. The archons thought that they do what they do by their power and will. But the Holy Spirit secretly brought about everything through them as he wished.

16b. Truth, which is from the beginning, is sown everywhere, and many see it being sown. But few who see it reap it.

17. Some said: "Mary conceived by the Holy Spirit." They err. They do not know what they say. When did a woman ever conceive by a woman? Mary is the virgin whom no power defiled. She is a great curse for the Hebrews, who are the apostles and the apostolic disciples. This virgin whom no power defiled is barren. The powers have defiled themselves. And the Lord would not have said: "My Father which is in heaven" unless he had had another father. But he would have said simply: "My Father."

18. The Lord said to the disciples: "... come into the house of

19.   The *Gospel* shows a knowledge of Greek and Syriac, which is part of the
       evidence for its Antiochene provenance. On 'names,' cf. 11 above. 'Christ' and
       'Messiah' are indeed words which mean 'Anointed' (see further 47).

21.   The theme of resurrection is introduced. As with the 'virgin birth,' the *Gospel*
       treats the subject on the basis of an existing popular conception which has to
       be corrected. here the notion that immortality will be conferred upon us
       arbitrarily as a result of Jesus' death and resurrection is challenged: rather,
       'death' is an experience which we will undergo unscathed if we have
       previously found the undying, eternal self within us. Being 'baptized into his
       death' (Paul, Romans 6:3) is an initiation which will show whether or not we
       have done so. Similar ideas, often derived from Paul, are developed in the
       esoteric Christian treatise from Nag Hammadi, *The Letter to Rheginus* (ed.
       M.L. Peel, *The Epistle to Rheginos*, London 1969); and see Welburn 1991,
       pp.215ff.

23.   The doctrine of resurrection expounded is neither the vulgar notion of
       coming back just as you were, nor the Gnostic one of a pure spirit resurrected
       from the body. It is based on Paul's teaching to the Corinthians, and cites 1
       Corinthians 15:50 — resurrection is a metamorphosis, a bodily, nay a fleshly
       event but in a transformed state of being, for 'flesh and blood' cannot rise
       again out of the ground. The influence of Paul's teachings, based on an
       explicit quotation from his writings, would fit Antioch, which was for long
       a centre of his mission (Acts 11:25f).
           Paul's resurrection teaching is developed from Jewish thought, and the
       present passage also has close parallels in the Talmud (notably tractate
       Sanhedrin 90b). For a detailed discussion of what is meant by the spirit 'in the
       flesh,' and its relation to what Rudolf Steiner called the *Phantom:* Welburn
       1991, 223ff. There are again close connections with the *Letter to Rheginus*.
           The saying of the Lord ('He who will not eat ...') is also recorded in the
       Gospel of John 6:53.

24.   Resurrection is connected with baptism 'into his death,' that is, an initiation.
       The theme of rising 'clothed' has an analogy to the ritual undressing to be
       baptized and 'putting on' the new identity of a Christian like a garment:
       again the symbolism is developed in Paul. The use of the phrase 'in the
       kingdom of heaven' to refer to the regenerate state points to the parable of
       the wedding-guest (Matthew 22:11-14), also alluded to in 27. The wed-
       ding-garment which he lacked, and was cast into outer darkness for not
       having, is the baptismal white robe, that is, he is one of those who have not
       first obtained the resurrection (see 21) and so perishes.
           In this world, garments express outwardly what we are; but the white
       robe, which we put on with baptism-initiation, is an ideal to which we have
       to live up.

the Father. Do not take or carry anything away in the house of the Father.

19. "Jesus" is a name that is hidden, "Christ" (or: "the Anointed") is a name that is manifest. Therefore "Jesus" does not exist in any language, but his name is "Jesus," as he is called. But "Christ" (or: "the Anointed") is his name — in Syriac it is "Messiah," but in Greek "Christ." Indeed all the others have it according to the language of each one of them. The "Nazarene" is the manifest of the hidden.

20. Christ has everything in him, whether man or angel or Mystery and the Father.

21. Those who say: "The Lord died first and then rose" err. For he rose first and then died. If anyone does not first obtain the resurrection, he will die. As God lives, this one was clay.

22. No one will hide a great and precious object in a great vessel. But many times has someone put countless myriads into a vessel worth a farthing. So it is with the soul. It is a precious thing and got into a despised body.

23. Some are afraid lest they rise naked. Therefore they desire to rise in the flesh. They do not know that those who wear the flesh are naked, those who prepare themselves to strip are not naked. "Flesh and blood shall not be able to inherit the kingdom of God." What is this which will not inherit? This which is upon us. But what is this which will inherit? It is the flesh of Jesus and his blood. Therefore he said: "He who will not eat my flesh and drink my blood has no life in him." What is it? His flesh is the Word and his blood is the Holy Spirit. He who has received these has food and has drink and clothing. I blame the others who say: "It will not rise." Then both are at fault. You say: "The flesh will not rise." But tell me what will rise, that we may honour you. You say: "The spirit in the flesh and this light also is in the flesh." This too is something that is in the flesh, for whatever you will say you say nothing apart from the flesh. It is needful to rise in this flesh, as everything is in it.

24. In this world those who put on garments are more precious than the garments. In the kingdom of heaven the garments are more precious than those who have put them on.

25.   Water and fire in the context of baptismal purification recalls the Mandean
        Mystery (above pp.39f), as does the distinction of hidden-manifest, water and
        water. The 'fire' = the oil, which is a spreading or 'sulphur' principle in
        alchemical terms.

26.   The theme of Jesus' different forms has Gnostic parallels, but the idea that
        God 'accommodates' himself to his creatures is a widespread Christian one.
        On not being able to see his greatness, cf. the Prologue to the Gospel of John
        1:5. The idea of the Word 'hiding itself' occurs in the statement of 'the Voice'
        in the Nag Hammadi *Trimorphic Protennoia* 45:21f ('And I hid myself in
        everyone and revealed myself within them') which is closely related to the
        Prologue. Again, ideas belonging to the background of the Gospel of John —
        rather than quoted from it. In 2 Peter 1:16 the Transfiguration is characterized
        as an initiation *(epopteia)*.
            The saying of Jesus is not known from elsewhere. The 'thanksgiving'
        (eucharistia), the themes of light, Holy Spirit and sharing with the angels recall
        Essene theology (and its Jewish-Christian continuation), but also anticipates
        technical terms soon to be introduced.

27.   See 24 and note.

28.   We spiral back to themes and patterns from the very opening of the *Gospel*:
        but the statements are now enriched. The opposition between natural and
        spiritual generation can now be developed into a conception of 'the perfect
        man,' who is a creative power within us (his 'children' are 'begotten all the
        time.') He is 'the heavenly man' in contrast to Adam, the natural man.

31.   On the birth of the Word from the mouth, cf. the teaching of Simon the
        Magus, p.165 above.
            The kiss which is the creative act ('kiss and give birth') of the perfect is
        probably the 'kiss of peace' known in the early Church (see 1 Thessalonians
        5:26). Here it is interpreted as a sign of our sharing in the 'perfect man.' The
        Nag Hammadi text *Eugnostus* 81,3ff mentions angels 'called "The church of
        the saints of light without shadow". Now when these kiss one another, their
        kiss becomes angels who are like them.' Cf. here the constantly begotten
        children of the 'perfect man.'
            We are to understand that the 'perfect' are in the condition of the angels
        through their initiation. Probably it is a sign of those who have participated
        in the sacrament of the 'bride-chamber,' which has not yet been mentioned
        as it belongs to the higher Christians who are united with the 'heavenly
        man.'

32.   Cf. 17 (and note). Mary Magdalene is mentioned again in 55, where it is said
        the Saviour often kissed her on the mouth — presumably the ritual kiss just
        described. This qualifies her as 'wife' or 'companion,' since it is the Mystery
        of the 'bride chamber' and in the mouth is begotten the Word. On Mary the
        sister of Mary his mother, cf. Matthew 27:56.
            Behind the figure of the Maries, of course, is an allusion to the Sophia —
        who appears explicitly in the sayings which follow (35,36).

25. By water and fire the whole place is purified, the manifest by the manifest, the hidden by the hidden. There are some that are hidden by the manifest. There is water in water, there is fire in anointing.

26. Jesus took them all secretly. For he did not reveal himself as he really was, but he revealed himself as they would be able to see him. To all creatures he revealed himself. He revealed himself to the great as great. He revealed himself to the small as small. He revealed himself to the angels as angel and to men as man. Therefore his Word hid itself from everyone. Some indeed saw him, while thinking that they were seeing themselves. But when he appeared to his disciples in glory upon the mountain, he was not small. He became great. But he made his disciples great that they should be able to see how great he is. He said on that day in the thanksgiving: "You who have joined the perfect, the light, with the Holy Spirit, join the angels with us also, the images."

27. Do not despise the lamb, for without it it is impossible to see the king. Nobody will be able to advance naked towards the king.

28. The children of the heavenly man are more numerous than those of the earthly man. If the children of Adam are numerous although they die, how much more the children of the perfect man who do not die but are begotten all the time.

29. The father produces a child, and the child is unable to produce a child; for he who has been begotten is unable to beget, but the child acquires brothers for himself, not children.

30. All who are begotten in the world are begotten by nature, and others by these. Those who are begotten by him are fed from there. But man feeds on the promise — that is the ... from above.

31. He is fed through the mouth. If the Word had come forth there, he would feed through the mouth and become perfect. For the perfect conceive through a kiss and give birth. Therefore we also kiss one another and receive conception by the grace which is among us.

32. Three were walking with the Lord always, Mary his

34.   The idea of the world-powers unknowingly serving the Spirit is not a Gnostic
       one: in Gnosticism the archons are blind but earthly man is genuinely in their
       power. The symbolism of 'your mother' in the otherwise unknown saying of
       the Lord recalls not so much Gnosticism as the Jewish-Christian *Gospel of the
       Egyptians* (see Hennecke-Schneemelcher 1963, pp.166f). Compare also the
       pattern of the marriage at Cana, where Jesus does the request of his mother,
       but says 'My time has not yet come' (John 2:4).

35.   Ménard refers to Jewish-Christian practices which continued the Old
       Testament requirement (Leviticus 2:13) of salt at sacrifices: 'We know that
       after his baptism, which stood in place of the old Jewish sacrifices, the
       neophyte took bread and salt, the two elements which make up the
       eucharistic feast' (Ménard 1967, p.153). However, a wider 'alchemical'
       symbolism is also evident in the *Gospel of Philip*, as will emerge in later
       sayings.

38.   A first reference to the dangers of initiation, which liberates energies which
       may 'burn' if not harmonized and spiritualized. That is why it is essential to
       grasp the opposition of natural and spiritual creativity: any blurring of the
       boundary may lead to destruction.

39.   Both names are forms of Achamoth = Wisdom, Sophia. Some Valentinian
       Gnostics made a similar distinction. But they were taking over earlier Jewish
       mystical ideas. E. Segelberg does not look to a Valentinian background but
       rather 'late Jewish exegetic tradition behind the Gospel of Philip' ('The
       Gospel of Philip and the New Testament,' in Logan and Wedderburn 1983).
       Ménard cites 1 *Enoch* 42, where the two figures are Wisdom and Iniquity.

40.   On good and evil as right and left, see 10 and note above.

mother and her sister and Magdalene who is called his companion. For Mary is his sister and his mother and his companion.

33. The Father and Son are simple names. The Holy Spirit is
a double name. For they are everywhere. They are above, they
are below, they are in the hidden, they are in the manifest. The
Holy Spirit is in the revelation, he is below, he is in the hidden,
he is above.

34. The saints are ministered unto by the evil powers. For
they are blind through the Holy Spirit, that they may think they
serve a man when they are at work for the saints. Therefore a
disciple one day asked the Lord for a worldly thing. He said to
him: "Ask your mother and she will give you from that which
belongs to another."

35. The apostles said to the disciples: "May our whole
sacrifice acquire for itself salt." They called the Sophia salt.
Without her no sacrifice is acceptable.

36. But the Sophia is barren and without child. Therefore she
is called salt, for salt is the place where they ... in their way is
the Holy Spirit. She is barren and her children are many.

37. What belongs to the father is the son's. And as long as the
son himself is small he is not entrusted with his own. When he
becomes a man, his father gives him all things that belong to
him.

38. Those that have gone astray whom the Spirit begets, go
astray also through him. Therefore through the same breath the
fire burns and is quenched.

39. Echamoth is one thing and Echmoth is another. Echamoth
is simply the Sophia. But Echmoth is the Sophia of death — that
is the Sophia of death, that is she who knows death which is
called the little Sophia.

40. There are animals which are subject to man like the calf
and the ass and others of this kind. There are others which are
not subject, which are alone in desert places. Man ploughs the
field with the animals that are subject and by this means he
feeds himself and the animals, whether those that are subject or
those that are not subject. So it is also with the perfect man.
Through powers which are subject he ploughs, arranging for

42. An interpretation of the story of Cain and Abel — and the first Old Testament reference in the *Gospel of Philip*. Unlike the Gnostics, who rejected the Old Testament or cited it only to show that it meant something different and opposite to the Jewish interpretation, the *Gospel* makes (limited) use of its materials. The idea that Eve was debauched by the serpent undoubtedly originates in Jewish legend, and appears e.g. in the *Book of the Blessed* (p.249 above) with its proto-kabbalistic background. The origin of human evil is thus explained. The same principle is applied in 1 John 3:8-10: 'He who does what is sinful is of the devil, because the devil has been sinning from the beginning. The reason the Son of God appeared was to destroy the devil's work. No-one who is born of God will continue to sin, because God's seed remains in him ... This is how we know who the children of God are and who the children of the devil are.'

43. The imagery of dyeing and of a colour-change through baptism connects with the alchemical strain in the *Gospel*. Cf. Steiner 1968, p.41. Similar imagery is found in the Syrian Fathers such as Jacob of Sarug: 'Black was I in sins, but . . . I have put away in baptism that hateful hue, for he hath washed me in his innocent blood who is the Saviour of all creatures' *(Canticle on Edessa)*. See further 54.

44. On 'firmly established,' see 11 above. The alchemy of the *Gospel* is concerned with a transformation of perception: the state of 'separateness' is that of the earthly man, who looks out upon the things around him 'but is not these.' Spiritual perception demands a change from within (he must 'become like them') in order to see. The perception of self is also reversed. Here below we look outward, and are trapped in our 'self' because we overlook our own limited perspective; in vision we are released from our self and so we are able to see ourselves truly.

46. Cf. 6 and note above.

47. Messiah is indeed equivalent in Semitic languages to Christ in Greek: both mean 'anointed.' It is also true that the name Jesus (Joshua) comes from a root in Hebrew meaning 'save' or 'redeem,' and that there is in Hebrew a word meaning to 'limit' or 'set bounds,' 'measure' which is spelled in a way very like Messiah. A Jewish-Christian background explains the knowledge shown by the *Gospel*. But the case of 'Nazarene' is more complicated. Certainly 'Nazara' does not mean 'truth' in any known language, as Robert Grant has pointed out. The name 'Nazorean' or 'Nazarene' occurs in the Gospel of Matthew 2:23 where an unknown prophecy is cited, 'He shall be called a Nazarene' (various spellings in the manuscripts). Although connected somehow with Nazareth in the birth-story, it is not a word meaning 'from Nazareth,' and evidently has deeper meanings — of the kind indicated here. The Mandeans probably provide the immediate setting for *Philip*: Nazorean is their name for their initiates, that is, those with knowledge (E.S. Drower, Oxford 1960, p.ix).

everything to come into being. For therefore the whole place exists, whether the good or the evil, and the right and the left. The Holy Spirit tends all and rules all the powers that are subject and that are not subject and those which are alone, for he ...

41. ... he was formed ... you would find that his children are noble creatures. If he was not formed but begotten, you would find that his seed is noble. But now he was formed and he begot. What nobility is this!

42. First arose adultery, afterwards murder. And he was begotten out of adultery, for he was the son of the serpent. Therefore he became a murderer even as his father also, and he killed his brother. But every intercourse which took place among those unlike one another is adultery.

43. God is a dyer. As the good dyes — they are called true — perish with the things that are dyed in them, so it is also with those God has dyed. Since his dyes are immortal, they become immortal through his tinctures. But God immerses those whom he baptizes in water.

44. It is impossible that anyone see anything of those firmly established unless he becomes like them. Unlike the case of man who is in the world, he sees the sun but is not sun, and sees the heaven and the earth and all the other things but he is not these — it is not so with the truth. But you saw something of that place, you became those. You saw the Spirit, you became Spirit. You saw Christ, you became Christ. You saw the Father, you will become Father. Therefore you see in this place everything, and you do not see yourself. But you see yourself in that place. For what you see you shall become.

45. Faith receives, love gives. Nobody will be able to receive without faith. Nobody will be able to give without love. Therefore that we may receive we believe; but that we may love, we give. For if someone gives but not in love, he has no benefit from that which he has given.

46. He who has not received the Lord is still a Hebrew.

47. The apostles who were before us called him thus: "Jesus the Nazorean, the Messiah," that is: "Jesus the Nazorean, the Christ." The last name is Christ, the first is Jesus, that in the

48.   The pearl is a symbol used in a highly developed fashion by the Gnostics as an image of the higher self. However, we should not overlook the use made of it in the New Testament, especially the Gospel of Matthew to which *Philip* has a particular affinity: see Matthew 7:6 and especially 13:46.

49.   Introduces the theme of the name of 'Christian,' which we know was first used at Antioch. It plays a central role in baptism and in other ways. The present saying may indicate that the community which produced the *Gospel* had known persecution. However, the 'name' is also of cosmic significance, and we should recall the ideas of the *Gospel* on language and 'names,' 11ff above. Participation in the 'name' leads to union with the Father. In the Mandean Mystery, the baptized also has pronounced over him the 'Name' of the divine Life with which he is to be united (p.39 above).

50.   Cf. 14 and note above.

51.   More resurrection ideas with a Jewish background: see *Midrash Rabbah* on Genesis (XIV, 7). According to Genesis, man (Adam) was moulded from earth, rather like an earthenware vessel (Gen.2:7). Hence it appears that when he dies, man is a broken pot which cannot be reassembled. Rabbi Yose argues, however, that God also 'breathed' the spirit of life into him. So he is really more like a glass vessel, which when melted down can be reblown. 'And if something which is made by the blowing of a human being can be repaired, how much more so with that which is made by the breath of the Holy One, blessed be he!' The Jewish passage is thus designed to correct a wrong notion of human nature, and offer an analogy which suggests a future resurrection.

        In the light of 23 above, the *Gospel of Philip* seems to be saying something slightly different. The 'vessel of earthenware' must correspond to the 'flesh and blood' which will not inherit the kingdom of heaven, that is, we will not rise out of our graves just as we were in life; such vessels do perish. The 'vessel of glass' is the 'spirit in the flesh' which will rise, transfigured, since it contains a living spirit (breath). The *Gospel* speaks of a transformation of the physical body, and the ideas immediately suggest alchemy with its 'living vessels' in which the spirit of the adept is reborn.

        The background is most probably to be found among the Mandeans, Living things like trees, animals and people are said to have 'Counterparts' or 'living images,' but artefacts such as pots, chairs, etc. would not have one. The *Gospel* will develop the teaching about 'images' (see already 11 above) at length in connection with rebirth later (e.g. 67). The 'glass vessel' would be 'living,' since it is produced by a breath-spirit, and have an 'image' with which we can be united in initiation as in an alchemical process and be regenerated. *Philip* has developed these Mystery ideas in Christian terms, the Jewish passage has used them analogically and so presents what is unlikely to be the source but is certainly a shared use of them.

53.   Introduces the Eucharist. The interpretation 'spread out' stresses the cosmic dimension.

54.   Seventy-two is the traditional Jewish number for the nations or languages of the world. The overcoming of differences and finding the archetypal Man is the result of baptism (dyeing); cf. 43 above. The Saying is not known from elsewhere, but must originally have spoken about baptism.

middle is the Nazarene. Messiah has two meanings: Christ as well as the measured one. Jesus in Hebrew is the redemption. Nazara is the truth. The Nazarene therefore is the truth. Christ has been measured. The Nazarene and Jesus have been measured.

48. If the pearl is cast down into the mire, it does not become more worthless, nor if it is anointed with balsam will it become more precious, but it has always the same value for its owner. So it is also with the children of God. Wherever they may be they have still the same value for their Father.

49. If you say: "I am a Jew," nobody will be moved. If you say: "I am a Roman," nobody will be upset. If you say: "I am a Greek, a barbarian, a slave, a free man," nobody will be disturbed. If you say: "I am a Christian," the whole heaven will shake. May it come to pass that I speak thus. He who hears him will not be able to bear it, for his name is great.

50. God is a man-eater. Therefore man is slain for him. Before man was slain they were slaying animals. For they for whom they slew were not gods.

51. Vessels of glass and vessels of earthenware are produced by fire. But the vessels of glass are made again, if they break. For they were produced by a breath. But the vessels of earthenware perish, if they break. For they were produced without breath.

52. An ass turning a millstone covered a hundred miles walking. When it was loosed, it found that it was in the same place. There are men who make many journeys and do not progress to any place. When evening came for them, they saw neither city nor village, neither creation nor nature, and power and angel. The wretches laboured in vain.

53. The Eucharist is Jesus. For he is called in Syriac Pharisatha, which is "he who is spread out." For Jesus came to crucify the world.

54. The Lord went into the dye-works of Levi. He took seventy-two colours, he cast them into the cauldron, and brought them all out white and said: "So also came the Son of Man as dyer."

55.   Christ is assimilated to a typical Mystery-god with a divine consort. See 17, 32 and notes above. The Saviour's saying is again unrecorded elsewhere; however, similar scenes of jealousy among the disciples are found in the New Testament Gospels and there is a closer parallel in *Gospel of Thomas* 114. Here however, the teaching concerns love rather than knowledge. Rather than entering into rivalries, the disciples should try to win Christ's love more and more.

57.   The Saying is partly identical with that preserved in the *Gospel of Thomas* 19, about the finding of one's eternal self. The version in *Thomas* continues with a mention of 'five trees in Paradise, which do not move in summer or winter, and their leaves do not fall. He who knows them shall not taste of death.' For the tree in Paradise symbol, see above pp.46ff and p.138 note 24. The 'five trees' which are ways to immortality show a ritual background of five sacramental stages is to be discerned behind *Thomas* as well as *Philip:* Welburn 1991, pp.189ff. In its present form, though, the *Gospel of Thomas* has turned away from sacramentalism in favour of an emphasis on the teaching of Jesus alone.

58.   The animals were part of man, but have separated from him and turned against one another. The animal natures in man are held in check by his ego 'which is not outwardly manifest but in secret,' whereas the animals have only external strength and act out their passions uncontrolled. The theme has been sounded already (14 etc.). in connection with the true or eucharistic food. Cf. *Gospel of Thomas* 7: 'Blessed is the lion which a man shall eat, and the lion become man ...' The theme connects also with that of sacrifices: man sacrificed animals to his false gods, his own animal natures: but the true sacrifice has become the Eucharist, based on wheat from the tilling of the ground.

59.   Becoming a Christian depends on the inner experience of initiation; only those who have the experience of the 'Holy Spirit' may 'take the name.' Those who claim to be Christians without going through the inner process are the ones who try to attend the 'marriage feast' (= kingdom of heaven) in the parable but have no wedding garment (Matthew 22:11-14: already alluded to in 24, 27 and notes above), only to be cast into outer darkness. Cf. 63 below.

60.   The mention of 'marriage' prepares the way for the later discussion of the 'Bride Chamber' sacrament. For the Christian 'Mystery' of marriage, cf. Ephesians 5:31f. The Mystery is not the sexual act ('the defilement of the appearance') but the inner wholeness which is the reattaining of Paradisal unity (71 below): there are parallels in the Mithraic 'Bride' initiation the Hermetic Mystery of union (above p.194 note 7), and so on.

       As a link with the creative origin (the archetypal Man who is the origin of everything, including the material world), the initiate is a crucial link in the chain of being. 'The existence of the world depends upon man.' For the world itself must 'become a child,' that is, be regenerated as in the ancient cyclic festivals in Babylon and elsewhere: see 99 below.

61.   Sex without the inner mystery is not just 'defilement,' it is giving oneself to the 'unclean spirits' instead of to Christ. The one who has attained the inner

55. The Sophia who is called barren is the mother of the angels and the companion of the Saviour. The Saviour loved Mary Magdalene more than all disciples. And he kissed her often on her mouth. The rest of the disciples were jealous of her. They asked and said to him: "Why do you love her more than all of us?" The Saviour answered and said to them: "Why do I not love you like her?

56. A blind man and one who sees, both being in the darkness, are not different from one another. When the light comes, then he who sees will see the light, and he who is blind will remain in darkness."

57. The Lord said: "Blessed is he who is before he came into being. For he who is came into being and will be."

58. The exalted position of man is not manifest but is in secret. Therefore he is lord over the animals which are stronger than he, which are great according to that which is manifest and that which is hidden. And this man gives them permanence. But if man separates from them, they kill one another and bite one another. And they ate one another because they did not find food. But now they found food because man tilled the ground.

59. If someone goes down into the water and comes up without having received anything and says: "I am a Christian," he has obtained the name on interest. But if he receives the Holy Spirit, he has the gift of the name. From him who has received a gift it is not taken away. But he who has received it on interest, it is demanded of him. So it is if someone is in a Mystery.

60. The Mystery of marriage is great. For through it the world became numerous. For the existence of the world rests upon man. But the existence of man rests upon marriage. Understand the undefiled intercourse, for it has great power. Its image is in the defilement of the appearance.

61. Among the unclean spirits there are male and female. The male are they that have intercourse with the souls which dwell in a female form. But the female are they that are mingled with those in a male form through a disobedient one. And no one

mystery (that is, as an inner state of wholeness) is above defilement. The *Gospel* speaks constantly of the inner state of 'marriage,' comparable to the state of the 'single one' in the *Gospel of Thomas* who has overcome the inner divisions and oppositions. Here the oppositions are especially male-female, desire-fear.

The sentence 'Then no one will be able to venture to go in to the man or the woman' implies that the holy person (who is explicitly said to be man or woman) is celibate. That is not a denial of sexuality (which would be blasphemy against the Mystery) but a resolution of inner energies and state of wholeness or innocence.

62.   Develops the theme of overcoming oppositions (desire-fear), and the mastery of natural energies. Overcoming fear is a central theme of initiations. For we must have the courage to become something other, and our present self must die.

63.   The initiate is one who overcomes the opposites, now presented in ultimate terms as death and life, good and evil, etc. Cf. 10 and notes above. The initiate must cross over the 'abyss' between life and death, the great 'void' which according to Zoroastrian thought the soul of the dead traverses to meet his 'image' (*daena*). The *Gospel of Philip* draws on a Mystery-background like that of the Mandeans and other Iranian-influenced Jewish groups. It presents the Iranian-Zoroastrian idea in pure form: the one who does not attain to the resurrection, and so has the spark of life within him (cf. 21, 90), will fall into the abyss of the 'middle' when he dies. This is the 'outer darkness' (69). The fate of those who do not obtain the resurrection is a problem which the *Gospel* leaves open: 'Only Jesus knows the end of this one' (107). The expression 'be found in the rest,' describing the state of being at one with one's true self, recalls the stages of spiritual knowledge characterized in the *Gospel of Thomas* and in the *Gospel of the Hebrews*. The version of Jesus' saying in the latter is phrased:

> He that seeks will not rest until he finds; and he that has found
> shall marvel; and he that has marvelled shall reign; and he that
> has reigned shall rest.

(Hennecke-Schneemelcher 1963, p.164)

Cf. *Gospel of Thomas* 2. On 'finding rest,' see also Matthew 11:28f.

shall be able to escape these when they seize him unless he receives a male power and a female, which is the bridegroom and the bride. But one receives from the image-like bridal chamber. When the foolish women see a man dwelling alone, they rush upon him and sport with him and defile him. So also foolish men, when they see a beautiful woman dwelling alone, they persuade her and force her, wishing to defile her. But if they see the man and his wife dwelling with one another, the women cannot go in to the man, nor can the men go in to the woman. So it is if the image and the angel are joined to one another. Then no one will be able to venture to go in to the man or the woman. Him who comes out of the world they cannot any longer detain because he was in the world. It is manifest that he is above the desire of the ... and fear. He is master over nature, he is superior to envy. If the evil one comes, they seize him and throttle him. And how will this one be able to escape the great powers of fear? How will he be able to hide himself from them? Often there are some who say: "We are faithful," that they may escape from the unclean spirit and demons. For if they had the Holy Spirit, no unclean spirit would cleave to them.

62. Be not afraid of the flesh, nor love it. If you are afraid of it, it will rule you; if you love it, it will swallow you up and throttle you.

63. He is either in this world or in the resurrection or in the places that are in the middle. Far be it from me that I should be found in them. In this world there is good and evil. Its good things are not good and its evil things are not evil. But there is evil after this world which is truly evil, which is called the middle. It is death. As long as we are in this world, it is fitting for us that we acquire the resurrection for ourselves, that when we strip off the flesh we may be found in the rest and not walk in the middle, for many go astray on the way. For it is good to come out of the world before man has sinned.

64. There are some who neither desire nor are able. But others if they desire derive no benefit, for they have not acted. For does a desire make them sinners? But not to desire does.

66.   The polarity of water and fire evokes the Mandean Mystery with its ordeals
        of water and fire. The distinction between the two forms of fire, one outward
        and one spiritual recalls the Mandeans and also Simon the Magus (pp.163f
        above). We have already seen (25) that the oil of the anointing is alchemically
        called fire. Baptism (water) and anointing (fire) produce a man of soul and
        spirit. The inner aspect of the fire, that is, its light-ether aspect, however,
        corresponds to a higher stage of initiation which is the Bride Chamber.

67.   The themes now come together in a new way around the initiation of the
        'higher Christian' in the Bride Chamber. The themes of death-rebirth, being
        united with the image (cf. Simon's 'becoming an image,') acquiring the 'name'
        of the Father, Son and Spirit (cf. 12 above) are drawn together and find their
        centre. Even though a person has received the names and is an initiated
        Christian, he may nevertheless go on to 'acquire them for himself,' that is, to
        undertake a conscious spiritual development on the basis of the gifts. If he
        receives this calling to the Bride Chamber (as in the parable often alluded to)
        and does not attend, he will lose even what he already has: 'the name also
        will be taken from him.'

        Becoming a son of the Bride Chamber goes beyond participation in the
        Christian life, focused around the Eucharist and the preliminary rites. Saying
        98 asserts that 'there is something higher than these,' that is, the further
        initiation of the Bride Chamber. The 'son' who is reborn there is not only
        joined to his eternal counterpart or 'image,' but penetrates through it to the
        truth: to the direct perception of spiritual things. He is united with the
        Mystery-god, just as the initiates were said to 'become Osiris or Bacchus' etc.
        'This one is no longer a Christian but a Christ.'

68.   Around half way through the *Gospel* we also reach the spiritual heart of the
        teaching: we are now ready to grasp the whole framework of the spiritual life
        which is expressed in the fivefold sacramentalism of the Christian community
        at Antioch. We have met all of them already, except the 'redemption.' H.G.
        Gaffron (1969, pp.191ff) has studied it and concluded that it is a death-rite
        comparable to the Mandean *masikta*. In the rite of the Mandeans, the priest
        accompanies the soul and escorts it into the other world. See Welburn 1991,
        pp.175f. It is a dangerous and holy undertaking which itself constitutes an
        exalted spiritual role, comparable to the later *consolamentum* or death-rite of
        the Cathars, after which the adept was a pure spirit even though still
        attached to the body.

69.   Versions of this Saying are also included in the *Gospel of Thomas* 22, fragments
        quoted from the *Gospel of the Egyptians* (Hennecke-Schneemelcher 1963, p.168)
        and so on.

        The subsequent Sayings quoted are preserved in the Gospel of Matthew
        6:6. *Philip* stands in particularly close relationship to the traditions in the
        Gospel of Matthew.

        The interpretation of the Sayings leads to a statement of the need for a
        complete reorientation of perception. The spiritual dimension of the cosmos
        cannot be found by looking ever further outward. It is outside or beyond the
        whole framework of inside-outside. By breaking through that limiting frame-
        work inwardly, the initiate also finds the answer to the cosmic riddle. That

Righteousness will hide from them both. And the desire is pleasing, the doing is not.

65. An apostolic disciple saw in a vision some who were imprisoned in a house of fire and who were bound in a house of fire, who were cast into a house of fire, having water in their hands. And they said to them: "These could have saved their souls, they did not wish. They have received the fire as punishment which is called the outer darkness, for it is black."

66. Out of water and fire the soul and the spirit came into being. Out of water and fire and light the son of the bridal chamber came into being. The fire is the anointing, the light is the fire. I do not speak of this fire that has no form, but of the other, whose form is white, which is beautiful light, and which gives beauty.

67. Truth did not come into the world naked, but it came in types and images. It will not receive it in any other way. There is a rebirth and an image of rebirth. It is truly fitting to be reborn through the image. What is the resurrection and the image? It is fitting that is rise through the image. It is fitting that the bridal chamber and the image through the image enter the truth, which is the restoration. It is fitting for those who do not only obtain the name of the Father and the Son and the Holy Spirit, but have acquired them for themselves. If someone does not acquire them for himself, the name also will be taken from him. But one receives them in the anointing of the brother and the power of the cross, which the apostles shall not call "the right" and "the left." For this one is no longer a Christian but a Christ.

68. The Lord has done everything in a Mystery, a baptism and an anointing and a Eucharist and a redemption and a bridal chamber.

69. And the Lord said: "I have come to make the things below like the things above and the things outside like the things inside. I have come to join them together at that place. He appeared at this place through types and images. Those who say: "... there is an above" err. For he who is manifest is that one ... who is called "he who is below." And he to whom belongs the

answer is the Pleroma (fullness). Though the term was used extensively and technically by the Gnostics, it belongs to the common heritage with Christianity in the New Testament (Gospel of John 1:16; Colossians 1:15-20).

70. R.McL. Wilson (1962) suggests that this passage refers to the condition of the dead, and the imagination of Christ's descent into hell to the souls who had lost their divine nature.

71. The mystery of marriage reproduces the original androgynous state and immortality of Adam-Eve.

72. The Saying is preserved in the Gospel of Matthew 27:46 and has parallels in Mark and Luke as well as here. The additional invocation 'Lord' is not known from elsewhere. On resurrection and the 'true flesh,' cf. above 23 and notes.

73. Here as elsewhere in the *Gospel* it is clear that all the stages of Christian life are open to women as well as men. Compare 61 above and note. For the meaning of 'beasts,' see 119 below: 'There are many beasts in the world which are of human form.'

74. Probably refers to the two stages, baptism and the Bride Chamber. In both there was evidently an anointing.

75. The aim of initiation is 'to see oneself' as in a spiritual mirror (cf. 44 above and note). This 'mirror' is the water of baptism: behind this idea is a cosmic myth of the divine Man and his image in the waters (see the Hermetic version, pp.197f above). Knowledge of oneself is the starting-point which leads to the Pleroma, to cosmic knowledge. But to see an image one needs not only a mirror but light, interpreted here as the anointing (see 66).

76. A mystical interpretation of the structure of the Temple in Jerusalem, such as has played a great part both in Judaism (see the Essene *Temple Scroll)* and in subsequent times down to modern Freemasonry. *Philip* interprets the stages

hidden is that one who is above him. For it is well said: "The inside and the outside and what is outside of the outside." Therefore the Lord called the perdition "the outer darkness." There is nothing else outside it. He said: "My Father who is in secret." He said: "Go into your chamber and shut your door upon yourself and pray to your Father who is in secret," which is he who is within them all. But he who is within them all is the Pleroma. After him there is no other within him. This is he of whom they say: "He who is above them."

70. Before Christ some came out whence they no longer could go in. And where they went they could no longer come out. But Christ came. Those who went in he brought out, and those who went out he brought in.

71. In the days when Eve was in Adam, there was no death. When she had separated from him, death arose. Again if he unites with her and receives death to himself, there shall be no death.

72. "My God, my God, why, Lord, have you forsaken me?" He spoke these words on the cross. For he separated that place, taking those who had begotten him from that ... Through God the Lord rose from the dead ..., but ... being perfect flesh, but this ... is true flesh ... is not true flesh, but an image-flesh of the true.

73. There is no bridal chamber for the beasts, nor for slaves, nor for women who are defiled, but it is only for free men and virgins.

74. Through the Holy Spirit we are reborn, but we are born through Christ. In the two we are anointed by the Spirit. When we were born we were united.

75. Nobody will be able to see himself, neither in water nor in a mirror without light. Nor again will you be able to see in light without water and mirror. Therefore it is fitting to baptize in the two, in the light and the water. But the light is the anointing.

76. There were three houses as places of sacrifice in Jerusalem. The one that opens to the west is called the holy. The other that opens to the south is called the holy of the holy. The

of progress through zones of increasing holiness in the Temple as an analogue of progression through the sacraments of Christian initiation. The outermost court could be entered even by Gentiles, while the innermost 'Holy of Holies' could be entered only by the priests. (The expression 'Holy of the Holy' remains to be explained). For the rending of the veil, cf. Matthew 27:51; also 125 below.

78.   A Mystery-version of the Fall, quite different from the traditional account of a 'punishment.' According to many Mysteries, humanity was originally destined to be divine and to possess divine knowledge. However, his original initiation failed, was interrupted, or its significance was not grasped (cf. 94 below). That is why man is now mortal and divided and yearns for divine knowledge which he does not have. The *Gospel of Philip* interprets Christ against this Mystery conception: he came to 'set right' the failed initiation of the beginning. For Eve should have been united with Adam in the Bride Chamber (79) and man would then have been deathless and illumined and in a state of permanent wholeness. Christ comes to provide the archetype of human birth (82). Thus the perspective is radically different from the 'historical' one of the Old Testament, a one-way movement from creation to the Last Day, from Fall to Last Judgment. History, for *Philip*, can be undone — at least for those who attain to the Bride Chamber.

       Did this 'Gnostic' version of the 'state of man' arise as a polemical turning upside-down of the biblical tale? It seems unlikely. Indeed, it seems to derive straight from a more original and mythological Adam-story known in ancient Babylonian texts, where primal Man is called Adapa. See notes to 94 below.

80.   On 'speaking words superior to the powers,' cf. *Apocalypse of Adam* (above, p.217).

81.   A reference to the Baptism of Jesus in the Jordan, as the archetype of the Mysteries (cf. 68) which were founded and are continued in the *Gospel* and its community. Note that it is treated as a cosmic and cyclic event, and as the descent of the cosmic Christ. The 'secret Mark' fragment also belongs to the setting of baptism and cosmic knowledge, presenting Jesus as the founder of the Mysteries by initiating-baptizing Lazarus (see below).

third that is open to the east is called the holy of the holies, the place where the high priest goes in alone. The baptism is the holy house, the redemption is the holy of the holy, the holy of the holies is the bridal chamber. The anointing has the resurrection and the redemption. The redemption is in the bridal chamber, but the bridal chamber is in that which is more exalted than they, in that which exists. You will not find ... are they who pray ... Jerusalem ... Jerusalem, they pray ... in Jerusalem, they look ..., who are called the holies of the holies ... veil was rent ... bridal chamber except the image ... above ... Its veil was rent from the top to the bottom; for it was fitting for some from below to go upward.

77. As for those who have put on the perfect light, the powers do not see them and cannot seize them. But one will put on the light in the Mystery, in the union.

78. If the woman had not separated from the man, she would not have died with the man. His separation became the beginning of death. Therefore Christ came that he might set right again the separation which arose from the beginning and unite the two, and give life to those who died in the separation and unite them.

79. But the woman is united to her husband in the bridal chamber. But those who have been united in the bridal chamber shall no longer be separated. Therefore Eve separated from Adam, because she was not united with him in the bridal chamber.

80. The soul of Adam came into being from a breath. Its union is the spirit ... that was given to him is his mother. They took his soul, they gave him a ... in its place, since, when he was united, he spoke words superior to the powers. They were envious of him, they separated the spiritual union. The spiritual which is hidden, they ... the ... to them alone ... bridal chamber, that men may defile themselves.

81. Jesus revealed ... Jordan the Pleroma of the kingdom of heaven. He who came into being before the All was begotten again. He who was anointed at first was anointed again, he who was redeemed redeemed again.

82. Gradually the full myth behind the Bride Chamber is unfolded. The initiation chamber is an image of 'the All,' like a Mithraic temple. In it is enacted the cosmic Mystery, the Father uniting with the archetypal 'image,' who is 'virgin earth' (83) (marriage of heaven and earth), womanhood or on the highest level the feminine aspect of God himself — see 17 and note above.

83. Christ provides the archetype of true birth.

84. Bringing round in 'spiral' fashion older themes (14, 40, 58, etc)., this saying unites them to the basic myth of the failed initiation in the beginning. Adam failed to 'eat the food' which brings about true, that is, human birth and is therefore an 'animal,' and worships the animal-powers. Similar themes appear in ancient Babylonia, for instance in the Gilgamesh story which reflects ideas about 'sacred kingship,' and so on. Gilgamesh seeks the 'Plant of Life,' but although he finds it fails to eat it and gain immortality; Enkidu, his companion, is of a half-animal nature and runs wild with the herds. See *Epic of Gilgamesh*, Harmondsworth 1964; and Welburn 1991, p.169.

85. In the Bride Chamber, man becomes a creative power united to God. In fact, he creates God just as God creates him, and transcends his creatureliness: the gods should therefore have man as their religion, as he worships the gods.

86. The cosmic and creative role of the initiate is now to be clarified. The *Gospel* makes a distinction between 'works,' 'images' and 'children' — though all are aspects of his creativity. They correspond to body, soul and spirit. Works stand in an external relationship, and are produced by outward exertion of his 'powers.' Children, on the other hand, are 'begotten' in intimate relationship, not as a task but as self-fulfilment and self-transcendence (on the connotations of 'rest,' see 63 and note above). Between them is the world of 'images' or Counterparts, and to these belongs 'the image-like man' in the halfway position between inner and outer, the 'appearance' and 'the truth.'

Human creativity thus mapped out furnishes an analogy to the patterns of divine creativity which the *Gospel* increasingly suggests. For 'children' = creative acts, see 28.

87. A characteristic contrast between the world and the 'kingdom of heaven' — cf. 24 above. See also Gospel of Matthew 20:25-28 and 9:15.

89. See Gospel of Matthew 3:15. The fragmentary Saying here also concerns baptism ('go down to the water ... redeem') but it is not clear whether it involves John as in Matthew.

82. If it is fitting to utter a Mystery, the Father of the All united with the virgin who came down, and edification illumined him. On that day he revealed the great bridal chamber. Therefore his body, which came into being on that day, came out of the bridal chamber. As he who came into being from the bridegroom and the bride, so Jesus established the All in it by means of these. And it is fitting that each one of the disciples enter his rest.

83. Adam came into being from two virgins, from the Spirit and from the virgin earth. Therefore Christ was born of a virgin, that he might set right the fall which occurred in the beginning.

84. There are two trees in the midst of Paradise. The one brings forth animals, the other brings forth men. Adam ate of the tree which brought forth animals; he became an animal and brought forth animals. Therefore they worship the animals ... of Adam. The tree ... is fruit ... Therefore they multiplied ... eat the ... fruit of the ... brings forth men ... worship the man ... God created man and men created God.

85. So it is in the world, as men create gods and they worship their creations. It would be fitting for the gods to worship men according to the truth.

86. The works of man arise from his power. Therefore they are called the powers. His works are his children who originated from rest. Therefore his power dwells in his works, but the rest is manifest in the children. And you will find that this penetrates unto the image. And this is the image-like man, doing his works by his power, but begetting his children out of rest.

87. In this world the slaves serve the free men. In the kingdom of heaven the free men will minister to the slaves. The children of the bridal chamber will minister to the children of the marriage. The children of the bridal chamber have one and the same name. The rest ... one another. They need not serve.

88. The contemplation ... and perception. More are ... contemplation. In those who are in ... glories of the ... are not.

89. ... go down to the water ... he will redeem him ... forth

90.   See 21, which applies to Christ; now it is applied to all who are baptized into
        his death. As with the interpretations of the 'virgin birth' (17) and Christ's
        death (21), the statement about baptism is not treated as wrong, and opposed
        to a special Gnostic doctrine: evidently it is the popular notion of its meaning
        which has to be corrected. Thus there are no grounds for seeing an opposi-
        tion between a Gnostic community using *Philip* and the 'great Church.'

91.   A legend explicitly given the authority of Philip. The Syrian Father Ephrem
        knew some version of it, perhaps, since the 'planting of the garden' suggests
        Paradise and the idea of the Messianic 'Plant' (above pp.46ff and p.138 note
        24, etc). Ephrem says in a hymn that the Tree of Life, when Adam fell, 'sank
        down into the virgin earth and was hidden, but it reappeared and sprang up
        on Golgotha.' Thus Christ on Golgotha = the new Tree of Life being offered
        to humanity. This goes beyond the Essene idea of the 'Tree which blossoms
        eternal' and the *Testament of Levi's* Priestly Messiah who gives humanity the
        fruit from the Tree of Life. As a Mystery-god, Christ becomes the Tree itself,
        and himself the 'food of immortality.' He is born in Paradise, in the Bride
        Chamber of the sacred marriage *(hieros gamos)* which takes place there, and
        the 'Trees in Paradise' are the sacraments which give communion with him.
        The grand pattern of the myth starts to become clear! Mithra too was a
        Mystery deity sometimes shown as the God in the Tree.

93.   See 14 above; and *Gospel of Thomas* 7:11.

94.   A further account of the 'failed initiation' in the beginning: Adam took as
        'law' what should have been 'freedom,' liberation; therefore instead of divine
        life he attained death. In the Babylonian myth of Adapa, the First Man, the
        gods offer the food and drink of immortality. However, the Man has been
        warned by the god Ea, his father, and when the gods ask, 'Ah, Adapa, why
        did you neither eat nor drink, stupid man; perverse mankind; you will never
        now have eternal life,' he replies, 'My master Ea ordered me, "You shall not
        eat, you shall not drink."' Thus by obedience to a god, taking his word as
        law, Man fails in his initiation-quest for the food of immortality. See *Poems
        of Heaven and Hell from Ancient Mesopotamia*, Harmondsworth 1971, pp.169-72.
        The 'failed initiation' myth thus explained the condition of humanity: only
        initiate-kings and spiritually awakened figures were said to 'have surpassed
        the First Man': see G. Widengren 1950, p.14.

who ... in his name. For he said: "Thus we shall fulfil all righteousness."

90. Those who say that men will die first and then rise err. If they do not first receive the resurrection while they are alive, they will not receive anything when they die. Thus also they speak of baptism, saying: "Great is baptism, for if men receive it they shall live."

91. Philip the apostle said: "Joseph the carpenter planted a garden, because he needed wood for his craft. It is he who fashioned the cross from the trees which he planted. And his seed was hanging on that which he had planted. His seed was Jesus, but the plant is the cross."

92. But the tree of life is in the midst of Paradise and the olive tree from which the anointing originated. Through it came the resurrection.

93. This world is an eater of corpses. All things that are eaten in it die again. The truth is an eater of life. Therefore none of those who feed on the truth will die. Jesus came from that place and he brought food from there. And to those who desire he gave life that they should not die.

94. God created a Paradise. Man lived in Paradise. There is ... and ... of God in ... Paradise is the place where they will say to me: "Man, eat this, or do not eat this according to your desire." This is the place where I shall eat all things, because there is the tree of knowledge. That one killed Adam. But here the tree of knowledge made man alive. The law was the tree. It is able to give the knowledge of good and evil. It neither cured him of evil nor did it establish him in the good, rather it created death for those who ate from it. For when he said: "Eat this, do not eat this," it became the beginning of death.

95. The anointing is superior to the baptism. For from the anointing we were called Christians, not because of the baptism. And Christ was called so because of the anointing, for the Father anointed the Son. But the Son anointed the apostles. And the apostles anointed us. He who has been anointed has the All. He has the resurrection, the light, the cross, the Holy Spirit. The Father gave him this in the bridal chamber, he received it.

96.   Also preserved as a Saying of the Lord in Gospel of John: 'I am in the Father, and the Father is in me' (14:10).

97.   Much is uncertain about the reconstruction and translation of the text here. Nor is it certain where the (unknown) Saying ends and commentary begins. Context: baptism.

98.   Apparently adds to the baptismal reference of 97. The 'higher' sacrament is the Bride Chamber (68).

99.   Applies the 'failed initiation' principle to the 'birth of the world' in a fashion parallel to the original mortal or failed birth of Man. The Creator of the material world remained on the level of works (see 86 above and notes), and did not attain to the union and spiritual begetting (creativity) of the Bride Chamber (= union with God). He did not beget imperishable 'children' (spiritual acts), but a perishable material 'thing.' Again, a very non-biblical reading of the Genesis creation-story! And once again it is not just a polemical, inverted version. For 99 implies that the world can 'become a child' — as happened in the Creation-festival at Babylon at the completion of the cycle of the year. The priests recited the births of the gods, and the beings of nature were described not as 'things' but as gods. When the yearly cycle ended, the world started again; it dissolved into chaos, but the gods created order as the cycle was re-established (cf. 81). It was not experienced as a repetition, but as the touching again of the creative source of the beginning. Just as Christ provides the archetype of true human birth, so his cosmic work is the re-establishing of the All.

101.   'When you were baptized into Christ,' says Paul, 'you have all clothed yourself with Christ' (Galatians 3:27). Some scholars (Stamm; Mollat; Tremel) among the commentators rightly intuited that Christ was felt as a living presence in the water, which the initiand 'puts on' by being immersed. This view is strikingly confirmed by *Philip*; since Paul assumes rather than argues his point, it probably belongs to the common background of baptism in the Mystery-rites.

102.   Cf Gospel of John: 'Flesh gives birth to flesh, but the spirit gives birth to spirit' (3:6) — the material belongs to the teaching to Nicodemus, connected with baptismal 'rebirth from above.' See also 113 below.
        The Law was an obstacle to the Gentiles (Greeks), but baptism creates a new 'chosen race,' namely 'the seed of the Son of Man.' Breaking down the barrier between Jew and Greek is an idea prominent in Paul, who pioneered the mission to the Gentiles: see especially Galatians 3:28ff.

96. The Father was in the Son and the Son in the Father. This is the kingdom of heaven.

97. The Lord has well said: "Some went into the kingdom of heaven laughing and came out a Christian and at once descended into the water. He came up, being lord over the All. Not because he thought that it is a game, but because he despised this ... the kingdom of heaven ... If he despises the world and disdains it as a game, he will come out laughing.

98. So it is also with the bread and the cup and the oil, even if there is something else more exalted than these.

99. The world originated through a transgression. For he who created it wanted to create it imperishable and immortal. He failed and did not attain to his hope. For the incorruption of the world did not exist, and the incorruption of him who created the world did not exist. For there is no incorruption of things but of children. And nothing will be able to receive incorruption unless it becomes a child. But he who is unable to receive, how much more will he be unable to give.

100. The cup of prayer contains wine and water, being appointed as the type of the blood over which thanks is given, and it is full of the Holy Spirit and belongs to the wholly perfect man. When we drink this, we shall receive for ourselves the perfect man.

101. The living water is a body. It is fitting for us to put on the living man. Therefore when he comes to descend into the water, he strips, in order that he may put on this one.

102. A horse begets a horse, a man begets man, a god begets god. So it is with the bridegroom and the bride. Their children originated from the bridal chamber. There was also no Jew who came forth from the Greeks as long as the law existed. And we too came forth from the Jews before we became Christian. You ... And these places were called ... the chosen race of the ... and the true man and the Son of man and the seed of the Son of man. It is called this true race. In the world these are the place where the children of the bridal chamber are.

103. While the union in this world is man and woman, the

104a. The translation and the division of the paragraphs here is far from certain.

104b. For the 'single one,' that is, the one who has overcome the divisions and oppositions in the Bride Chamber, cf. *Gospel of Thomas* 75: 'Jesus said, "There are many standing at the door, but the single ones are they who shall enter the Bride Chamber."' Also 104.

105.   The sense can perhaps be restored from *Gospel of Thomas* 67: 'Jesus said, "He who knows the All but fails to know himself lacks everything."' This is related to the famous Gnostic 'holy word' already cited by the Hermetic author of *Poimandres* (above, p.201): 'He who knows himself knows all things in himself.' But both *Thomas* and *Philip* seem to change the emphasis rather deliberately: cosmic knowledge should not lead people not 'to enjoy the things they have.' The old Mystery-knowledge is being modified to give a role to the earthly self of the Christian. Cf. Welburn 1991, pp.193f.

107.   See 63 above.

108.   A strikingly un-Gnostic paragraph: Gnosticism stresses the contrast between the spirit and the body, the one holy the other extraneous and defiled. However, the *Gospel* stresses the purifying effect of the Eucharist even on the physical nature. As Segelberg points out, there is no justification for Wesley Isenberg's rendering of 'holy man' as priest (in his version for Robinson 1988, p.155): see Segelberg in Logan and Wedderburn 1983, p.210. In fact the passage differs not only from Gnostic ideas but also from the orthodox notion of the validity of the rite through the office held and the words recited. Here it depends upon the personal holiness of the one officiating. The absence of the terminology of priesthood and the undefined role of the 'holy man' is in fact major evidence for the early situation of the *Gospel of Philip* in Christian evolution.

109.   See the introductory discussion of this passage.

110.   'He who sins is the slave of sin' is preserved as a Saying of the Lord in the Gospel of John 8:34. The phrase 'love covers over a multitude of sins' occurs in 1 Peter 4:8. W. Isenberg offers an alternative rendering of the section, which he believes also alludes to 1 Corinthians 8:1 ('love edifies' or 'builds up.') Taken in that light, the passage amounts to a rejection of *gnosis* altogether in favour of love. This seems to me too remote from the general teaching of the *Gospel* with its high reverence for *gnosis*, though modified in emphasis by love (cf. 115). It remains better to interpret it in the manner of Schenke and Ménard, as here.
        Gnostic 'freedom' in the absolute sense is understood as cosmic exaltation — being 'lifted up above the whole place,' and so free from the conditions and necessities of this world. Cosmic ascension is a deeply rooted theme among the Mandeans and in the Mysteries which lie behind them (Babylonia, Iran) or are related to them (Mithraism, etc).

place for the power and the weakness, in the aeon the likeness of the union is something other.

104a. But we call them by these names. But there are others that are exalted above every name which is named, and they are superior to the strong, for where there is force there are those that are better than the strength.

104b. As for those, it is not the one, yet it is the other. But they are both this single one. It is this one who will not be able to overcome the fleshly mine.

105. For all who have the All it is not fitting that they all know themselves. Some, if they do not know themselves, will not enjoy the things they have. But those who have come to know themselves will enjoy them.

106. Not only will they not be able to seize the perfect man, but they will not be able to see him, for if they see him, they will seize him. In another way no one will be able to acquire for himself this grace, except he put on the perfect light and become himself perfect. Everyone who puts it on will go ... this is the perfect ...

107. It is fitting that we should become ... before we come ... He who will receive the All ... these places, he will not be able ... that place, but he will go into the middle as imperfect. Only Jesus knows the end of this one.

108. The holy man is altogether holy, including his body. For if he has received the bread, he will make it holy, or the cup, or all the rest which he receives he purifies. And how will he not purify the body also?

109. Even as Jesus perfected the water of baptism so he poured out death. Therefore we descend into the water, but we do not unto death, in order that we should not be poured out. When the wind of the world blows, it makes the winter come. When the Holy Spirit blows, the summer comes.

110. He who has the knowledge of the truth is free. But the free does not sin. For he who sins is the slave of sin. The mother is the truth, but the knowledge is the father. Those to whom it is not permitted to sin, the world calls free. Those to whom it is not permitted to sin, the knowledge of the truth lifts

111.   Perhaps simply continues from 110.

The mention of the good Samaritan (see Gospel of Luke 10:25ff) raises a problem. All other allusions to traditions held in common with the New Testament Gospels can be explained from Matthew and a shared background with John; but the Good Samaritan is only in Luke. Yet it seems unlikely that the author or compiler of *Philip* knew Luke's Gospel. Segelberg wants to explain it on the basis that the parable 'is such an impressive text that once heard it could readily be reproduced. It does not therefore indicate that the Gospel of Philip knew the whole of the Gospel' (op.cit. p.206). Or possibly the oral tradition which lay behind Luke's literary work reached Philip-territory independently of the Gospel.

112.   Robert M. Grant (1961, p.135) cites a passage from the early Greek philosopher Empedocles containing similar ideas; but probably they represent the 'common knowledge' of Hellenistic times. The specific use here made of them is metaphorical: they point to the inner birth-process of the Bride Chamber, the birth of the Christ within. To bring this about we must have our hearts set on the Lord and his image will become reality.

It is possible, as suggested by Ménard (1967, p.229) that there is also allusion made to the myth about Sophia, that she longed to give birth apart from her consort in the Pleroma, and succeeded only in producing an 'abortive' world instead of a living, spiritual one (cf. 99 above).

113.   Picks up themes from 44: being united with the world in spiritual perception. Now it emerges that in its fullest, intensest form that is a 'marriage union,' a *hieros gamos*. In the process we also find out what we are — whether we are spirit or merely an animal nature.

Behind the latter part of the saying lie the ideas concerning the origin of the animal natures out of man: see 58 and notes above. Hence man is always able to become an animal by eating the 'tree' of nature rather than spirit (84) and indeed does so unless he takes on real human form in the image of Christ who was born as the archetype of human nature. Cosmologically, this corresponds to the domination of the world by the separating tendencies, the animal-archons who are worshipped as 'powers' by the natural man.

up the hearts, which means it makes them free, and makes them be lifted up above the whole place. But love edifies. But he who has become free through the knowledge is a slave for love's sake to those who have not yet been able to take up the freedom of the knowledge. But the knowledge makes them worthy in that it causes them to become free. Love does not take anything, for how can it take although everything belongs to it? It does not say: "This is not thine" or "this is mine," but it says: "It is thine."

111. The spiritual love is wine and fragrance. All enjoy it who will anoint themselves with it. They also enjoy who stand apart from them, as long as the anointed stand there. If those who are anointed with ointment stop standing beside them and depart, those who are not anointed and only stand apart from them remain again in their stench. The Samaritan gave nothing to the wounded man except wine and oil; it is nothing other than the ointment. And he healed the wounds. For love covers a multitude of sins.

112. As for him whom the woman loves, those to whom she will give birth resemble him. If it is her husband, they resemble her husband. If it is an adulterer, they resemble the adulterer. Often if a woman sleeps with her husband of necessity, but her heart is with the adulterer with whom she usually has inter-course, she gives birth to whom she will give birth resembling the adulterer. But you who are with the Son of God, do not love the world, but love the Lord, that those to whom you give birth shall not resemble the world but shall resemble the Lord.

113. Man mingles with man, horse mingles with horse, ass mingles with ass, races mingle with their kinsfolk. Likewise the spirit mingles with the spirit, and the word has intercourse with the word, and the light has intercourse with the light. If you become man, man will love you. If you become spirit, the spirit will unite with you. If you become word, the word will mingle with you. If you become light, the light will have intercourse with you. If you become those from above, those from above will rest upon you. If you become horse or ass or calf or dog or sheep or another of the animals which are outside and below,

114.   Distinguishes between inner slavery (an attitude of mind) and the one who though outwardly a slave has the potential for freedom within him.

115.   The alchemy of the four elements again, this time applied to the Christian virtues. To the traditional three is added *gnosis,* corresponding to the light, that is, to the illumination in the Bride Chamber.
        Despite the allegorical application, the underlying metaphor of plant growth and 'ripening' is deeply rooted in the Mysteries. On Christ assimilated to a Mystery corn-god, cf. 15 and note above.

116.   A hymn of praise to Grace and to Jesus Christ, rather as love prompted a celebration in the manner of Paul (see 110). The reconstruction of the meaning, unfortunately, becomes more difficult as the passage progresses.

117.   The question turns to the practicality of Christian love and grace: can it really be put into practice? How do we reconcile its theory with the actual distress which human beings always seem to cause each other?

118.   Various points are worth noting: the *Gospel* envisages a situation: a situation where people are in contact with believers and with non-believers on a regular basis. The Church from which it comes is not a closed community, but a part of urban Antioch (according to the best theory of its place of origin). Its advice is not directed toward a group of like-minded Gnostic idealists.
        The *Gospel* admits that with the exception of Jesus, even the best of men will cause grief to some, even though he has only good intentions. The wicked distress themselves because of what he stands for.

119.   Further practical application, now concerning teaching. The teaching is not an abstract doctrine to be given in the same form to everyone, but according to 'the state of soul of each one': it was only later that the drive towards a defined 'orthodoxy' required that all Christians acknowledge certain identical propositions. But the *Gospel of Philip* appeals to one 'who understands the discipleship.'
        The idea that 'there are many beasts in the world which are of human form' belongs to the Mystery conception that initiation for the first time bestows fully human existence. Compare the words of the Lord in Matthew: 'Do not give dogs what is sacred; do not throw your pearls to pigs. If you do, they may trample them under their feet, and then turn and tear you to pieces' (7:6).

neither man nor spirit nor word nor light nor those from above nor those from within will be able to love you. They will not be able to rest in you and you have no part in them.

114. He who is a slave unwillingly will be able to become free. He who has become free by the favour of his master and has sold himself into slavery will no longer be able to become free.

115. The husbandry of the world is through four kinds. They gather them into the barn through water and earth and wind and light. And the husbandry of God is likewise through four, through faith and hope and love and knowledge. Our earth is the faith in which we take root. The water is the hope by which we are nourished. The wind is the love by which we grow. But the light is the knowledge by which we ripen.

116. Grace is ... earthly, it is Lord over ... the highest heaven ... Blessed is he who did not grieve any soul. This is Jesus Christ. He encountered the whole place and did not burden anyone. Therefore blessed is such a one, because he is a perfect man. For this is the Word.

117. Ask us about him, as it is difficult to set this one upright. How shall we be able to accomplish this great thing? How will he give rest to everyone?

118. First of all it is not fitting to grieve anybody, whether great or small, whether unbeliever or believer; then to give rest to those who are at rest in the good. There are some to whose profit it is to give rest to him who is well. He who does good is unable to give rest to these, for he does not come according to his will. But he is unable to grieve unless he causes them to distress themselves. But he who is well grieves them sometimes. he is not like this, but their wickedness grieves them. He who has the nature gives joy to the good. But some through this grieve badly.

119. A master of the house acquired all things, whether children or slaves or cattle or dogs or pigs or wheat or barley or chaff or grass or castor oil or meat and acorns. But he was wise and knew the food of each one. he set bread before the children and oil and meat. But he set castor oil and corn before

120.   The use of the title 'Son of Man' in the *Gospel of Philip* has been studied by
       F.H. Borsch (1970) who argues that the *Gospel* and related traditions preserve
       a use of the concept 'Son of Man' employed by Jesus but lost from the
       orthodox line in Christianity. On this saying, see Borsch pp.81ff. He argues
       that the use of 'Son of Man' does not derive from the Church tradition,
       therefore, but goes back to Mysteries 'in which it was the great hero made in
       the image of Man (often Adam) and his son (often Seth) ... who were known
       by these designations' (1970 p.83). The Mandean writings include many
       references to such figures.

       The further reference to a 'son of the Son of Man,' however, is unusual. It
       evidently refers to the individual who takes up the creative and begetting
       power of the Son of Man: he is further transformed and so may be described
       as a 'son' of the Son of Man. Cf. 102 above.

121.   On becoming 'an offspring,' cf. Gospel of John 1:14 (the 'unique offspring' of
       God whose glory has been made visible) and its parallel in the *Trimorphic
       Protennoia* from Nag Hammadi Codex XIII 46:20f ('glory of the offspring of
       God.') It seems once more that by taking up the power to become a 'child'
       (cf. John 1:12) through initiation, the initiate not only becomes spiritually
       creative but shares in the divine nature, changing himself and becoming more
       than a creature. On the opposition hidden/open, see 58.

122.   The symbolism of 'marriage' is worked out at length. The change which
       comes about in the Christ-initiate is not an external one, but one 'in secret.'
       It is not just that he has been made into something different: that would
       mean little enough; rather, into his power has been put the creative power of
       changing himself. This is the power of the 'marriage,' which must not be
       defiled by being looked upon from outside — that is to say, any attempt to
       meddle in the sphere of the 'marriage,' the inner union of creative forces, and
       to influence or control another person on this level is a desecration. For it
       'belongs to the will' and to the highest freedom we have as 'children of God.'
       The imagery of violating the intimacy of the marriage is employed (with
       reference to oriental customs). But the marriage is the union of bride and
       bridegroom within, releasing our self-creating and transforming power. It is
       another version of the violated marriage feast for which the guest is not
       properly clad. The only right way of utilizing the spiritual resources within
       is by attaining knowledge (through initiation) and so one's own freedom.
       Then one becomes 'the bridegroom and the bride.'

the slaves. And he set barley and chaff and grass before the cattle. He threw bones to the dogs, but he threw acorns to the pigs and scraps of bread. So it is also with the disciple of God. If he is wise, he understands the discipleship. The bodily forms will not deceive him, but he will look to the state of the soul of each one and will speak with him. There are many beasts in the world which are of human form. If he recognizes them, he will throw to the pigs acorns, but to the cattle he will throw barley and chaff and grass. To the dogs he will throw bones. To the slaves he will give the first, the basic principles, to the children he will give the perfect teachings.

120. There is the Son of man and there is the son of the Son of man. The Lord is the Son of man, and the son of the Son of man is he who is created by the Son of man. The Son of man received from God the power to create. It is also his to beget.

121. He who has received the power to create is a creature. He who has received the power to beget is an offspring. He who creates cannot beget. He who begets is able to create. But it is said: "He who creates begets." But his offspring is a creature, because the offspring are not his children but his works. He who creates, works visibly and is himself visible. He who begets, works secretly and he is hidden ... the image. He who creates creates openly. But he who begets begets the children secretly.

122. Nobody will be able to know the day when the man and the woman have intercourse with one another except them alone, for the marriage of the world is a mystery for those who have taken a wife. If the marriage of defilement is hidden, how much more is the undefiled marriage a true mystery. It is not carnal but pure. It does not belong to lust, but to the will. It does not belong to the darkness or the night, but it belongs to the day and the light. If a marriage is laid bare, it has become fornication. And the bride has committed fornication not only when she receives another man's seed, but even if she leaves her bedchamber and is seen. Let her appear only to her father and mother and the friend of the bridegroom and the children

123.   A metaphorical re-interpretation of circumcision, but less critical than *Gospel of Thomas* 53.

The ideas in the body of the paragraph work on the same principle as the treatment of the 'marriage' in 122. If something 'hidden' is brought into the open, its power is destroyed and evaporated. This applies as much to evil in us as to the good and creative. Hence it is precisely what we must do with our hidden (that is, unobserved or unacknowledged) evil — even as it is what we must not do with the inviolable self of another: drag it out into the open and master it.

The saying of Jesus is known from Gospel of Matthew 3:10.

The *Gospel of Philip* clearly distinguishes mere repression of the evil within us (= cutting it off, but it will sprout again) and the real transformation which comes through knowledge. Until we have achieved that knowledge, we do not have even authentic existence (the basic Mystery-idea again; and cf. particularly 4). When it dissolves the power which our lack of awareness gave to the hidden evil in us, the hidden 'truth' can be revealed in the right way, not as a violation through interference with our will, but as the discovery of what was always there within us ('it rests within itself' — cf. 21, 90 on the 'living' essence which survives the death-ordeal of initiation and so is revealed). Its revelation is described as 'glorification': a term used in the Mysteries, in the Gospel of John and in the *Trimorphic Protennoia* from Nag Hammadi Codex XIII: see Welburn 1991, pp.266ff. The connection with the tradition of John is confirmed by the citation of the saying which also appears in John 8:32 on the liberating power of truth. The revelation of the 'glory' is connected with becoming a child or offspring of God (121); that is, not just a creature or product of divine power, but a self-creative being.

of the bridegroom. To these it is permitted to enter daily the bridal chamber. But as for the others, let them desire even to hear her voice and to enjoy her ointment, and let them feed from the crumbs that fall from the table like the dogs. Bridegrooms and brides belong to the bridal chamber. No-one will be able to see the bridegroom and the bride unless he becomes this.

123. When Abraham ... that he should see that which he was to see, he circumcised the flesh of the foreskin, showing us that it is fitting to destroy the flesh ... of the world. As long as their ... hidden, they exist and are alive. When they became visible, they died according to the example of the visible man, for as long as man's bowels are hidden, the man is alive. If his bowels are exposed and come out of him, the man will die. So it is also with the tree. Whilst its root is hidden it sprouts and lives. If its root is exposed the tree withers. So it is with everything begotten in the world, not only with the visible but also with the hidden. for as long as the root of evil is hidden, it is strong. But if it becomes known, it has dissolved. But if it becomes visible, it has perished. Therefore the Word says: "Already the axe is laid to the root of the trees." It will not be cut off. That which will be cut off will sprout again. But the axe delves down to the bottom until it brings up the root. But Jesus severed the root of the whole place, but others only partially. As for us, let each one of us dig for the root of evil which is in him and let him pluck it out of his heart by its root. But it will be plucked out if we recognize it. But if we are ignorant of it, it takes root in us and brings forth its fruits in our heart. It is lord over us, we are its slaves. It takes us captive so that we do the things we do not want, and the things we want we do not do. It exerts power because we have not recognized it. As long as it exists, it is effective. The ... is the mother of the ... the ignorance ... Those that are from ignorance neither existed nor exist nor will they exist ... they will be perfected when the whole truth is revealed. For the truth is like the ignorance: while it is hidden it rests within itself. But when it is revealed and recognized, it is glorified. Inasmuch as it is stronger than the ignorance and

124.   A fundamental Christian contrast between worldly and spiritual, applied to
       the outer meaning (types and symbols) and the inner reality (the Bride-
       chamber). For the thought, cf. 1 Corinthians 1:26ff.

125.   The mention of 'the holy of the holy' (124; cf. 76) brings once more the image
       of the Temple as an analogy to the progress of the Christ-initiate to the goal,
       the Bride Chamber. This section interprets the tradition (Gospel of Matthew
       27:51; allusion to Matthew 23:37f was suggested by R.M. Grant in addition)
       that with the fulfilment of the Christian Mystery the veil of the Temple in
       Jerusalem was split 'from top to bottom.' The veil is given a cosmic meaning,
       since the Temple was understood in Jewish esotericism as a cosmic symbol,
       and the analogy is with the initiation centre which Jesus constituted as an
       image of the All (82 above and notes). Access to the Temple, that is,
       initiation, is the gaining of cosmic knowledge and the rending of the veil.
          Just as literal circumcision is left behind, and its spiritual meaning fulfilled
       in Christianity (123) so the revealing to Christians of what was kept secret in
       the 'Holy of Holies' of the Temple (= God's direct presence) is the end of
       Judaism (cf. 6). It is not that the outer parts of the Temple, and the lesser
       mysteries, were revealed: in that case, any who were of the priesthood, with
       the right to enter the Holy of Holies, could have kept something back. But
       the veil was rent from top to bottom, and the 'Holy of Holies,' God's
       presence, is now completely accessible to individuals who enter the Bride
       Chamber, its Christian equivalent. The Godhead did not shrink back into its
       most secret sanctuary, but was totally revealed in the Mystery of the Cross,
       with its cosmic meaning (on Pleroma, cf. 69 above and notes. Note also that
       in 126 it is said that in the end every individual will be 'filled,' that is, attain
       cosmic knowledge of the 'fullness,' revealed in Christ (as in Gospel of John
       1:16; Colossians 1:15-20).
          The Flood imagery, and the idea of entering into the forbidden zones of
       the Temple, which has a cosmic meaning and is also the Paradise from which
       man was expelled, all appear elsewhere in Syriac Christian literature
       (Ménard 1967, p.243). This, together with other resemblances, shows once
       more that the *Gospel* belongs to the development which produced mainstream
       Christianity in its region, not to a special Gnostic offshoot.
          In fact, it becomes increasingly evident in the last sections that the attain-
       ment of the Bride Chamber is not only for the few, though it is so at present.
       In the coming times, 'the perfect light will pour out upon everyone' — cf. the
       Testament of Levi (pp.137f above). The Christian historical dimension has a
       reality leading to a universal redemptive process ('the slaves will be free and
       the prisoners will be ransomed' — cf. 9), not just for a Gnostic élite.

the error, it gives freedom. The Word said: "If you know the truth, the truth will set you free." Ignorance is a slave, knowledge is freedom. If we know the truth, we shall find the fruits of the truth in us. If we unite with it, it will receive our fulfilment.

124. Now we have the revealed things of the creation. We say: "They that are strong are honoured. But the hidden are the weak that are despised." So it is with the revealed things of the truth. They are weak and despised. But the hidden are strong and honoured. But the mysteries of the truth are revealed as types and images. But the bed-chamber is hidden. It is the holy in the holy.

125. The veil at first concealed how God ordered the creation. But when the veil is rent and the things within become visible, this house will be left deserted, or rather will be destroyed. But the whole divinity will not flee from these places into the holy of the holies, for it will not be able to mingle with the unalloyed light and the faultless Pleroma, but it will be under the wings of the cross and under its arms. This ark will be its salvation when the flood of water prevails over them. If some are in the tribe of the priesthood, these will be able to enter within the veil with the high priest. Therefore the veil was not rent only above, since they would be open only for those from above. Nor was it rent only below, since it would have appeared only to those from below, but it was rent from the top to the bottom. Those from above opened for us who are from below that we might enter into the secret of the truth. This truly is the honoured that is strong. But we shall enter there by means of despised types and weaknesses. They are indeed despised compared with the perfect glory. There is glory that excels glory. There is power that excels power. Therefore the perfect and the hidden things of the truth have been opened for us. And the holy of the holies has been revealed, and the bed-chamber has invited us in. While it is hidden, evil is brought to nought, but it was not taken from the midst of the seed of the Holy Spirit. They are slaves of wickedness. But when it is revealed, then the perfect light will pour out upon everyone,

127.   The whole *Gospel* ends on a strongly Christian, not a Gnostic note: the consciousness of the Christ-initiate sees spirit in matter, the cosmic Pleroma in the fulfilment of the Christ-mystery (cf. 125 and notes). Rather than the Gnostic dualism of matter and spirit, and the rescue of the spirit alone, it points to the presence of the Christ in the earthly world. Indeed, unless he attains to the knowledge of Christ here on earth through initiation, he will not be able to attain it in the next world ('the other place.') But if he does, he possesses the peace which enables him to live untroubled in this world, as well as the knowledge of what he will find in the next.

Title. At the end, as often in the ancient world. The use of the term 'Gospel' to mean a literary work is late, and may not originally have been so applied to *Philip*.

and all those who are in it will receive the anointing. Then the slaves will be free and the prisoners will be ransomed.

126. Every plant that my Father in heaven has not planted will be plucked out. Those who are separated will be united and will be filled. All who shall enter into the bedchamber will kindle the light. For they do not kindle as at marriages which we do not see because they happen at night. The fire burns only at night and goes out. But the mysteries of this marriage are completed in the day and the light. That day or its light does not set.

127. If someone becomes a child of the bridal chamber, he will receive the light. If someone does not receive it while he is in these places, he will not be able to receive it in the other place. He who will receive that light will not be seen, nor can he be seized. And no one will be able to molest such a one even if he lives in the world. And also when he departs from the world, he has already received the truth in the images. The world has become the aeon, for the aeon is for him the Pleroma, and it is thus that it is revealed to him alone, not hidden in the darkness and the night, but hidden in a perfect day and a holy light.

The Gospel according to Philip.

9. *The Secret Gospel according to Mark*

They arrived at Bethany. And a certain woman, whose brother had died, was there. And coming before Jesus she prostrated herself and said to Him, 'Son of David, have mercy on me.'

The disciples rebuked her. But Jesus was angry, and went with her into the garden, where the tomb was. And straightaway a great cry was heard from the tomb. Jesus went and rolled the stone away from the door of the tomb. And straightaway He entered, and there was the youth. He stretched forth His hand and raised him, grasping his hand. And the youth looked at Him, and loved Him. And he began to entreat Him, that he might be with Him.

And going out of the tomb, they came to the house which belonged to the youth — for he was rich. And after six days, Jesus told him what to do, and in the evening the youth came to Him, wearing nothing but a linen cloth. And he remained with Him that night. For Jesus taught him the mystery of the Kingdom of God.

And thence arising, He returned to the other side of the Jordan.

The story sounds familiar. At least, the whole first part of it needs only the addition of the name Lazarus to merge into the most familiar and the greatest of the 'miracles' narrated by the Gospels. The actual words, however, and the latter part of the episode in particular may give us pause. The impression of familiarity is checked and undermined.

That is because the story does not come from any of the four Gospels in the New Testament, but from one of those 'other' Gospels which existed in early Christian times but were rejected by the orthodox Church — one of those known under the name of New Testament Apocrypha, or Apocryphal Gospels. Or rather — well, the case is really rather complicated, even scandalously so. Yet it has shed a quite extraordinary light on one of the central events of Christianity, as well as on the activities of the early Church authorities. It has brought out into the open a mystery of death and of rebirth.

In describing it we shall not be able to avoid some of the scandal, so we may as well face it head-on. The text was recovered as recently as 1958, and fully published as late as 1973, by an American scholar called Morton Smith whose behaviour over the discovery has not always been exemplary. Indeed, there have even been accusations that Smith could have forged the text; but I think we may dismiss these outcries which seem to incline to the hysterical. One can only wish, however, that Smith had behaved a little better and called in corroborative scholarly experts to authenticate the document he found in the Judean monastery of Mar Saba thirty years ago. He did not, and the Archimandrite of the Jerusalem Greek Patriarchate, with jurisdiction over Mar Saba, has perhaps not helped things much by spiriting away the text to the patriarchal library and so making it for the present totally inaccessible. Yet it is certain that the text exists. It is certain, too, that the Gospel passage we have quoted exists there as a quotation within a letter from the early Church Father, Clement of Alexandria to one Theodore, otherwise unknown. And what Clement says about it is a further scandal. For he counsels Theodore that this is a 'secret Gospel,' and when asked about it: '... one should not concede that the secret Gospel is by Mark, but should even deny it on oath. For "Not all true things are to be said to all men".'

Readers of Clement will know that this principle is a favourite notion of his. But firstly what is this, 'that the secret Gospel is by Mark'?

Clement cites the passage as from the original version of the Gospel of Mark, not from an apocryphal work. Yet this version of Mark is certainly not the one we possess in the New Testament either! In that sense it is most definitely an apocryphal text. The Gospel of Mark accepted by the Church and included in the New Testament canon contains no trace of the Lazarus-episode, found otherwise only in the Gospel of John. Over the last fifteen years, since the text was published, scholarly enterprise has tried out most of the possible explanations for the odd state of affairs thus revealed, often with the design of steadying the rocking boat of established traditions. The great Catholic scholar R.E. Brown thought that it was merely a late addition to canonical Mark, written up on the basis of Chapter 11 in the Gospel of John to bolster belief in the agreement of all the four Gospels, removing the disconcerting silence of three of them over the great event in the Fourth. Morton Smith himself advanced a most fantastic and complex family tree for the passage, supposed to reflect the orgiastic practices of Jesus' first disciples (!) modified in expression by the use of the original Marcan Gospel, so that it is at once primary and secondary: a view which has persuaded almost nobody. Time has shown the most simple and coherent explanation to be that the 'secret Mark' is actually the original text of the Gospel and not an addition at all. It is the esoteric Gospel of which our canonical Mark is a carefully abridged and edited version.*

The style of the passage is the same restless, excited Greek as the Gospel of Mark we know. Events happen 'straightaway,' or are interrupted by 'and' or 'but' at almost every sentence. The Christ-Event cannot be told, in Mark's view, in balanced, formal narrative prose; Christ is a reality constantly breaking in, disrupting the organized order of things to which the Pharisees and the powers of the world adhere. It is as if mundane consciousness sees the surface of things, but behind the surface is the shining light of Christ, and where the surface cracks open we are dazzled by flashes of significance.

Moreover, the passage of the 'secret Gospel' fits convincingly into the text of Mark, Chapter 10. There we find the appearance, and the even more surprising disappearance, of a rich youth. Coming before Jesus he asks, '... what must I do to inherit eternal life?' Jesus replies, '... go, sell what you have, and give to the poor, and you will have treasure in heaven; and come, follow me.' But his call is not taken up: the young man's face falls, '... for he had great possessions.' Now if the episode were merely what the textual critics say, a peg on which to hang Jesus' sayings about wealth and the Kingdom of God, that last phrase ('and come, follow me') is redundant, and shows up Jesus with an unfulfilled saying. It would have been enough for him to pronounce 'go sell what you have ...' and then launch into the saying about the camel and the needle's eye when the youth slunk off. The next saying makes matters worse.

---

* Cf. Morton Smith, *The Secret Gospel*, Clearlake, California 1982. The text is better discussed in J.D. Crossan, *Four Other Gospels*, Minneapolis 1985, pp.91ff; also in M.W. Meyer, *The Ancient Mysteries. A Source-Book*, San Francisco 1987, pp.231ff.

Jesus continues mantically, '... for all things are possible with God.'
And yet nothing happens. The youth does not, by divine grace, go
through the eye of the needle and become a follower of Jesus — in
the canonical Mark. But that is precisely what we do see in the
longer, original text. This explains, too, why 'the youth' is introduced in the fragment as if he were already familiar, when all that
the 'secret' passage had said of him was an allusion to his being the
brother of the woman at Bethany.

The rich youth of Mark 10, in short, turns out to be the figure we
know as Lazarus. Far-reaching conclusions can be drawn from that
fact alone: but here I want to stay with the Gospel of Mark, Chapter
10, where we now insert the longer text after 10:34. With the help
of the original Gospel, we thus discover that the youth did indeed
enter upon the terrible struggle to tear free of the bonds tying him
to worldly wealth. In no merely metaphorical sense he had to 'die
to the world,' so that it had no remaining power over his soul. For
a modern man, such a struggle would still be a very difficult one.
Yet the crisis for such a man today would be an inner one. What we
must appreciate when dealing with the ancient world, however, is
that people then felt and experienced things much more as a unity:
a crisis of the soul affected them right into their limbs, producing
psycho-somatic illness. We know from accounts among the Essenes,
who put their initiates through similar ordeals, that they went
through a bodily as well as psychic collapse:

> I am forsaken in my sorrow,
> and without any strength.
> For my sore breaks out in bitter pains
> and in incurable sickness impossible to stay;
> my heart laments within me
> as in those who go down to Hell.
> My spirit is imprisoned with the dead
> for my life has reached the Pit;
> my soul languishes within me
> day and night without rest.

Thus one of the initiation-poems from the Dead Sea Scrolls, the
writings of the Essene sect at Qumran. The rich youth no doubt
suffered 'sickness unto death' in his agony of inner transformation;
but in the Essene poems too the sickness is not finally unto death,
but leads to a new inner birth, a birth to 'eternal life.'

I stress the real, even the physical character of the young man's death-experience, because the 'secret Gospel' goes on to confirm for the first time historically something known to Rudolf Steiner by his spiritual investigations: namely that the so-called 'miracle' of the raising of Lazarus was an event belonging to the Mysteries, a ritual rather than a literal 'death' and raising. Jesus completes the raising of Lazarus to life with six days of Mystery instruction and a rite which is clearly a baptism (also much used by the Essenes). Yet this knowledge of the ritual rather than literal nature of his death and resurrection must not lead us to think it was all some solemn mummery. The ritual completes and heals the wound, the 'incurable sickness' that reached even to the physical body.

The realization that baptism was involved enables us also to speak, as I have done above, of 'rebirth' as well as 'resurrection.' For in early Christianity baptism was above all the rite of rebirth. Candidates for baptism into the Mystery of Christianity during the early phase of the Church had to undergo a period of fasting and instruction; then they were baptized on the night before the Easter dawn, naked, until they were clothed in white robes, like new-born children or like Eve and Adam in Paradise. They were fed on milk and honey, rather than solid food. But these things were only the outer sign, of course, of the rebirth taking place within them. At the same time, we need hardly suppose that every initiate underwent the severe trauma of Lazarus. That seems to have been a higher initiation. In John indeed it is called a glorification, again a term known from the ancient mysteries. But we see that it is no accident to find also in Mark, Chapter 10, the famous discourse of Jesus on becoming as little children so as to enter the Kingdom of Heaven.

It is no accident, either, that following the inserted 'secret' text, at the end of Chapter 10 we find James and John wishing to enter into Jesus' 'glory.' Jesus in reply asks them, '... Are you able to drink the cup that I drink, or to be baptized with the baptism with which I am baptized?' Many biblical scholars have suspected, from Jesus' words, that he must have performed rites of baptism, though that flies in the face of Churchly tradition and the Gospel texts as they have been transmitted. The 'secret Gospel' confirms their suspicion. It shows that the element of the Mystery-activity of Jesus has been suppressed from the orthodox text. (And we can see that in a similar context the text of the Gospel of John 4:1f has been tampered with.) How could this come about?

The loss of the longer text of Mark results from two different factors. Firstly, we must understand the original character of the Gospels. They were no published books in the modern sense, available from bookshops and libraries. Their contents were communicated to those entering upon the Christian 'way,' as it was called, as part of their instruction. But full access to the understanding of Christ was possible only to those who in Paul's words had been baptized into his death. The evidence is that the secret passage from the original Mark was read to Christian initiates on that Easter night of their baptism. Concerning the highest initiation-baptism performed by Jesus, it was read to them at the most solemn moment of their embarking on the Christian life through inner rebirth. And that was the only time it was read. Its special character thus already separated it from the rest of the Gospel, from which readings were made through the rest of the year.

The second decisive factor, alas, brings us once more into the sphere of scandal. Our information comes once more from the Letter of Clement in which the 'secret Gospel' is embedded. And it introduces into the story a famous, or infamous, figure, Carpocrates.

Of direct spiritual knowledge William Blake was to say that 'the righteous will turn it to righteousness, and the wicked to wickedness.' When esoteric knowledge falls into the wrong hands, it is not only likely to be misunderstood: it will have a warped and destructive effect on the soul. There have without doubt been those in the history of Christianity who have grasped at spiritual freedom (that 'freedom in Christ' proclaimed by Paul) who had not developed the inner strength or maturity to be really free. Forces were nevertheless unleashed, and they have been controlled by the results, rather than being able to control the forces. So-called 'libertine' and orgiastic practices are attested for the second century, with Carpocrates as a leader of the movement connecting them with Christian 'freedom.' Clement adds detail to the reports:

> Since the foul demons are always devising destruction for
> the race of men, Carpocrates, instructed by them and
> using deceitful arts, so enslaved a certain presbyter of the
> Church in Alexandria that he got from him a copy of the
> secret Gospel, which he interpreted according to his blas-
> phemous and carnal doctrine and, moreover, polluted,
> mixing with the spotless and holy words utterly shameless

lies. From this mixture is drawn off the teaching of the
Carpocratians.

Clement is rightly horrified that such knowledge should fall into
the wrong hands. That is why he advises Theodore to deny any
reports about the Gospel, even on oath.

But there is an equally horrifying story implicit in what Clement
says. The demons after all had their victory. The Church, to fight off
the stains of libertine accusation, ended by suppressing the original
truth of the Gospel. They were manoeuvred into sealing up the
esoteric knowledge of Christ which the event of his death on
Golgotha brought into history and briefly opened to the light of
day. The 'secret Mark' is the most convincing evidence so far
discovered that the Mystery-background, the environment in which
Jesus' message appears in the *Gospel of Thomas* and the *Gospel of
Philip*, is also that of our familiar Gospels and that in which Jesus
himself lived and moved. The Gospel of John preserved the
knowledge that the disciples came from the circles of the Baptist
and the world of the esoteric baptizing sects of which he was the
most striking representative. The evidence of a connection between
Jesus and the Essenes thus comes to meet the evidence of wider
activities in the obscure domain of the Mysteries connected with the
life and death that became a new Mystery and a turning-point in
spiritual history.

Does that mean that we can lay Jesus to rest, so to speak, in his
historical niche? Philip Davies, an expert on the Dead Sea Scrolls,
suggested recently that there is nothing left of Jesus' claim to ori-
ginality. 'Everything about Jesus, his life and his teaching and even
his death, fits in to one of a number of patterns that we can see
already being established in the thoughts and beliefs of people of
his time.'* That is true. And yet it is contradicted by the sense of
bafflement, of contradiction, of the incredible 'scandal of the Cross'
which we meet everywhere in the earliest Christian writings. The
content of the life and teachings of Jesus had indeed been prepared,
had crystallized in the Mysteries of the Jordan valley and the Dead
Sea. But the way in which it was fulfilled, as an event in history
that could give new meaning to people's earthly lives, broke open
the framework of the Mysteries. It was so unexpected, so hard to

* P. Davies, in the 'Horizon' publication *Resurrecting the Dead Sea Scrolls*, BBC London
1993, p.24.

comprehend, that what the Essenes had thought would be the End turned out to be only a new beginning.

Perhaps we have not yet got beyond the beginning. In order to preserve the sense of a new beginning, the Church (perhaps understandably) concealed the knowledge of the background in the Mysteries; in order to maintain the novel doctrine of a new manifestation of God upon earth, a 'new creation' in Christ, it suppressed the link with the cosmic Mysteries and their inner processes. Now it is possible to see that we need to rediscover that dimension once more. Yet we do not therefore need to turn away from Christianity — rather we are rediscovering the very forces which were at work in Christian origins. Without the Mystery-dimension, Christianity itself is conquered by history and becomes a transient phenomenon, a hopeless attempt to reduce the unfath-omable to human terms as dogma and outward authority. At the same time, it is nonsense to suppose that we can ever reverse the step which took us as individuals to shape our own lives, to take the risk of giving our own meaning to the unique and unrepeatable series of events which is our own life-history, and collectively the history in which we all find our unique relationship to God. We cannot put off modernity by some wilful act and sink ourselves in the unselfconscious wholeness of the world. Nor do we need to. Christianity remains the only religion which, in its beginnings, shows a way of reconciling these deep and contradictory elements in our nature. Now that its beginnings have so mysteriously been restored to us, the hope that it offered in a divided world may once more become ours.

Source: The Gospel of Mark *in the New International Version Chapter 10, with the insertion of the original section from the Letter of Clement, translated by A.W. from the original Greek.*

1.   Genesis 1:27.

2.   Genesis 2:24.

❋ The Gospel of Mark ❋

Jesus then left that place and went into the region of Judea and across the Jordan. Again crowds of people came to him, and as was his custom, he taught them.

Some Pharisees came and tested him by asking him, "Is it lawful for a man to divorce his wife?"

"What did Moses command you?" He replied.

They said, "Moses permitted a man to write a certificate of divorce and send her away."

"It was because your hearts were hard that Moses wrote you this law," Jesus replied. "But at the beginning of creation God 'made them male and female.'[(1)] 'For this reason a man will leave his father and mother and be united to his wife, and the two will become one flesh.'[(2)] So they are no longer two but one. Therefore what God has joined together, let man not separate."

When they were in the house again, the disciples asked Jesus about this. He answered, "Anyone who divorces his wife and marries another woman commits adultery against her. And if she divorces her husband and marries another man, she commits adultery."

People were bringing little children to Jesus to have him touch them, but the disciples rebuked them. When Jesus saw this, he was indignant. He said to them, "Let the little children come to me, and do not hinder them, for the kingdom of God belongs to such as these. I tell you the truth, anyone who will not receive the kingdom of God like a little child will never enter it." And he took the children in his arms, put his hands on them and blessed them.

As Jesus started on his way, a man ran up to him and fell on his knees before him. "Good teacher," he asked, "what must I do to inherit eternal life?"

"Why do you call me good?" Jesus answered. "No-one is good — except God alone. You know the commandments, 'Do not murder, do not commit adultery, do not steal, do not give

3.   Exodus 20:12-16; Deuteronomy 5:16-20.

false testimony, do not defraud, honour your father and mother'."[3]

"Teacher," he declared, "all these I have kept since I was a boy."

Jesus looked at him and loved him. "One thing you lack," he said. "Go, sell everything you have and give to the poor, and you will have treasure in heaven. Then come, follow me."

At this the man's face fell. He went away sad, because he had great wealth.

Jesus looked around and said to his disciples, "How hard it is for the rich to enter the kingdom of God!"

The disciples were amazed at his words. But Jesus said again, "Children, how hard it is to enter the kingdom of God. It is easier for a camel to go through the eye of a needle than for a rich man to enter the kingdom of God."

The disciples were even more amazed, and said to each other, "Who then can be saved?"

Jesus looked at them and said, "With man this is impossible, but not with God; all things are possible with God."

Peter said to him, "We have left everything to follow you!"

"I tell you the truth," Jesus replied, "no-one who has left home or brothers or sisters or mother or children or fields for me and the gospel will fail to receive a hundred times as much in this present age (homes, brothers, sisters, mothers, children and fields — and with them persecutions) and in the age to come, eternal life. But many who are first will be last, and the last first."

They were on their way up to Jerusalem, with Jesus leading the way, and the disciples were astonished, while those who followed were afraid. Again he took the Twelve aside and told them what was going to happen to him. "We are going up to Jerusalem," he said, "and the Son of Man will be betrayed to the chief priests and teachers of the law. They will condemn him to death and will hand him over to the Gentiles, who will mock him and spit on him, flog him and kill him. Three days later he will rise."

They arrived at Bethany. And a certain woman, whose

brother had died, was there. And coming before Jesus she prostrated herself and said to him, "Son of David, have mercy on me."

The disciples rebuked her. But Jesus was angry, and went with her into the garden, where the tomb was. And straightaway a great cry was heard from the tomb. Jesus went and rolled the stone away from the door of the tomb. And straightaway he entered, and there was the youth. He stretched forth his hand and raised him, grasping his hand. And the youth looked at him, and loved him. And he began to entreat him that he might be with him.

And going out of the tomb, they came to the house which belonged to the youth — for he was rich. And after six days, Jesus told him what to do, and in the evening the youth came to him, wearing nothing but a linen cloth. And he remained with him that night. For Jesus taught him the mystery of the kingdom of God.

And thence arising he returned to the other side of the Jordan. Then James and John, the sons of Zebedee, came to him. "Teacher," they said, "we want you to do for us whatever we ask."

"What do you want me to do for you?" he asked.

They replied, "Let one of us sit at your right and the other at your left in your glory."

"You do not know what you are asking," Jesus said. "Can you drink the cup I drink or be baptized with the baptism I am baptized with?"

"We can," they answered.

Jesus said to them, "You will drink the cup I drink, and be baptized with the baptism I am baptized with, but to sit at my right or left is not for me to grant. These places belong to those for whom they have been prepared."

When the ten heard about this, they became indignant with James and John. Jesus called them together and said, "You know that those who are regarded as rulers of the Gentiles lord it over them, and their high officials exercise authority over them. Not so with you. Instead, whoever wants to become great

among you must be your servant, and whoever wants to be first must be slave of all. For even the Son of Man did not come to be served, but to serve, and to give his life as a ransom for many."

They they came to Jericho. As Jesus and his disciples, together with a large crowd, were leaving the city, a blind man, Bartimaeus (that is, the Son of Timaeus), was sitting by the roadside begging. When he heard that it was Jesus of Nazareth, he began to shout, "Jesus, Son of David, have mercy on me!"

Many rebuked him and told him to be quiet, but he shouted all the more, "Son of David, have mercy on me!"

Jesus stopped and said, "Call him."

So they called the blind man, "Cheer up! On your feet! He's calling you." Throwing his cloak aside, he jumped to his feet and came to Jesus.

"What do you want me to do for you?" Jesus asked him.

The blind man said, "Rabbi, I want to see."

"Go," said Jesus, "your faith has healed you." Immediately he received his sight and followed Jesus along the road.

Bibliography

Borsch, F.H. *The Son of Man in Myth and History*, London 1967.

——, *The Christian and Gnostic Son of Man*, London 1970.

Brown, R.E. *The Gospel according to John* in the 'Anchor Bible' Commentaries, Vol.I, London 1971.

Bultmann, R. *Theology of the New Testament*, Vol.II, London 1955.

Burgmann, H. *Die essenischen Gemeinden von Qumran und Damascus*, Frankfurt am Main 1988.

Charlesworth, J.H. (ed.) *The Old Testament Pseudepigrapha*, London (Vol.I) 1983, (Vol.II) 1985.

Corbin, H. *Spiritual Body and Celestial Earth*, Princeton 1977.

Davies, P.R. *Qumran*, Guildford 1982.

Drower, Lady E.S. *Water into Wine*, London 1956.

——, *The Thousand and Twelve Questions*, Berlin 1960.

——, *The Secret Adam*, Oxford 1960.

Eisenman R. and J. Wise, *The Dead Sea Scrolls Uncovered*, Longmead 1992.

Eliade, M. *Patterns in Comparative Religion*, London 1958.

Festugière, A.J. *La Révélation d'Hermès Trismégiste*, Paris 1986.

Fowden, G. *The Egyptian Hermes*, Cambridge 1986.

Gaffron, H.G. *Studien zum koptischen Philippusevangelium unter besonderer Berücksichtingung der Sakramente*, Bonn 1969.

Gaster, T.H. *The Scriptures of the Dead Sea Sect*, London 1957.

Grant, R.M. *Gnosticism. An Anthology*, London 1961.

——, 'The Mystery of Marriage in the Gospel of Philip,' in the journal *Vigiliae Christianae* 15, 1961.

Hengel, M. *Judaism and Hellenism*, London 1974.

Hennecke-Schneemelcher, *New Testament Apocrypha*, Vol.I, London 1963.

Hick, J. (ed.) *The Myth of God Incarnate*, London 1977.

Isser, S.J. *The Dositheans*, Leiden 1976.

Jeremias, J. *Der Lehrer der Gerechtigkeit*, Göttingen 1963.

Logan and Wedderburn *The New Testament and Gnosis*, Edinburgh 1983.

Mahé, J.P. *Hermès en Haute-Égypte*, Québec 1982.

Marcovich, M. *Studies in Graeco-Roman Religions and Gnosticism*, Leiden 1988.

Ménard, J. *L'Évangile selon Philippe*, Strasbourg 1967.

Merkelbach,R. *Mithras*, Königstein 1984.

Pritchard, J.B. (ed.) *The Ancient Near East*, Vol.II, Princeton 1975.

Pryke, John *The Scrolls and Christianity*, London 1969.

Robinson, J.M. (ed.) *The Nag Hammadi Library in English*, Leiden 1988.

Russell, D.S. *The Method and Message of Jewish Apocalyptic*, London 1964.

Schiffman, L.H. (ed.) *Archaeology and History of the Dead Sea Scrolls*, Sheffield 1990.

Schmithals, W. *Gnosticism in Corinth*, Nashville 1971.

Scholem, G. *On the Kabbalah and its Symbolism*, New York 1969.

Scott, W. (ed.) *Hermetica*, II, Boston 1985.

Steiner, R. *Genesis. Secrets of the Bible Story of Creation*, London 1959.

——, *The Gospel of St Matthew*, London 1965.

——, *The Easter Festival in relation to the Mysteries*, London 1968.

Stone, M.E. (ed) *Jewish Writings of the Second Temple Period*, Assen & Philadelphia 1984.

Vermaseren, M.J. *Mithras, The Secret God*, London 1963.

Vermes, G. *The Dead Sea Scrolls in English*, Harmondsworth 1987.

Welburn, A. *The Beginnings of Christianity*, Edinburgh 1991.

Widengren, G. *The Ascension of the Apostle and the Holy Book*, Uppsala 1950.

——, *The King and the Tree of Life in Ancient Near Eastern Religion*, Uppsala 1951.

Wilson, R.McL. *The Gospel of Philip*, London & New York 1962.

——, *Gnosis and the New Testament*, Oxford 1968.

Zaehner, R. *Teachings of the Magi*, London 1975.

Index to biblical references

Old Testament

Index